International Review of Social History

PUBLISHED FOR THE INTERNATIONAAL INSTITUUT VOOR
SOCIALE GESCHIEDENIS, AMSTERDAM

EXECUTIVE EDITOR
Aad Blok, *Internationaal Instituut voor Sociale Geschiedenis, Cruquiusweg 31, 1019 AT Amsterdam, The Netherlands*

EDITORIAL COMMITTEE
Ravi Ahuja, Dennis Bos, Ulbe Bosma, Jan-Bart Gewalt, Marjolein 't Hart, Karin Hofmeester, Marcel van der Linden (Chair), Michael Zeuske

EDITORIAL STAFF
Angèle Janse, *Editorial Assistant*

CORRESPONDING EDITORS
Friedhelm Boll, *Friedrich Ebert Stiftung, Bonn*
Eileen Boris, *University of California, Santa Barbara*
David De Vries, *Tel Aviv University*
Nancy Green, *EHESS, Paris*
Michael Hall, *Universidad Estadual de Campinas*
David Howell, *University of York*
Elina Katainen, *Helsinki*
Amarjit Kaur, *University of New England, Armidale*

Reinhart Kößler, *Bochum*
Friedrich Lenger, *Justus-Liebig-Universität, Giessen*
Paolo Malanima, *Università degli Studi di Reggio Calabria*
Siegfried Mattl, *Institut für Zeitgeschichte, Wien*
Prabhu Mohapatra, *New Delhi*
Irina Novičenko, *Center for Social History, Moscow*
Lars Olsson, *Linnaeus University, Växjö*
Ricardo D. Salvatore, *Universidad Torcuato di Tella*
Lucy Taksa, *University of New South Wales, Sydney*

ADVISORY BOARD
Eileen Boris, *University of California, Santa Barbara*
Ute Frevert, *Yale University*
Manuel Pérez Ledesma, *Universidad Autonoma de Madrid*
Richard Price, *University of Maryland*
Wilfried Reininghaus, *Nordrhein-Westfälisches Staatsarchiv Münster*

SUBSCRIPTIONS
International Review of Social History (ISSN 0020–8590) is published in three parts in April, August and December plus one supplement in December. Three parts plus one supplement form a volume. The subscription price (excluding VAT) of volume 55 (2010) which includes electronic access and delivery by air where appropriate is £148 net (US$253 in the USA, Canada and Mexico) for institutions; £47 net (US$66 in the USA, Canada and Mexico) for individuals ordering direct from the publisher and certifying that the journal is for their own personal use. Single parts and the supplement are £39 (US$66 in the USA, Canada and Mexico) plus postage. An electronic only price available to institutional subscribers is £126 (US$217 in USA, Canada and Mexico). EU subscribers (outside the UK) who are not registered for VAT should add VAT at their country's rate. VAT registered subscribers should provide their VAT registration number. Japanese prices for institutions are available from Kinokuniya Company Ltd, P.O. Box 55, Chitose, Tokyo 156, Japan.

Orders, which must be accompanied by payment, may be sent to a bookseller, subscription agent or direct to the publisher: Cambridge University Press, The Edinburgh Building, Shaftesbury Road, Cambridge CB2 8RU; or in the USA, Canada and Mexico: Cambridge University Press, Journals Fulfillment Department, 100 Brook Hill Drive, West Nyack, New York 10994–2133. Periodicals postage paid at New York, NY and at additional mailing offices. Postmaster: send address changes in USA, Canada and Mexico to International Review of Social History, Cambridge University Press, 100 Brook Hill Drive, West Nyack, New York 10994–2133.

Information on International Review of Social History and all other Cambridge journals can be accessed via journals.cambridge.org

T0364207

**international
review of
social history**

Special Issue 18

Globalization, Environmental Change, and Social History

Edited by Peter Boomgaard and Marjolein 't Hart

CAMBRIDGE UNIVERSITY PRESS
Cambridge, New York, Melbourne, Madrid, Cape Town,
Singapore, São Paulo, Delhi, Tokyo, Mexico City

Cambridge University Press
The Edinburgh Building, Cambridge CB2 8RU, UK

Published in the United States of America by Cambridge University Press, New York

www.cambridge.org
Information on this title: www.cambridge.org/9781107401518

A catalogue record for this publication is available from the British Library

ISBN 978-1-107-40151-8 Paperback

CONTENTS

Globalization, Environmental Change, and Social History

Edited by
Peter Boomgaard and Marjolein 't Hart

Notes on Contributors

Globalization, Environmental Change, and Social History:
An Introduction
Peter Boomgaard and Marjolein 't Hart   1

The El Dorado of Forestry: The Eucalyptus in India, South
Africa, and Thailand, 1850–2000
Brett M. Bennett   27

The Mid-Atlantic Islands: A Theatre of Early Modern Ecocide?
Stefan Halikowski Smith   51

Environmental Change and Globalization in Seventeenth-
Century France: Dutch Traders and the Draining of French
Wetlands (Arles, Petit Poitou)
Raphaël Morera   79

The Colonial Famine Plot: Slavery, Free Trade, and Empire in
the French Atlantic, 1763–1791
Joseph Horan   103

Environmental Changes, the Emergence of a Fuel Market, and
the Working Conditions of Salt Makers in Bengal, c. 1780–1845
Sayako Kanda   123

Industrial Life in a Limiting Landscape: An Environmental
Interpretation of Stalinist Social Conditions in the Far North
Andy Bruno   153

"Pumpkins Just Got in There": Gender and Generational
Conflict and "Improved" Agriculture in Colonial Zimbabwe
Guy Thompson   175

Hydro-businesses: National and Global Demands on the São
Francisco River Basin Environment of Brazil
Lucigleide Nery Nascimento and Mimi Larsen Becker   203

NOTES ON CONTRIBUTORS

Mimi Larsen Becker, Department of Natural Resources and the Environment, University of New Hampshire, James Hall, Durham, NH 03824, USA; e-mail: mimi.becker@unh.edu

Brett M. Bennett, Department of History, The University of Texas at Austin, GAR 1.104 B7000, Austin, TX 78712, USA; e-mail: brebenne@mail.utexas.edu; utxaustinbennett@yahoo.com

Peter Boomgaard, Koninklijk Instituut voor Taal-, Land- en Volkenkunde, PO Box 9515, 2300 RA Leiden, The Netherlands; e-mail: boomgaard@kitlv.nl

Andy Bruno, History Department, University of Illinois at Urbana-Champaign, 309 Gregory Hall, 810 S. Wright St, Urbana, IL 61801, USA; e-mail: arbruno2@illinois.edu

Stefan Halikowski Smith, Department of History, Swansea University, Singleton Park, Swansea SA2 8PP, United Kingdom; e-mail: S.Halikowski-Smith@swansea.ac.uk

Marjolein 't Hart, Leerstoelgroep Economische en Sociale Geschiedenis, Faculteit der Geesteswetenschappen, Universiteit van Amsterdam, Spuistraat 134, 1012 VB Amsterdam, The Netherlands; e-mail: M.C.tHart@uva.nl

Joseph Horan, Department of History, Florida State University, 401 Bellamy Building, PO Box 3062200, Tallahassee, FL 32306, USA; e-mail: jwho4h@fsu.edu

Sayako Kanda, Faculty of Economics, Keio University, 2-15-45 Minato-ku, Mita, Tokyo 108-8345, Japan; e-mail: kanda@a7.keio.jp

Raphaël Morera, CDHTE-CNAM, 5, rue du Vertbois, 75003 Paris, France; e-mail: morera.raphael@g.mail.com

Lucigleide Nery Nascimento, Department of Natural Resources and the Environment, University of New Hampshire, James Hall, Durham, NH 03824, USA; e-mail: LNN_UNH@hotmail.com

Guy Thompson, Department of History and Classics, University of Alberta, Edmonton, Alberta, T6G 2H4, Canada; e-mail: Guy.Thompson@ualberta.ca

IRSH 55 (2010), Supplement, pp. 1–26 doi:10.1017/S0020859010000477
© 2010 Internationaal Instituut voor Sociale Geschiedenis

Globalization, Environmental Change, and Social History: An Introduction

PETER BOOMGAARD

Koninklijk Instituut voor Taal-, Land- en Volkenkunde, Leiden

E-mail: boomgaard@kitlv.nl

MARJOLEIN 'T HART

Faculteit der Geesteswetenschappen, Universiteit van Amsterdam

E-mail: M.C.tHart@uva.nl

Throughout the ages, the activities of humankind have weighed considerably upon the environment. In turn, changes in that environment have favoured the rise of certain social groups and limited the actions of others. Nevertheless, environmental history has remained a "blind spot" for many social and economic historians.[1] This is to be regretted, as changes in ecosystems have always had quite different consequences for different social groups. Indeed, the various and unequal effects of environmental change often explain the strengths and weaknesses of certain social groups, irrespective of their being defined along lines of class, gender, or ethnicity.

This Special Issue of the *International Review of Social History* aims to bring together the expertise of social and environmental historians. In the last few decades of the twentieth century, expanding holes in the ozone layer, global warming, and the accelerated pace of the destruction of the tropical forests have resulted in a worldwide recognition of two closely related processes: globalization and environmental change.[2] The contributions to this volume provide striking case studies of such connections in earlier periods, revealing a fruitful interconnection between social and environmental history. This introduction provides a historiographical context for the essays that follow, focusing on the relevant notions connected

---

1. See Ted Steinberg, "Down to Earth: Nature, Agency, and Power in History", *The American Historical Review*, 107 (2002), pp. 798–820, 805.
2. Thomas E. Lovejoy and Lee Hannah (eds), *Climate Change and Biodiversity* (New Haven, CT, 2006); Alfred W. Crosby, *Children of the Sun: A History of Humanity's Unappeasable Appetite for Energy* (New York [etc.], 2006).

with globalization and environmental change, and stressing the existing interactions between environmental and social history. We are particularly interested in the consequences of processes induced by globalization, how transnational forces and agents changed the socio-ecological space, and how that affected relationships between different classes in history.

GLOBALIZATION AND GLOBAL HISTORY

Globalization is a concept that needs further elaboration. The rise of the internet, the shifts in the power of sovereign national states, the intricate intertwining of global markets, and the enormous numbers of people migrating across regions and continents trying to escape wars, environmental degradation, or disasters have prompted several scholars to explain these recent trends using new definitions of globalization. The description by the political scientists David Held and Anthony McGrew nicely captures our understanding:

> Simply put, globalization denotes the expanding scale, growing magnitude, speeding up and deepening impact of interregional flows and patterns of interaction. It refers to a shift or transformation in the scale in human organization that links distant communities and expands the reach of power relations across the world's major regions and continents.[3]

In history, as well as in the social sciences, debates abound on the timing or start of globalization. In contrast to some scholars, we are not inclined to use globalization as a term limited to a new epoch that started in the 1980s or 1990s,[4] neither do we think that the rapid globalization in the nineteenth century precludes all early modern globalization,[5] nor do we see a specific date (1492 or 1571 have been suggested, for example) in the early modern period from which globalization truly took off.[6] Rather, we wish to look upon globalization as a set of highly variegated processes that can be labelled in different ways, ranging from "thick" to "thin" globalization and from "diffused" to "expanded". These categories are

---

3. David Held and Anthony McGrew, "The Great Globalization Debate: An Introduction", in *idem* (eds), *The Global Transformations Reader: An Introduction to the Globalization Debate*, 2nd edn (Cambridge, 2003), p. 4. "Regions" refer to certain larger areas within a continent, usually encompassing several nation-states, for instance south-east Asia or the European Community.
4. Kenichi Ohmae, *The End of the Nation State: The Rise of Regional Economies* (New York, 1995); Martin Albrow, "A New Decade of the Global Age, 1996–2006", *Globality Studies Journal: Global History, Society, Civilization*, 8 (2007), pp. 1–26.
5. Kevin H. O'Rourke and Jeffrey G. Williamson, "When Did Globalisation Begin?", *European Review of Economic History*, 6 (2002), pp. 23–50.
6. Dennis O. Flynn and Arturo Giráldez, "Path Dependence, Time Lags and the Birth of Globalisation: A Critique of O'Rourke and Williamson", *European Review of Economic History*, 8 (2004), pp. 81–108.

derived from *Global Transformations*, the influential study by David Held *et al.* in which they observe variations in the extensity, the intensity, the velocity, and the impact of global connections.[7]

"Thick" globalization then refers to processes that share an expanding scale, growing magnitude, and an acceleration as well as a deepening of their impact. A case in point is the growing interconnection of the world markets in the late nineteenth century under the auspices of the British Empire. Thin globalization typically relates to developments that can be defined by an expanding scale while the other three characteristics are weak. A good example is the long-distance trade along the Eurasian silk route in the medieval period. The impact of diffuse globalization is likewise rather shallow, yet its velocity and intensity are high; the worldwide spread of Coca-Cola may serve as an illustration. Finally, expanded globalization refers to developments in which the impact is high, yet the intensity and velocity are limited, as represented by the colonization of Latin America and the Caribbean in the early modern period. This distinction in different categories allows us thus to investigate environmental impacts that can be substantial even before the rise of imperialism or other obvious "thick" globalizations.

In line with these thoughts, it would be preferable to speak about "globalizations" instead of one "globalization", not as a single process but as a multitude of uneven developments.[8] Implicit in numerous conceptualizations of globalization is the assumption that it inevitably entails homogenization, that all societies will increasingly look the same.[9] Although convergence is indeed often strong, globalization also leads to divergence, which is best illustrated perhaps by the division in world power. A set of elite groups in the core regions maintain excellent relations with the new nodes of power, while other groups and regions become increasingly marginalized. For example, when the world financial markets experienced rapid interconnection in the late twentieth century

---

7. David Held *et al.*, *Global Transformations: Politics, Economics, and Culture* (Cambridge [etc.], 1999), pp. 17–23.
8. See also Wolf Schäfer, "From the End of European History to the Globality of World Regions: A Research Perspective", *Globality Studies Journal: Global History, Society, Civilization*, 1 (2006), pp. 1–9, 6. This resembles the debates regarding modernization, in which it has become common ground to study "modernizations" instead of the one master trajectory in history towards modern society. The latter inevitably led to the misguided supposition of the superiority of the Western path of development. See Christopher Bayly, *The Birth of the Modern World, 1780–1914: Global Connections and Comparisons* (Oxford, 2004); Julia Adams, Elisabeth S. Clemens, and Ann Shola Orloff (eds), *Remaking Modernity: Politics, History, and Sociology* (Durham, 2005).
9. Many historians follow this assumption, above all economic historians. See among others O'Rourke and Williamson, "When Did Globalisation Begin?", and Flynn and Giráldez, "Path Dependence, Time Lags and the Birth of Globalisation".

the number of financial experts actually acquainted with the development was quite small; they were termed the "new economic hit men", and included major investors such as George Soros.[10]

The social scientist Manuel Castells stressed that globalization effectuates a sharpening of class distinctions and even the emergence of new classes. He observed that in the age of the internet, certain business managers moved rapidly towards the upper echelons of society, while at the bottom a new "fourth class" found itself deprived of digital ways to make money. Castells summarizes these trends as follows: elites are cosmopolitan and global, "ordinary people" remain oriented towards the local.[11] Comparable processes are observed in different fields: for example, James Scott noted that in a Malaysian village the new profits of the green revolution went disproportionately to the wealthier farmers.[12] Thus, marginalized people remain localized, strengthening divergence.

Divergence can also be the result of resistance to global trends. A growing consciousness of typically local and national interests results in movements wishing to stress differing and alternative paths, such as nationalist parties and fundamentalist Islam, to mention but a few. Movements that do not oppose globalization yet aspire to blend global tendencies within local traditions and solutions are called glocal, which can also reinforce divergent trends.[13]

Historians have also recognized the thick globalization of the last few decades of the twentieth century, above all its impact on the role of sovereign states. Not that the nation-state is withering away, but its functions have undergone major transformations, and historians have become more attentive to the workings of transnational trends and agents in earlier periods.[14] As the global connections changed and intensified, as regional and intercontinental structures expanded, historians increasingly looked back on the development of their own nation-states as constructs that were strongly linked to a specific phase in world history. This stimulated the rise of a distinct group of world historians, as exemplified by the establishment of the *Journal of World History* in 1990.[15] Within world

10. Niall Ferguson, *The Ascent of Money: A Financial History of the World* (New York [etc.], 2008), pp. 314–327.

11. Manuel Castells, *The Rise of the Network Society*. I: *The Information Age: Economy, Society and Culture*, 2nd edn (Cambridge [etc.], 2000), pp. 296ff.

12. James Scott, *Weapons of the Weak: Everyday Forms of Peasant Resistance* (New Haven, CT, 1985), pp. 56, 305.

13. Roland Robertson, *Globalization: Social Theory and Global Culture* (London, 1992).

14. Patrick O'Brien, "Historiographical Traditions and Modern Imperatives for the Restoration of Global History", *Journal of Global History*, 1 (2006), pp. 3–39, 38.

15. Jerry H. Bentley, "A New Forum for Global History", *Journal of World History*, 1 (1990), pp. iii–v, noted the increased awareness of historians regarding the changing position of the nation-state.

history a further specialization occurred, with one group studying the world as a whole (world historians) and another focusing on global connections and comparisons across regions and continents (global historians). Although the *Journal of World History* harboured both species, the *Journal of Global History* was founded in 2006 with explicit reference to the second group.[16] In calling attention to global connections, this Special Issue is strongly embedded within this latter trend of historiography, stressing further that globalization is a multifaceted process with both convergent and divergent trends that do not necessarily have to be "thick" to have a significant impact on localized societies.

ENVIRONMENTAL HISTORY

Since the start of the new millennium, environmental change has acquired an undisputed position in the historiography. It is invoked frequently by historians of all sorts and trades to explain the rise and decline of former civilizations such as that of the Fertile Crescent and of the Mayas. Also, short-term effects, such as weather conditions during major historical battles, have received increased attention.[17] But this is a rather recent phenomenon. For a long time, history traditionally studied the actions of humans in the past, with only scant attention paid to the environment, which was more often than not viewed as immovable and unchangeable.

Nowadays, environmental history is quite generally defined as the study of the interaction between humans and nature, or between society and nature, in the past.[18] The field received major stimuli with the growing awareness since the 1960s and 1970s of the impact of industrial pollution and nuclear waste.[19] The historical world witnessed a major institutionalization with the establishment of the American Society for Environmental History in 1975, followed by the publication of a journal, the *Environmental Review* (renamed *Environmental History* in the 1990s).

16. William Gervase Clarence-Smith, Kenneth Pomeranz, and Peer Vries, "Editorial", *Journal of Global History*, 1 (2006), pp. 1–2; O'Brien, "Historiographical Traditions", p. 7.
17. Jared Diamond, *Collapse: How Societies Choose to Fail or Succeed* (New York, 2005); Ian Whyte, *World Without End? Environmental Disaster and the Collapse of Empires* (London [etc.], 2008).
18. Wolfgang Behringer, *Kulturgeschichte des Klimas: Von der Eiszeit bis zur globalen Erwärmung* (Munich, 2007), p. 119; Timo Myllyntaus, "Environment in Explaining History: Restoring Humans as Part of Nature", in *idem* and Mikko Saikku (eds), *Encountering the Past in Nature: Essays in Environmental History* (Athens, OH, 2001), pp. 141–160, 143–145; Richard White, *The Organic Machine: The Remaking of the Columbia River* (New York, 1996), p. ix: "we cannot understand human history without natural history and we cannot understand natural history without human history. The two have been intertwined for millennia."
19. Alfred Crosby, "The Past and Present of Environmental History", *The American Historical Review*, 100 (1995), pp. 1177–1189, 1187–1188.

Since then, North America has always been home to a prominent group of environmental historians.[20] Europe followed in 1988 with the European Association for Environmental History, which published the *Environmental History Newsletter* before it became involved in the distribution of the journal *Environment and History* (published from 1995), of which Richard Grove was the founding editor, supported by colleagues from Europe, Africa, Asia, Australia, and the USA. Both journals set the academic standard for the field. The approach was strongly interdisciplinary, with contributions from historians, natural scientists, social scientists, and geographers, to mention only the most important. A couple of worldwide bestsellers rendered the field of study well known, notably Alfred W. Crosby's *Columbian Exchange* (1972) and *Ecological Imperialism* (1986); Donald Worster's *The Ends of the Earth* (1988); Clive Ponting's *A Green History of the World* (1991); Richard Grove's *Green Imperialism* (1995); Jared Diamond's *Guns, Germs and Steel* (1997); and John McNeill's *Something New Under the Sun* (2000). The creation of a new Italian historical journal in 2008, *Global Environment*, shows the strength and resilience of the environmental history approach.[21]

Environmental history at its best shares three characteristic tendencies with global history: the long-term perspective, the transnational and transcontinental connections, and the interdisciplinary approach. First, many topics in environmental history require a long-term perspective. Pollution is often a matter of one or more generations, most ecological catastrophes have long-term repercussions, and erosion and climatic changes usually span decades or even centuries. Not surprisingly, the *longue durée* of the *Annales* tradition comes to the foreground again.[22] Second, in spatial terms environmental history frequently transgresses national borders. Pollution does not stop at human-made frontiers; neither does erosion, let alone climate change. Like global historians, numerous environmental historians look beyond Eurocentric or Western-centric approaches by focusing on developments in Asia, Africa, Latin America, Australasia, and even the oceans. The relationship between

20. J. Donald Hughes, *What is Environmental History?* (Cambridge, 2006); Sverker Sörlin and Paul Warde, "The Problem of the Problem of Environmental History: A Re-Reading of the Field and Its Purpose", *Environmental History*, 12 (2007), pp. 107–130, 108.

21. The *bollettino* called *I Frutti di Demetra* serves Italian-speaking environmental historians. The Low Countries have shared a *Jaarboek voor Ecologische Geschiedenis* since the 1990s. See also Marjolein 't Hart, "Tussen dierenliefde en milieubeleid. Tien jaar ecologische geschiedschrijving in de Lage landen", *Jaarboek voor Ecologische Geschiedenis*, 10 (2007), pp. 23–44.

22. Fernand Braudel, *La Méditerranée et le Monde Méditerranéen à l'époque de Philippe IIe* (Paris, 1949); Emmanuel Le Roy Ladurie, *Histoire du climat depuis l'an mil* (Paris, 1967); Richard White, "American Environmental History: The Development of a New Historical Field", *Pacific Historical Review*, 54 (1985), pp. 297–335; J.R. McNeill, "Observations on the Nature and Culture of Environmental History", *History and Theory*, 42 (2003), pp. 5–43, 14.

colonialism/imperialism and ecological decline has received increased attention in the past two decades.[23] Third, the interdisciplinary approach is strong not only among world historians, but also in environmental history as the latter incorporates insights from a range of fields, including biology, chemistry, geology, and archaeology.[24] Characteristically, the youngest journal in the field of environmental history, *Global Environment*, carries the subtitle *A Journal of History and Natural and Social Sciences*.

As much of environmental history was and is linked to the growing concerns of the green social movement, the field is strongly problem-oriented. Topics typically deal with the spread of epidemic disease, the consequences of climatic change, the far-reaching effects of natural disasters, the reduction in ecological diversity, and humans overburdening the ecosystem, as witnessed by air, soil, and water pollution and the impoverishment and erosion of the soil.[25] Improved knowledge of El Niño climatic cycles has stimulated new research.[26] Such environmental causes carry an enormous weight, but it is the social, economic, cultural, and political context that can explain the actual impact and consequences in full. Why are comparable disasters less destructive than others, why are some societies more resilient than others, why are certain classes or groups hurt more than others? Such questions call for a strong association of environmental studies with social history.

SOCIAL HISTORY AND ENVIRONMENTAL STUDIES

Despite the potential links between social and environmental history, the two fields still retain their own preferences, leaving several obvious interconnections underdeveloped. Most social historians tend to look at nature, at the environment, as a given, as a constant entity that needs no further research. On the other hand, many environmental historians – often preoccupied with getting the necessary details from the natural sciences right – are inclined to look upon society as a homogeneous entity. The effects of disastrous floods or volcano eruptions, for example, are

23. David Arnold, *The Problem of Nature: Environment, Culture and European Expansion* (Oxford [etc.], 1996); Ramachandra Guha, *The Unquiet Woods: Ecological Change and Peasant Resistance in the Himalaya*, 2nd edn (Berkeley, CA, [etc.], 2000), p. xiii; John Richards, *The Unending Frontier: An Environmental History of the Early Modern World* (Berkeley, CA, [etc.], 2003); William Beinart and Lotte Hughes, *Environment and Empire* (Oxford, 2007).
24. J. Donald Hughes, "Three Dimensions of Environmental History", *Environment and History*, 14 (2008), pp. 319–330.
25. Myllyntaus, "Environment in Explaining History", p. 149.
26. Mike Davis, *Late Victorian Holocausts: El Niño Famines and the Making of the Third World* (London, 2001); Ross Couper-Johnston, *El Niño: The Weather Phenomenon that Changed the World* (London, 2001).

frequently studied only for societies as a whole, without taking into account the different groupings within those societies.[27] Even many of the environmentalist works within the widely acclaimed Annales School tended to overlook all sorts of societal differences.

Having said that, it should be pointed out that in several areas meaningful interaction can be found between social history and environmental studies. In this section we can stress only those that are of direct interest to this volume, centring, first, around the notion of vulnerability; secondly, imprudent environmental policies, related to the concept of unintended consequences; and, thirdly, social protests related to environmental policies (or the lack thereof), including the movement for environmental justice.

Vulnerability has recently become a major topic in environmental studies. Many disasters that seem purely "natural", such as earthquakes and floods, are often significantly aggravated by particular social policies or processes. Indeed, natural hazards turn into true disasters only if there is a high degree of vulnerability among a significant part of the population. Repeatedly, risks from natural catastrophes are greater for the poor, for racial and ethnic minorities, the less educated, and the politically powerless.[28] At the same time, those groups at the lower end of the social hierarchy often suffer disproportionably from environmental degradation.

Studies related to El Niño have become commonplace in this regard. Worldwide droughts had occurred before, yet since the late eighteenth century considerable segments of the peasant class were increasingly living at subsistence levels in monoculture environments, with the result that any small fluctuation in harvests or grain prices had disastrous consequences. With the changing forms of production and consumption, what mattered above all was the question of which groups had access to the existing resources.[29] In early nineteenth-century South Africa, for example, droughts destabilized above all the already marginalized indigenous

27. Alan Taylor, "Unnatural Inequalities: Social and Environmental Histories", *Environmental History*, 1:4 (1996), pp. 6–19, 7; Stephen Mosley, "Common Ground: Integrating Social and Environmental History", *Journal of Social History*, 39 (2006), pp. 915–933, 922.

28. Terry Cannon, "Vulnerability Analysis and the Explanation of 'Natural' Disasters", in Ann Varley (ed.), *Disasters, Development and Environment* (Chichester, 1994), pp. 13–31; Greg Bankoff, Georg Frerks, and Dorothea Hilhorst (eds), *Mapping Vulnerability: Disasters, Development and People* (London, 2004); Greg Bankoff, "Constructing Vulnerability: The Historical, Natural and Social Generation of Flooding in Metropolitan Manila", *Disasters*, 27 (2003), pp. 224–238; Michael Dorsey, "Globalizing Justice: Against Environmental Racism in the Age of Globalization", in Natalia Arias and Ivonne Yánez (eds), *Resistance: A Path Towards Sustainability* (Quito, 2000), pp. 37–50; Ted Steinberg, *Acts of God: The Unnatural History of Natural Disaster in America* (New York, 2000).

29. Davis, *Late Victorian Holocausts*, pp. 277ff.; Amartya Sen, *Poverty and Famines: An Essay on Entitlement and Deprivation* (Oxford, 1982); on subsistence in a global context see Marcel van der Linden, *Workers of the World: Essays Toward a Global Labor History* (Leiden, 2008), pp. 324ff.

agrarian communities and, at the same time, strengthened the establishment of British rule over the territories.[30]

Climatic changes did not always need to have so much effect. The degree of vulnerability mattered, as Emanuela Guidoboni showed for the sixteenth-century Po Valley. There, communities had grown increasingly vulnerable due to the deforestation and cultivation of mountain slopes, while recurrent near-famine conditions had already weakened the peasant class too. In such circumstances the increase in rainfall during the "Little Ice Age" – which was not actually that exceptional – resulted in floods with an extremely high number of casualties.[31] Another example is the rapid spread of the plague in fourteenth-century Europe, which cannot be attributed solely to the deathly germs. Prior to the plague's arrival, living standards had been lowered, not least by a series of volcanic eruptions that impacted climatic circumstances and thus increased vulnerability.[32]

Yet vulnerability can also result in social movements that reduce such risks. In eighteenth-century colonial Mexico, floods brought about an increased awareness and willingness to cooperate among riverine populations. The organizations transcended even traditional lines of ethnicity and class. Likewise, Greg Bankoff has noted the emergence of mutual associations in twentieth-century Manila, in particular in areas prone to earthquakes and typhoons, which significantly enlarged the resilience of these communities. Such associations proved helpful in all spheres of life.[33]

A second concept that will be discussed in this context pertains to that of unintended consequences. Nowadays, Iceland is dominated by sterile wasteland, but at the time of its initial settlement wasteland accounted for only one-fifth of the surface area. Overgrazing and concomitant erosion rendered Iceland a harsh place to live, reducing its population from some 80,000 in the twelfth century to well below 30,000 in the eighteenth

---

30. Charles Ballard, "Drought and Economic Distress", *Journal of Interdisciplinary History*, 17 (1986), pp. 359–378.
31. Emanuela Guidoboni, "Human Factors, Extreme Events and Floods in the Lower Po Plain (Northern Italy) in the 16th Century", *Environment and History*, 4 (1998), pp. 279–308.
32. M.G.L. Baillie, "Putting Abrupt Environmental Change Back into Human History", in Paul Slack (ed.), *Environments and Historical Change: The Linacre Lectures 1998* (Oxford, 1999), pp. 46–75, 64–70.
33. Georgina H. Endfield, Isabel Fernández Tejedo, and Sarah L. O'Hara, "Conflict and Cooperation: Water, Floods, and Social Response in Colonial Guanajuato, Mexico", *Environmental History*, 9 (2004), pp. 221–247; Greg Bankoff, "Dangers to Going it Alone: Social Capital and the Origins of Community Resilience in the Philippines", *Continuity and Change*, 22 (2007), pp. 327–355, 341; see also Enakshi Ganguly Thukral and Machindra D. Sakate, "Baliraja: A People's Alternative", in Enakshi Ganguly Thukral (ed.), *Big Dams, Displaced People: Rivers of Sorrow, Rivers of Change* (New Delhi, 1992), pp. 143–154. Regarding situations in which water is a scarce resource – thus requiring cooperation, yet in which conflicts abound – see Helga Haftendorn, "Water and International Conflict", *Third World Quarterly*, 21 (2000), pp. 51–68.

century, from being rather well-to-do farmers to becoming poor cottiers and fishermen. Another famous example is the case of the Aral Sea. Driven by the short-term performance planning of the Soviet regime, aimed at achieving self-sufficiency of cotton production in central Asia, planners did not consider the possible long-term impact of their ideas. The consequences were disastrous for all communities in the area.[34]

In the social sciences, the concept of unintended consequences was popularized by Robert K. Merton as the "unanticipated consequences of purposive social action". Whereas humans usually act on the basis of opinion and estimate, most knowledge stems from comparable actions in the past.[35] Here the particularities of the environment come to the forefront. The consequences of policies implicating the environment are frequently noticeable only after decades and are then often irreversible. Iceland's settlers did not realize the vulnerability of the island, as the environment in their home communities had not suffered from pasture at all. Decisions that worked well in the past may well be utterly destructive in later periods or in other settings; in this context the phrase "other things being equal" is often wrong as the environment is actually changing all the time.

A well-studied theme in this respect deals with conservation by colonial governments. In *Green Imperialism* Richard Grove established the growing awareness among colonial administrators of the possible detrimental effects of deforestation in particular. Within these colonial semi-scientific networks Grove even discovered the roots of Western environmentalism.[36] Although the latter is a rather contested viewpoint, the fact remains that conservation schemes in the colonies preceded those in the homelands themselves.

Such conservation policies carried consequences, of course, that were at least partially unintended.[37] The establishment of national parks and

---

34. Whyte, *World Without End?*, pp. 123, 201; Joachim Radkau, *Nature and Power: A Global History of the Environment* (Cambridge, 2008), pp. 154, 166. For an excellent introduction to the environmental effects of colonization policies in the early modern period, see Richards, *The Unending Frontier.*

35. Robert K. Merton, "The Unanticipated Consequences of Purposive Social Action", *American Sociological Review*, 1 (1936), pp. 894–904, 899. For an insightful elaboration regarding unintended consequences in state policies, see James Scott, *Seeing Like a State: How Certain Schemes to Improve the Human Condition Have Failed* (New Haven, CT, 1998).

36. Richard Grove, *Green Imperialism: Colonial Expansion, Tropical Islands Edens and the Origins of Environmentalism, 1600–1860* (Cambridge, 1995). On criticism regarding Grove's interpretations on the origins of environmentalism, see Radkau, *Nature and Power*, p. 128; S. Ravi Rajan, *Modernizing Nature: Forestry and Imperial Eco-Development, 1800–1950* (Oxford, 2006), p. 68.

37. Naturally, the effects of colonial policies were not always unintended. In the mid-nineteenth century, in order to improve the thrift of the colonized subjects, the British colonial secretary, Earl Grey, developed a tax system that was to fall in particular on those with the lowest incomes in the tropics. The scheme aimed to encourage positive working attitudes, as he

national forests in the US drove numerous Native Americans from their traditional grounds.[38] In twentieth-century Java the regulations to limit hunting implied that only those able to pay for a licence to hunt were allowed to do so, whereas large groups that previously had access were denied the right to those resources.[39] In a similar fashion, the German colonial regime in northern Tanzania undermined the position of the wealthier indigenous farmers, thereby upsetting the social networks that had allowed many people to survive drought and famine in earlier periods.[40] British engineers in India thought to improve the water management of the Indus with new dams and dykes and encouraged the founding of new settlements close to the river borders. However, those areas were also prone to flooding, which was the reason the local population had refrained from constructing houses there before. The result was increased vulnerability of the local population to natural hazards.[41]

Such policies, well-intended or not, provoked at times violent protests.[42] Complaints against the German colonial forest policy fed the Maji Maji rebellion of 1905–1907 in Tanzania.[43] Prior to the emergence of the *Zapatista* movement in Mexico, the small peasants in Chiapas had suffered from

---

was convinced that tropical life made people too content with subsistence (in contrast to people in temperate zones). The new hut and poll taxes, in addition to direct taxes on "provision grounds" (the lots formerly assigned in the Caribbean by the master to have the slaves provide their own food, after emancipation usually in the hands of former slaves and their descendants) disproportionably burdened the locals. This kind of pseudo-scientific reasoning actually continued until the next century. See Philip D. Curtin, "The Environment Beyond Europe and the European Theory of Empire", *Journal of World History*, 1 (1990), pp. 131–150, 148–149.

38. Robert H. Keller and Michael F. Turek, *American Indians & National Parks* (Tucson, AZ, 1998).

39. Peter Boomgaard, "Oriental Nature, Its Friends and Its Enemies: Conservation of Nature in Late-Colonial Indonesia, 1889–1949", *Environment and History*, 5 (1999), pp. 257–292, 273.

40. John R. McNeill, *Something New Under the Sun: An Environmental History of the Twentieth-Century World* (New York [etc.], 2000), p. 207.

41. Benjamin Weil, "The Rivers Come: Colonial Flood Control and Knowledge Systems in the Indus Basin, 1840s–1930s", *Environment and History*, 12 (2006), pp. 3–29, 14; see also Beinart and Hughes, *Environment and Empire*, p. 138, on the British perception of irrigation as a cure-all, even though famines persisted. On colonial policy to reduce vulnerability see Ravi Ahuja, "State Formation and 'Famine Policy' in Early Colonial South India", *Indian Economic and Social History Review*, 39 (2002), pp. 351–380.

42. Richard Grove, *Ecology, Climate and Empire: Colonialism and Global Environmental History, 1400–1940* (Cambridge, 1997), pp. 208–211. Not always, though, as shown by Grace Carswell, "Soil Conservation Policies in Colonial Kigezi, Uganda: Successful Implementation and an Absence of Resistance", in William Beinart and Joann McGregor (eds), *Social History & African Environments* (Oxford [etc.], 2003), pp. 131–154, thanks largely to the fact that the colonial government used local chiefs to implement their policies – as a result, local conditions were taken into account more.

43. Thaddeus Sunseri, "Reinterpreting a Colonial Rebellion: Forestry and Social Control in German East Africa, 1874–1915", *Environmental History*, 8 (2003), pp. 430–451.

ecological marginalization.[44] In South Africa, a series of protests followed the introduction of the government's policy to prevent the spread of the deadly East Coast fever. The best solution was the regular dipping of all cattle, preferably every week, to kill off the ticks that transmitted the disease. The new regulations, however, interfered strongly with the traditions of the inhabitants of Transkei, as cattle constituted their main form of accumulation and status, and dipping (at the state-owned tanks) increased the costs enormously (a fee per head of cattle was to be paid at every dipping), while trade and transport were hindered considerably. Numerous grievances were voiced – including the suspicion that the whites allowed the disease to rage deliberately in order to undermine African society, forcing young men to work in the new enterprises of the colonists. Violent attacks on state officials followed in 1914.[45]

The leading work in this field is Ramachandra Guha's path-breaking *The Unquiet Woods*. With the commercialization of the forests in the Himalayas, access to the means of production was radically altered. The British did not recognize communal rights but wished to deal only with individual farmers, which threatened, in particular, the traditional rights of grazing and fuel gathering. In the waves of protest that followed, official buildings were set fire to and the forest blocks targeted by the authorities for cutting down destroyed. After Indian independence, commercialization continued, however. A disastrous flood in 1970 fuelled the rise of a new movement that stressed the ruinous effects of deforestation. In the village of Reni, female peasants started to embrace trees in order to prevent them being felled in 1974 (see Figure 1). This non-violent means of protest was soon adopted elsewhere and the Chipko movement (*chipko* means "to hug") proved extremely successful, bringing commercial forestry in the area to a standstill. Thereafter, environmentalist movements in various other countries started to regard "Chipko" as a benchmark for inspiration, providing a bridge between localized protest and global action.[46]

In the US, the awareness of inequalities in access to the available resources, coupled with increased environmental degradation, nourished the movement for environmental justice in the 1980s. Activists regarded environmental protection as an unalienable right of man, and called for sustainable development with equal access to existing resources. The participants,

44. Philip Howard, "The History of Ecological Marginalization in Chiapas", *Environmental History*, 3 (1998), pp. 357–377.
45. Colin Bundy, "'We Don't Want Your Rain, We Won't Dip': Popular Opposition, Collaboration and Social Control in the Anti-Dipping Movement, 1908–16", in William Beinart and Colin Bundy, *Hidden Struggles in Rural South Africa: Politics and Popular Movements in the Transkei and Eastern Cape, 1890–1930* (London [etc.], 1987), pp. 191–221.
46. Guha, *The Unquiet Woods*, pp. 27–56, 152–184, 198–199; Beinart and Hughes, *Environment and Empire*, p. 277. Chipko also inspired the early Greenpeace movement.

Figure 1. Chipko movement: children and women embracing a tree, 1987.
Photograph: The Right Livelihood Award.

largely low-income women and blacks, differed from those in the mainstream environmental movement, which was predominantly middle-class, male, and white.[47] The principles of environmental justice were picked up in other countries, and became a true global social movement. The indigenous rights movement swelled in the 1980s and gained a strong foothold in international forums in the 1990s.[48]

In turn, this movement inspired social historians to look at environmental degradation in relation to class, gender, and ethnicity.[49] Some scholars focused on the impact of global economic trends on spatial allocations. The worldwide drive towards industrialization was so overriding that the entrepreneurial class frequently won in the struggles over the use of urban space, the local authorities failing or unwilling to implement existing environmental laws.[50] Other scholars noted the consequences of global economic trends on trade-union policies. The major concessions that activists achieved at the Anaconda copper smelter in Montana (including the right to refuse to work in unsafe conditions without loss of pay) were curtailed with the global recession of the 1970s. That same depression caused the collapse of the coalition between lower-class black activists and middle-class environmentalists in the metal works in

---

47. Giovanna Di Chiro, "Nature as Community: The Convergence of Environment and Social Justice", in William Cronon (ed.), *Uncommon Ground: Toward Reinventing Nature* (New York, 1995), pp. 298–320, 300, 307.

48. Joan Martinez-Alier, *The Environmentalism of the Poor: A Study of Ecological Conflicts and Valuation* (Cheltenham [etc.], 2002), pp. 168ff.; Arias and Yánez, *Resistance: A Path Towards Sustainability*; Beinart and Hughes, *Environment and Empire*, pp. 327ff. Patricia Widener applied a truly transnational perspective in analysing the various protests along a pipeline owned by a multinational corporation in the oil exploitation in Ecuador: the Amazon, the Andes, and Pacific Coast; Patricia Widener, "Global Links and Environmental Flows: Oil Disputes in Ecuador", *Global Environment Politics*, 9 (2009), pp. 31–57. The brutal exploitation of the surrounding environment of two communities by the same international company is studied in Frank Meyer, "Expanding the Frontiers of Labour History: Kjartan Fløgstad's Synthesis of Local, Global, and Environmental History", *International Review of Social History*, 54 (2009), pp. 95–109.

49. Carolyn Merchant, "Shades of Darkness: Race and Environmental History", *Environmental History*, 8 (2003), pp. 380–394; *idem*, "Gender and Environmental History", *Journal of American History*, 76 (1990), pp. 1117–1121; Robert Bullard (ed.), *Confronting Environmental Racism, Voices from the Grassroots* (Boston, MA, 1993); Dolores Greenberg, "Reconstructing Race and Protest: Environmental Justice in New York City", *Environmental History*, 5 (2000), pp. 223–250; Angela Gugliotta, "Class, Gender, and Coal Smoke: Gender Ideology and Environmental Injustice in Pittsburgh, 1868–1914", *Environmental History*, 5 (2000), pp. 165–193. See also Shirley Bradway Laska, "Environmental Sociology and the State of the Discipline", *Social Forces*, 72 (1993), pp. 1–17.

50. Geneviève Massard-Guilbaud, "The Struggle for Urban Space: Nantes and Clermont-Ferrand, 1830–1930", in Dieter Schott, Bill Luckin, and Geneviève Massard-Guilbaud (eds), *Resources of the City: Contributions to an Environmental History of Modern Europe* (Aldershot, 2005), pp. 113–131.

Gary, Indiana.[51] Among geographers, the far-reaching social implications of globalizing capitalism and the new implications of "space" led to the emergence of critical geographical studies.[52]

TRANSNATIONAL AGENTS, ENVIRONMENTAL CHANGE, AND SOCIAL CONSEQUENCES

As argued earlier, globalization, though often perceived as a recent phenomenon, is actually a much older process, going back many centuries and even millennia. In a similar vein, people often associate environmental problems with the past fifty years or so, while it would not be difficult to provide examples of such problems, created by environmental change, originating several thousand years ago. Therefore, globalization and environmental change, often operating in tandem, are age-old but often underestimated historical processes. This volume presents case studies that touch on five major themes of great importance for environmental historians: species transmission, agricultural policies, energy usage, mining, and water management.

Possibly one of the oldest and most ubiquitous examples of environmental change is the spread of plants and animals from their region of origin to other parts of the globe (species transmission). Originally, the plants were mainly, if not exclusively, domesticated ones that produced food, fodder, oil, and fibres to be used for textile or rope, dyes, perfumes, and medicine, while the animals were also domesticated, and served humankind as food (or were at least a source of food), companions, means of transportation, traction, and as beasts of burden. Later, ornamental plants would come to play a considerable role in these plant migrations, as would trees that were to be planted in deforested regions. Perhaps the best-known episode in this global movement of plants and animals is the so-called Columbian Exchange, the term coined for the post-1492 migration of crops and animals from the New World to Africa and Eurasia, and from the Old World to the New, as documented by Alfred Crosby. Thus, potatoes, tomatoes, and paprikas were introduced to Europe, maize (corn) and cassava to Africa, and maize, sweet potatoes, chillies, and tobacco to Asia, while wheat, rice, cattle, and horses came from the Old World to the New.[53]

51. Laurie Mercier, *Anaconda: Labor, Community, and Culture in Montana's Smelter City* (Urbana, IL, 2001), pp. 195–197; Andrew Hurley, *Environmental Inequalities: Class, Race, and Industrial Pollution in Gary, Indiana, 1945–1990* (Chapel Hill, NC, 1995), pp. 147–149.

52. David Harvey, *Spaces of Capital: Towards a Critical Geography* (New York, 2001); Andrew Herod, "The Practice of International Labor Solidarity and the Geography of the Global Economy", *Economic Geography*, 71 (1995), pp. 341–363.

53. Alfred W. Crosby, *The Columbian Exchange: Biological and Cultural Consequences of 1492* (Westport, CT, 1972); *idem, Ecological Imperialism: The Biological Expansions of Europe, 900–1900* (Cambridge, 1987).

Such introductions were often deliberate attempts, undertaken by European merchant companies and colonizers, to generate a larger flow of commodities from the regions under their control. However, the introduction of various carbohydrate-rich crops, such as cereals, and roots and tubers, is less well documented. Sometimes they were introduced in order to increase food security in areas where the Europeans aimed at a shift from labour-intensive food crops to equally labour-intensive export crops. More often, we do not know when and why seeds or cuttings from these crops were brought over to other areas, and we can only conclude that at a certain moment they began to be successfully cultivated in regions where they did not occur before.[54]

The environmental changes brought about by these plant and animal migrations were far-reaching. Landscapes changed beyond recognition. This was the case, for instance, when the new crops were cultivated commercially on large estates (plantations), as happened with sugar, coffee, cacao, tobacco, tea, rubber, and oil palm. But it also occurred in the case of cereals such as maize, which now covers, often almost as a monoculture, large areas in Eurasia where smallholder agriculture is predominant. In many cases, the new crops "colonized" hitherto uncultivated areas, particularly in the ecologically vulnerable uplands, which often led to deforestation and erosion. Similar environmental damage was caused in areas where large ruminants had been absent before their post-1492 introduction.[55]

The increasing popularity of environmental history and the recent trend towards global warming have led to a growing emphasis in historical studies on climate change in the past, and a gradually warmer climate between 1670 and 1800 is now sometimes cited as the main factor behind increased rates of population growth.[56] However, it is also likely that the newly introduced, "alien" food crops, with high carbohydrate content, often yielding more calories per unit of land and/or per unit of labour, or being cultivated in places that were too cold or too steep for other crops, contributed to these higher growth rates, probably at least partly also because their presence led to crop diversification, and therefore lower famine risk.[57] Thus, the Columbian Exchange may have contributed to

---

54. Peter Boomgaard, "Maize and Tobacco in Upland Indonesia, 1600–1940", in Tania Murray Li (ed.), *Transforming the Indonesian Uplands: Marginality, Power and Production* (Amsterdam, 1999), pp. 45–78; Peter Boomgaard, "In the Shadow of Rice: Roots and Tubers in Indonesian History, 1500–1950", *Agricultural History*, 77 (2003), pp. 582–610.
55. Richards, *The Unending Frontier*.
56. Anthony N. Penna, *The Human Footprint: A Global Environmental History* (Chichester, 2010), pp. 98–103.
57. See for instance Geoffrey C. Gunn, *First Globalization: The Eurasian Exchange, 1500–1800* (Lanham, MD, [etc.], 2003), p. 204; Behringer, *Kulturgeschichte des Klimas*, p. 226; Cormac Ó Gráda, *Famine: A Short History* (Princeton, NJ, 2009), pp. 70–72.

higher population densities, during an epoch in which population growth rates and densities were generally speaking relatively low, which was the usual state of affairs in most areas of the world prior to 1950.

Some transmissions were truly unintended, such as the mosquito that travelled with the slave ships to the Caribbean sugar-plantation economies carrying the deadly Yellow Fever. The blacks themselves had inherited immunity to this disease, but the Europeans had not. The hidden transmission caused the death of numerous British soldiers sent to these islands to crush slave resistance, and furthered the cause of the Haitian rebels in the early nineteenth century: as soon as the spring rains facilitated the multiplication of the mosquitoes, French soldiers sent by Napoleon were decimated by Yellow Fever.[58]

In this volume, we encounter several examples of species transmission. It is the main theme of Bennett's essay on the introduction of eucalyptus species, originally trees growing in Australia, into South Africa, India, and Thailand, mainly between 1850 and 2000. The trees were often introduced because forestation or reforestation was deemed necessary by functionaries of the (indigenous, colonial, and postcolonial) forest departments, and eucalypts were fast-growing species. Bennett argues that the trees had many disadvantages, particularly for local smallholders, of which a voracious appetite for water was one. Thus, the continued planting of these trees sparked off local protest movements, for instance in Thailand in recent times. Both the need for reforestation and the fact that so many forestry experts opted for the same solution can be seen as features of the globalization process.[59]

Another example of the introduction of alien species is to be found in the essay by Halikowski Smith, dealing with the "discovery" and colonization of the mid-Atlantic islands – the Canary Islands, Madeira, the Azores, Cape Verde – in the fifteenth and sixteenth centuries by the Portuguese and the Spaniards. Various "new" crops were introduced, including sugar cane and grapes as commercial crops, and various cereals

---

58. J.R. McNeill, *Mosquito Empires: Ecology and War in the Greater Caribbean, 1620–1914* (New York [etc.], 2010). Equally unintended was the spread of the *Aedes albopictus*, also known as the Asian tiger mosquito, carrying a number of viruses that were causative agents of epidemic diseases, including Dengue Fever, which can be life-threatening and for which no vaccine yet exists. Several decades ago, this disease was typically found in tropical areas only. But with the globalization of the used-tyres economy, the Asian tiger mosquito seems to have been a frequent passenger in the tyre casings. Rubber tyres thus spread Dengue Fever worldwide. Donald Kennedy and Marjorie Lucks, "Rubber, Blight, and Mosquitoes: Biogeography Meets the Global Economy", *Environmental History*, 4 (1999), pp. 369–383, 377; Wouter van der Weijden, Rob Leewis, and Pieter Bol, *Biological Globalisation: Bio-Invasions and their Impacts on Nature, the Economy and Public Health* (Utrecht, 2007), pp. 157–158.

59. Eucalypts were planted not only in a colonial or tropical context, but also in Europe, for instance in Spain and Italy.

as subsistence crops (though some of these were exported, creating food shortages). The introduction of these crops was preceded by the large-scale and rapid deforestation of the islands; the introduction of livestock had similar effects. These islands were usually underpopulated – if not empty – when the European settlers arrived. However, the environmental effects of rapid deforestation, brought about not only by the free settlers themselves but also by black slaves and white convict and indentured labourers often imported to the islands in order to speed up the land-clearing process, and the combination of too many hectares planted with export crops and a lack of food crops, caused overpopulation and emigration. Soon, the production of sugar on these islands was no longer profitable, and sugar cane migrated onwards to Brazil and later to the Caribbean.[60] It may be mentioned as an aside that deforestation was a problem that would continue to plague the islands, and for which on Madeira eucalypts were planted as a remedy.[61]

The essay by Horan takes the story up on the eighteenth-century Caribbean sugar plantations, where the slave population was now having problems very similar to those experienced a few centuries earlier on the mid-Atlantic islands. French sugar planters – and presumably those of other nationalities as well – were having so much trouble feeding their black slaves adequately, largely because sugar took up so much space (and time), that the production of food crops, or the collection of foodstuffs in the uncultivated areas, including hunting, was at times insufficient. This situation led to undernourishment, malnutrition, famine, high morbidity, and high mortality. Thus the introduction of a new crop – sugar – was the cause of the introduction of black slaves while the expansion of sugar led to high mortality among the slaves and therefore to the perpetuation of the slave trade. The sustained and increasing supply of cane sugar from the West Indies (and elsewhere) was, of course, a response to increasing global demand.[62]

The food supply problem, which appears to have become more acute as time went by, no doubt because sugar became increasingly a monoculture and covered larger sections of the islands (although there were considerable differences between the islands), lies at the root of the famous

---

60. José Padua established an intricate relationship between the exploitative views connected with slavery and racism and the rigorous deforestation of the tropical forests in Brazil: to the colonizers, both labour and environment seemed inexhaustible resources; José Augusto Padua, "European Colonialism and Tropical Forest Destruction in Brazil", in J.R. McNeill, J.A. Padua, and Mahesh Rangarajan (eds), *Environmental History: As if Nature Existed* (Oxford, 2010), pp. 130–150.
61. Personal observation of one of the authors.
62. Sidney W. Mintz, *Sweetness and Power: The Place of Sugar in Modern History* (New York, 1985); Richards, *The Unending Frontier*, pp. 412–460.

story – not told by Horan – of Captain William Bligh, who, in 1776, was
sent out by London to Tahiti, in the Pacific, to collect breadfruit plants
which then were to be transported to the Caribbean. This tree took little
time to grow, its carbohydrate-rich fruit was easily harvested, and could
feed many people; the plant was therefore ideal for the Caribbean situation (see Figure 2). The journey, however, ended in the infamous mutiny
on the *Bounty*, and Bligh was forced to leave his ship in a boat. He lived to
tell the tale, however, and returned to the Pacific many years later, taking
347 breadfruit plants to the West Indies, where they became a success.[63]
The comparison is perhaps not entirely fair, but it would appear that
while, according to Horan, the French planters did not do much more
than complain that the French merchants who monopolized the trade
with the French West Indies were involved in a conspiracy ("famine plot")
against the colonists in order to keep food prices high, the British
authorities actually tried to do something about it.

Changing agricultural policies and practices should be mentioned as the
second theme that goes to the heart of environmental history. Throughout
history, rulers and governments have attempted to influence their peasantry
and their larger landowners (aristocracy) with regard to the crops they were
growing, the time they started planting, cropping and land-use patterns, and
the places where new arable lands were cleared. It goes without saying that
such attempts – if successful – changed the landscape considerably.[64]

Many of the essays included in this volume address the environmental
effects of agricultural developments in the remote or recent past to a
greater or lesser extent – Halikowski Smith, Morera, Horan, Kanda, and
Nascimento and Becker. However, only in the contribution written by
Thompson are changing agricultural policies and practices the main
theme. He discusses changes in agricultural practices, largely as a consequence of colonial and postcolonial policies, in post-1930 Rhodesia/
Zimbabwe. Thompson shows how measures in agriculture, designed by
the colonial agricultural extension services, and backed by the colonial
civil service, in addition to better access to markets through the construction of roads, led to the introduction of new technology (ploughs for
example), new cropping and land-use patterns, and shifts from subsistence
to market crops. These policies represented globally held notions, or at

---

63. See for instance Gunn, *First Globalization*, p. 76.
64. A few examples are Carville Earle, "The Myth of the Southern Soil Miner: Macrohistory,
Agricultural Innovation, and Environmental Change", in Donald Worster (ed.), *The Ends of the
Earth: Perspectives on Modern Environmental History* (Cambridge, 1988), pp. 175–210; Clive
Ponting, *A Green History of the World* (London, 1991), pp. 37–116; Helen Wheatly (ed.),
Agriculture, Resource Exploitation, and Environmental Change (Aldershot, 1997); McNeill,
Something New Under the Sun, pp. 212–227; J. Donald Hughes, *An Environmental History of
the World: Humankind's Changing Role in the Community of Life* (London, 2002), pp. 30–140.

Figure 2. This is the breadfruit tree (*Artocarpus altilis*), which was taken by Captain William Bligh from the Pacific to the Caribbean in the late eighteenth century. Here it was planted in order to feed the slaves on the plantations.
Source: G.E. Rumphius, Herbarium Amboinense/Het Amboinsche Kruid-boek *(Amsterdam, Changuion [etc.], 1741–1750), I, plate xxxiii, opposite p. 114.*
Courtesy KITLV, Leiden.

least notions held by most Western agronomists, regarding changes that would improve yields in tropical agriculture, standards of living, and local food security (and would probably produce higher tax returns as well). In Rhodesia, all this occurred in combination with the land-segregation policies of the colonial regime.

Many of the new practices represented environmental change, as was the case with more "waste" land coming under cultivation, fields with single crops taking the place of intercropped arable lands, the application of manure, and the increased need for weeding. These shifts in agricultural practices, in turn, changed specific rights, obligations, and workloads, leading to gender and generational conflicts, and new relations between men and women, and fathers and sons.[65]

Another major theme in environmental history is the use of energy, and the way in which, on the one hand, increasing energy consumption led to environmental changes, while on the other hand environmental changes (such as deforestation) led to a shift from biomass (firewood, charcoal, peat, straw, grass, cow dung) to fossil fuels (coal, oil, gas). Although locally some types of biomass fuel became scarce at an early stage, it is in principle a renewable energy source, while fossil fuels are not – they will eventually run out.

Britain was the first country where the growing use of firewood and charcoal caused the forest cover to shrink so much that by the late eighteenth century there was no longer sufficient biomass fuel, which had also become very expensive. This led to a shift from firewood and charcoal to coal for many households and industrial processes. At the same time, differential access to the new fuel resources hardened existing class distinctions.[66] The shift played an important role in the Industrial Revolution and in "the Rise of the West". In the twentieth century, a gradual shift from coal to oil occurred, and the availability of cheap oil led to high economic growth rates. Fuel consumption, therefore, is an important theme in environmental history,

---

65. Recurrently, colonial administrators undervalued the productive role of female peasants. In the land settlements schemes of Malawi in the 1950s, the administrators tried to abolish matrilocality, which had long ensured women's access to land, as they regarded it as an obstacle to growth by preventing the rise of a male breadwinner class; John McCracken, "Conservation & Resistance in Colonial Malawi: The 'Dead North' Revisited", in Beinart and McGregor, *Social History & African Environments*, pp. 155–174, 168. In Kenya, women resisted official orders to plant maize only and continued to grow drought-resistant millet: Beinart and Hughes, *Environment and Empire*, p. 287.
66. Wrigley stated that class positions were henceforth no longer defined merely by access to land and capital goods, but also by access to the new energy resources; E.A. Wrigley, "Meeting Human Energy Needs: Constraints, Opportunities, and Effects", in Slack, *Environments and Historical Change*, pp. 76–95, 88. Wrigley noted also that the shift from biomass to fossil fuels rendered poverty more than before a social-political issue. In pre-industrial societies, access to the energy stored in the environment was limited, which reduced the possible range of actions. With the new energy systems, it had become possible to reduce poverty significantly. Failure or unwillingness to reduce poverty thus became, more than before, a moral issue.

and many scholars have emphasized increasing and changing energy consumption as a driving force in history.[67] Moreover, in numerous instances collecting biomass fuel (together with land clearing for agriculture) caused, as we have seen, deforestation, while the production of fossil fuel led in many cases to ruined landscapes and pollution. Production and consumption of all types of fuel feature prominently in the global warming debate.

Fuel consumption is addressed, as an aside, in various contributions in this volume, for instance by Halikowski Smith, Horan, and Bennett, but only in Kanda's essay is it the main theme. Her essay deals with the ways in which changes in local and global demand for salt and other commodities influenced the use of biomass and fossil fuels, the demand for which, in turn, caused problems for the salt makers in India in the first half of the nineteenth century. Salt-making was a British "colonial" – East India Company – monopoly, which had to compete for fuel with other types of "industrial" enterprise promoted, undertaken, or monopolized by the Company (opium, silk, indigo, sugar cane), and with modern water transport – steamers – introduced by the British. This competition led to scarcity and a rise in fuel prices, but local circumstances dictated what type of fuel would become scarce – sometimes it was locally produced coal, but in other places firewood was more expensive and harder to obtain than coal, while elsewhere markets developed for grasses, stalks, and straw, which until then had usually been "free goods".[68]

In the 1840s, many Indian salt makers stopped being active in this trade because the salt they produced had become too expensive due to the high fuel prices. Not much later, cheap salt would be imported from Britain. Thus the local scarcity of biomass fuels led, as it did in Britain earlier, to coal mining, but the shift from biomass to coal was much more localized and had totally different economic and social consequences than it did in Britain. Part of the explanation for these differences is no doubt that India was a quasi-colony around that time, while England was not.[69]

---

67. I.G. Simmons, *Changing the Face of the Earth: Culture, Environment, History* (Oxford, 1989); Ponting, *A Green History of the World*, pp. 267–294; McNeill, *Something New Under the Sun*; Edmund Burke III, "The Big Story: Human History, Energy Regimes, and the Environment", in *idem* and Kenneth Pomeranz (eds), *The Environment and World History* (Berkeley, CA [etc.], 2009), pp. 33–53.

68. The redistribution of colonial forest endowments usually resulted in a worsening position of the poor, if only for the loss of cheap fuel. Only the wealthier farmers had the means to buy the wood that was henceforth sold on the market; Rabindra Nath Chakraborty, "Links Between Income Distribution and Environmental Degradation in Rural India", in Stig Toft Madsen (ed.), *State, Society and the Environment in South Asia* (Richmond, 1999), pp. 165–199, 190.

69. See for instance Michael Mann, "Ecological Change in North India: Deforestation and Agrarian Distress in the Ganga-Yamuna Doab 1800–1850", in Richard H. Grove, Vinita Damodaran, and Satpal Sangwan (eds), *Nature and the Orient: The Environmental History of South and Southeast Asia* (Delhi [etc.], 1998), pp. 396–420, 398.

Kanda's contribution deals with fuel, but also with extractive industries, or, in other words, "mining" (salt, coal). Mining ought to be another important theme in environmental history, although in few textbooks is it paid more than scant attention.[70] Many, if not most, extractive industries all over the world have in common the fact that they were (and are) unhealthy and dangerous – and hence often carried out by slaves, convict labour (often chain gangs), *corvée* and other forms of compulsory labour, or by those at the bottom of the heap who have no alternatives – and that they destroy the local landscape, turning it into what is often called a "moon landscape". In addition, mining operations often poison down-river areas with the chemicals they use (for instance in gold, silver, and mercury mines) and the sludge they produce. It goes without saying that this state of affairs caused health problems among the miners and the inhabitants of adjacent areas, problems often reinforced by the creation of pockets of stagnant water, a sure source of malaria and other mosquito-transmitted diseases.[71]

In this volume, the contribution by Bruno also addresses the conditions under which mining took place, in this case in the Khibiny Mountains in the Soviet Union (close to the border with Finland) in the 1930s. It tells the story of a group of *kulaks* – relatively well-off peasants, deemed class enemies by the Soviet state – who were stripped of their property, and forced to migrate to this inhospitable region, where they had to work in the apatite mines, in compulsory labour therefore. Apatite is a form of calcium phosphate which can be used to manufacture phosphate fertilizer.

The "special settlers" had to work under appalling conditions, not only because of the low temperatures, but also owing to the lack of food, proper housing, drinking water, waste disposal, and other features of elementary hygiene. This population, already quite vulnerable under "normal" circumstances, was therefore hit even harder than others when harvests in the grain-producing areas of the Soviet Union failed, as was the case in 1932–1933. Death from starvation was now added to diseases caused by malnutrition, such as scurvy and rickets. Water that had to be used for drinking, washing, and bathing was polluted with the waste products of the mines, and with human waste. Thus, the silver mines in classical Athens, the gold and coal mines in seventeenth- to nineteenth-century Sumatra, and the apatite mines in Stalinist Russia had in common

---

70. For a brief overview of mining and its impact on the environment during the past two centuries, see McNeill, *Something New Under the Sun*, pp. 31–35. A recent case study is Jason W. Moore, "Silver, Ecology, and the Origins of the Modern World, 1450–1640", in Alf Hornborg, J.R. McNeill, and Joan Martinez-Alier (eds), *Rethinking Environmental History: World-System History and Global Environmental Change* (Lanham, MD [etc.], 2007), pp. 123–142.
71. Radkau, *Nature and Power*, pp. 237, 244.

that they were run largely by unfree labour, in addition to being a source of pollution to their natural environment, which undermined the health of the labourers.

A last theme of great importance to the environmental historian is the multifaceted role of water in history. As Bruno's contribution to this volume shows, the absence of clean, unpolluted water is a threat to human health. But even clean water can be harmful to humans, as it might be a home to mosquito larvae that could eventually turn into disease carriers, as was shown in an earlier part of this introduction.[72] At the same time, water had (and has) many competing uses – it is needed for irrigation, for transport, it is a home to fish and other organisms, and it powers hydroelectric plants.[73]

In this volume, Nascimento and Becker sketch the development of a river system in twentieth-century Brazil, the São Francisco River Basin, from the 1930s, and more in detail after c.1950. Their contribution demonstrates how population growth, urbanization, and the desire for "development" and industrialization (linked to growing global demand and supported by global capital flows) led to an emphasis on hydroelectric power plants, the construction of which competed with the river's other functions, including being a source of irrigation, a means of transportation (shipping), a spawning ground for fish, and a provider of fertile silt.

This policy obviously caused considerable environmental change, transforming the physical structure of the river bed, and the type of agriculture and livestock keeping, and therefore the landscape in the watershed area. While this policy stimulated migration of people from outside the watershed to a number of towns and cities in the region, it also drove away – or at least put out of business – small fishermen, boat and ship owners, and smallholder agriculturalists. Elsewhere, similar trends were noted: the spread of perennial irrigation strengthens the dependency on export cash crops at the expense of subsistence food crops.[74]

The essay by Morera also deals with water management, this time in seventeenth-century France. Here, Dutch capital (with links to the Dutch East India Company), Dutch technology (windmills), and Dutch know-how were being employed to drain wetlands, thus stimulating local agriculture. Those who financed this enterprise obtained various rights to local lands and waters, thanks to the support of the local aristocracy-cum-bureaucracy, who had a stake in the positive outcome and whose position

---

72. Whether irrigation furthered the spread of malaria depended on many aspects, such as the proliferation of fish and frogs that eat the larvae of the mosquito.
73. Peter H. Gleick (ed.), *Water in Crisis* (New York, 1993); McNeill, *Something New Under the Sun*, pp. 118–191; Peter Boomgaard (ed.), *A World of Water: Rain, Rivers and Seas in Southeast Asian Histories* (Leiden, 2007).a
74. Beinart and Hughes, *Environment and Empire*, p. 144.

was strengthened by these activities. This was to the detriment of many smallholder peasants and fishermen in those regions, as is shown by various recorded conflicts and law suits. The reclamation of moors and swamps became a truly global trend in the eighteenth century, stretching from Europe to China, altering physical space and reinforcing the position of local elites at the same time.[75] In the French case, it was not so much a matter of global demand (although some of the products of these "polders" were exported), but of the global supply of capital in combination with the global spread of new technology and know-how.

CONCLUSION

All the contributions to this Special Issue focus on the links between environmental and social history, especially in connection with changes induced by long-term processes of globalization. Invariably, they reflect fruitful recent and ongoing research. The field is still rather young, dating largely from the past two decades, as this introduction demonstrates.

The authors illustrate the far-reaching consequences of global processes for social relations, which are not necessarily limited to the late nineteenth or twentieth centuries. Morera, for example, shows how the ruling classes in France managed to strengthen their position with the support of the networks of Dutch capitalists in the seventeenth century while thoroughly transforming the environment. In the early modern period, therefore, transnational agents also left long-lasting footprints in the environment that predisposed the position of social classes and groups. Such footprints were exceptionally large on the islands in the Caribbean and the mid-Atlantic, as Horan and Halikowski Smith make clear, although the term "ecocide" might be too strong a term to describe what happened. The notion of expanded globalization seems quite appropriate in these cases.

This volume also reveals both convergent and divergent trends in global history. Convergence was at times strong, as exemplified by Bennett (eucalypt trees being planted in several regions around the world), Morera (water management in France and Holland), Thompson (agricultural colonial policies in British colonies), Nascimento and Becker (irrigation agriculture and global consumer demands), and Halikowski Smith (sugar plantations on numerous Atlantic islands). In other cases divergence dominates, for example among the 60,000 or so salt workers of the British East India Company in Bengal, with highly localized problems and solutions to the worldwide rise in fuel prices depending upon regional environmental circumstances (Kanda's contribution). Horan notes equally different approaches and outlooks among British and French

---

75. *Ibid.*, p. 146; Radkau, *Nature and Power*, p. 197.

plantation owners in the Caribbean, although the global setting of sugar plantation slavery posed quite similar problems.

Within these different global trends transnational agents operated, at times with unintended consequences. Nascimento and Becker show how the emphasis on irrigation and hydropower rendered large groups in Brazil more disaster-prone than before by limiting their access to water resources. An increased unequal exposure to risk was encountered among the "special settlers" of the Soviet Khibiny Mountains in Bruno's contribution and the slaves on the French Caribbean plantations in Horan's article. The problems following the planting of eucalypts in South Africa, India, and Thailand shown in Bennett's article, undoubtedly another unintended consequence of conservation policies, caused the rise of social protests – protests that were also reported to have occurred after the draining of the swamps in seventeenth-century France, as Morera demonstrates.

Globalization thus not only increased the vulnerability of marginalized groups, it also fuelled the formulation of environmental concerns and the formation of environmental interest groups. In the twenty-first century, globalization continues to give rise to transnational protest, as exemplified by the Chipko movement and the plea for environmental justice gaining global dimensions.

IRSH 55 (2010), Supplement, pp. 27–50 doi:10.1017/S0020859010000489
© 2010 Internationaal Instituut voor Sociale Geschiedenis

The El Dorado of Forestry: The Eucalyptus in India, South Africa, and Thailand, 1850–2000*

BRETT M. BENNETT

College of Humanities and Languages, University of Western Sydney

E-mail: utxaustinbennet@yahoo.com

SUMMARY: This article argues that because of the perceived and real biological characteristics of the different species of the genus *Eucalyptus*, imperialists and settlers, and later governments and the elites of developing nations, planted eucalypts widely and created new socio-ecological systems that encouraged and reinforced divergent patterns of economic, social, and ecological development. Planting eucalypts changed local ecologies and encouraged a movement towards market-based capitalism that benefited settlers, large landowners, urban elites and middle classes, and capital-intensive industries at the expense of indigenous groups living in and near forests. This article analyses the globalization of eucalypts in four broad phases: first, an enthusiastic expansion and planting from 1850–1900; secondly, failure in the tropics from 1850–1960; thirdly, increased planting and success rates in the tropics from 1960–2000, and fourthly, a growing criticism of eucalypts that began in the late nineteenth century and blossomed in the 1980s during an intense period of planting in India and Thailand.

INTRODUCTION

The different species of the genus *Eucalyptus* should be considered the fountain of youth and the El Dorado of forestry: for over 150 years people believed eucalypts could cure tropical diseases while also providing a source of continuously renewable wealth. Eucalypts were planted in a variety of climates in Australia, Asia, Africa, Europe, South America, and North America. Foresters and botanists were impressed by their quick growth, hard wood, and ability to grow quickly where other trees cannot. Governments, industrialists, and large landowners sought to grow the trees for fuel, poles, pulpwood, and, more importantly, profits. Yet the

* I would like to thank the Social Science Research Council, the National Science Foundation (Grant #0924930), and the University of Texas at Austin for generously funding research on this topic. Peter Boomgaard provided invaluable editorial advice during the revising of this article.

social and ecological effects caused by 150 years of eucalyptus planting reveal that the initial beliefs that encouraged people to create vast forests of eucalypts are as much myth as reality.

The initial hope that eucalypts would be a wonder wood was dampened when people living in and near newly made eucalyptus plantations began complaining about their negative ecological effects and inability to grow in tropical areas. Over the next 150 years many rural people, scientists, and environmental activists tried to stop the planting of eucalypts for a variety of ecological, social, and cultural reasons. Today, there is considerable opposition to the planting of eucalypts, although the size of eucalyptus plantations continues to expand across the developing world.

This essay provides a historical analysis of the globalization and the socio-ecological effects of eucalyptus plantations in India, South Africa, and Thailand. It argues that the widespread planting of eucalypts during the nineteenth and twentieth centuries caused immense social, ecological, and economic changes among peoples living in the regions of India, South Africa, and Thailand where eucalypts were planted extensively.

Because of the perceived and real biological characteristics of eucalypts, imperialists and settlers, and later governments and the elites of developing nations, planted eucalypts widely and created new socio-ecological systems that encouraged and reinforced divergent patterns of economic, social, and ecological development. Planting trees changed local ecologies and encouraged a movement towards market-based capitalism that benefited settlers, large landowners, urban elites and middle classes, and capital-intensive industries at the expense of indigenous groups living in and near forests. This larger process of social and ecological change also encouraged the rise of regional criticisms of eucalypts which were linked through global scientific and environmentalist networks. In effect, the massive plantings of eucalypts, and the responses against them, helped to create a more common social, economic, and ecological system spanning the greater Indian Ocean region.

Since the mid-nineteenth century the planting of eucalypts has been part of a broader global development where humans have manipulated and homogenized the natural environment in order to encourage economic growth and facilitate social control.[1] Certain ecological, social, and economic patterns have been reinforced as a response to the attempt to create a more homogenized world – the planting of eucalypts being one of them.[2] *Eucalyptus* is a ubiquitous genus because its various species developed

---

1. Historians are beginning to see the trend towards developmentalism as a more general feature of the modern world. See Kenneth Pomeranz, "Introduction", in Edmund Burke III and Kenneth Pomeranz (eds), *The Environment and World History* (Berkeley, CA, 2008).

2. Donald Worster calls these new ecological patterns "agro-ecologies"; Donald Worster, "Transformations of the Earth: Toward an Agroecological Perspective in History", *Journal of American History*, 76 (1990), pp. 1087–1106.

biological characteristics that allow them to grow throughout much of the world.[3] But eucalypts succeeded not merely because of their unique biological traits. In fact, the long-term success of eucalypts in the tropical world is a result of a century of testing and experimentation that led to better species selection and the creation of hybrids that prospered in tropical climates. Thus, the cultural and economic desire to plant these trees, coupled with a century of scientific experimentation, meant that eucalypts became the tree that many initially wanted them to be.

This article analyses the globalization of eucalypts in four broad phases: first, an enthusiastic expansion and planting of eucalypts from 1850–1900; secondly, a failure of eucalypts in the tropics from 1850–1960; thirdly, a period of scientific, social, and industrial change that allowed for the increased planting and success rates of eucalyptus species planted in the tropics from 1960 to the present; fourthly, a growing criticism of the ecological and social effects of eucalyptus plantations which began slowly in the late nineteenth century and blossomed in the 1980s during an intense period of eucalyptus planting in India and Thailand.

This does not mean that eucalypts had the same histories in South Africa, India, and Thailand. The justification for planting eucalypts and the social reception and ecological effects of their planting depended on a number of historically and regionally contingent factors. Yet support for and criticisms against eucalypts usually required access to global networks of science and environmental activism. In this sense, the history of the eucalyptus, while encompassing specific nations and regions, is truly global.

GLOBALIZING EUCALYPTS

Eucalypts are trees that live on photosynthesis, water, and nutrients from soil. *Eucalyptus* is a genus of trees in the *Myrtaceae* family that includes around 700 species, almost all of which evolved in Australia. Eucalypts evolved a specific adaptation to Australia's peculiarly nutrient poor and dry conditions which botanists call sclerophyll, in which leaves are small, tough, waxy, and have less nutrition.[4] Mammals in Australia evolved mechanisms to digest and live on the low nutritional, often toxic, and tough qualities of eucalyptus leaves and bark. But most mammals outside

---

3. Alfred Crosby, *Ecological Imperialism: The Biological Expansion of Europe, 900–1900* (Cambridge, 1986). In the second edition of *Ecological Imperialism*, Crosby cited the genus as the one example of species from the "Neo-Europes" that successfully spread and colonized Europe. This account places the ecological success of the tree in the context of its biological ability to flourish in a variety of locations and climates. See Prologue and p. 166.
4. For a discussion of the larger evolutionary history of Australia and its plants see Eric Rolls, "The Nature of Australia", pp. 35–45, and Tim Flannery, "The Fate of Empire in Low- and High-Energy Ecosystems", pp. 46–59, in Tom Griffiths and Libby Robin (eds), *Ecology and Empire: Environmental History of Settler Societies* (Edinburgh, 1997).

Australia cannot eat vegetation with such low nutritional content. In ideal growing conditions, many species of eucalyptus thrive. Yet, as this article shows, over the past 150 years people often failed to find these ideal conditions. Even when ideal environmental conditions could be found, the social and ecological consequences of their planting often offset any economic gain.

Despite these biological characteristics, it is almost impossible that eucalypts would have colonized the lands surrounding the Indian Ocean during the nineteenth and twentieth centuries without the help of humans. The history of the spread of eucalypts, then, is also profoundly social. Human desires to improve the productivity of nature dovetailed with the perceived characteristics of the genus. Despite the destruction of Australia's native eucalyptus forests by an expanding frontier of settlers, botanists in Australia during the nineteenth century enthused about the characteristics of the genus and its individual species.[5]

Ferdinand von Mueller, the state botanist for Victoria for most of the mid to late nineteenth century (1853–1896), and Joseph Maiden, director of the Sydney Botanic Gardens and Herbarium from 1896–1924, helped to popularize the genus during that period by sending hundreds of thousands of eucalyptus seeds to private individuals and botanical gardens throughout the British Empire and the rest of the world.[6] From botanical gardens in Melbourne and Sydney, eucalypts spread to gardens in Mauritius, Cape Town, Durban, Pietermaritzburg, Grahamstown, Calcutta, Ootacamund, and Bangkok and then throughout India, southern Africa, and Thailand.[7] Once diffused from these gardens, foresters, farmers, and villagers all planted eucalypts through individual and state-sponsored programs.

SOUTH AFRICA 1850–2000

The introduction of eucalypts into South Africa is intrinsically bound up with settler colonialism. Only in the broadest sense can their initial planting be considered as being directly related to the processes of

5. Tom Griffiths, *Forests of Ash: An Environmental History* (Melbourne, 2001), pp. 32–87; John Dargavel, *Fashioning Australia's Forests* (Melbourne, 1995), pp. 16–59.
6. For Mueller see A.M. Lucas, "Baron von Mueller: Protege Turned Patron", in R.W. Home (ed.), *Australian Science in the Making* (Sydney, 1988), pp. 133–152. For Maiden see Jodi Frawley, "Botanical Knowledges, Settling Australia: Sydney Botanical Gardens, 1896–1924" (unpublished Ph.D., University of Sydney, 2009).
7. See Robin Doughty, *The Eucalyptus: A Natural and Commercial History of the Gum Tree* (Baltimore, MD, 2000), pp. 24–59, 189–191. Key works on botanical gardens include Richard Drayton, *Nature's Government: Science, Imperial Britain, and the "Improvement" of the World* (New Haven, CT, 2000); Donal McCracken, *Gardens of Empire* (London, 1997); and Lucile Brockway, *Science and Colonial Expansion* (New York, 1979).

capitalism or a market-based economy. Its proponents at first sought eucalypts for agricultural and economic sustainability, not for export. Capital-intensive and market-based plantations of eucalypts became popular beginning in the late nineteenth and early twentieth centuries, especially following the two world wars. Plantings of eucalypts were, nonetheless, common features of the South African landscape by the late nineteenth century. Describing South Africa to British readers, the Liberal British politician and historian, James Bryce, noted that any visitor to South Africa

> [F]inds them [eucalypts] now everywhere, mostly in rows or groups round a house or a hamlet, but sometimes also in regular plantations. They have become a conspicuous feature in the landscape of the veldt plateau, especially in those places where there was no wood, or the little that existed has been destroyed. Kimberley, for instance, and Pretoria are beginning to be embowered in groves of eucalyptus; Buluwayo is following suit; and all over Matabililand and Mashonaland one discovers in the distance the site of a farm-steading or a store by the waving tops of the gum-trees.[8]

European settlers planted exotic trees because the few indigenous forests in South Africa became increasingly scarce resources. The desire to plant fast-growing exotic species of trees became more pressing as British migration to southern Africa in the nineteenth century expanded the European population in the Cape and Natal, and some groups of Afrikaners moved into the interior to found new settlements.

The first eucalyptus species planted widely in South Africa was the *E. globulus*, the "blue gum". It came via an Indian Ocean network, from Australia to Mauritius to the Cape Colony, likely in 1828.[9] By the mid-nineteenth century the *E. globulus* had established itself throughout most of Southern Africa, from the Cape all the way into the Transvaal.[10] Eucalypts found many champions in the mid to late nineteenth century. One of the genus's most outspoken advocates, John Croumbie Brown, a Scottish-born colonial botanist who worked in Cape Town from 1862–1866, recommended planting eucalypts because of their supposed superior biological qualities: eucalypts were seen as the "fittest" trees because they so easily grew where other native trees would not.[11] As in

---

8. James Bryce, 1st Viscount Bryce, *Impressions of South Africa* (New York, 1897), pp. 29–30.

9. See John Noble, *History, Productions, and Resources of the Cape of Good Hope* (Cape Town, 1886), p. 150.

10. Its first recorded entry into Natal was in 1846. See *Bulletin of Miscellaneous Information (Royal Gardens, Kew)*, vol. 1900, no. 157/168 (1900), pp. 12–15. Soon after, "[T]he growth of these exotics became a prominent feature in the Colony. Every farm had its plantation, which embraced numerous species", pp. 13–14.

11. Richard Grove, "Scottish Missionaries, Evangelical Discourses and the Origins of Conservation Thinking in Southern Africa 1820–1900", *Journal of Southern African Studies*, 15

India, some advocated the planting of *E. globulus* to stave off malaria, especially in areas such as the north-eastern Transvaal and Mashonaland.[12]

For a time, the blue gum became synonymous with the expansion of European settlements and trade in South Africa.[13] Settlers hoped that they would provide health for Europeans and rough timbers and poles for housing, trade, the railways, and mining. Like elsewhere in the British Empire in the nineteenth century, the popularity of *E. globulus* declined as the trees died from premature dieback because of drought and fungus. Other species of eucalyptus, such as *E. grandis, E. saligna, E. maculata,* and *E. paniculata,* increasingly replaced *E. globulus* in the twentieth century.

Planting trees was part of the mid to late nineteenth-century European mindset of conservation: trees supposedly brought rain, agriculture, and civilization.[14] As elsewhere in Africa, many European settlers thought that any landscape devoid of trees was the result of wanton destruction by Africans, not a result of natural ecological processes.[15] Throughout South Africa, Europeans generally criticized the timber usage of Africans. In Lesotho, British missionaries and foresters blamed the Africans for deforesting the landscape, even though it is likely that much of Lesotho's ecology was not suited to vast forests.[16]

(1989), p. 184, as cited in William Beinart and Peter Coates, *Environment and History: The Taming of Nature in the USA and South Africa* (London, 2002), p. 41.

12. This belief continued in some circles until the end of the nineteenth century. Missionaries hoped eucalypts would render Mashonaland healthy. See William Brown, *On the South African Frontier: The Adventures and Observations of an American in Mashonaland and Matabeleland* (New York, 1899), p. 309; William Parr Greswell, *Geography of Africa South of the Zambesi* (Oxford, 1892), p. 363. For the Transvaal, see M.A. Carey-Hobson, *At Home in the Transvaal* (Aberdeen, 1896), p. 51.

13. The South African forest research officer R.J. Poynton suggested in the 1950s that the *E. globulus* "was at one time perhaps the most ubiquitous exotic tree in South Africa". See his *Notes on Exotic Forest Trees in South Africa* (Pretoria, 1957), p. 35.

14. For a description of how desiccationist narratives helped create forestry legislation and state control in South Africa, see Gregory Barton, *Empire Forestry and the Origins of Environmentalism* (Cambridge, 2002), pp. 99–104; William Beinart, *The Rise of Conservation in South Africa: Settlers, Livestock, and the Environment 1770–1950* (New York, 2003), pp. 95–98. For a discussion of early conservation efforts in the Cape Colony, see Richard Grove, "Early Themes in African Conservation: The Cape in the Nineteenth Century", in David Anderson and Richard Grove (eds), *Conservation in Africa: Peoples, Policies and Practice* (Cambridge, 1987), pp. 21–38; Richard Grove, "Scotland in South Africa: John Croumbie Brown and the Roots of Settler Environmentalism", in Griffiths and Robin, *Ecology and Empire*, pp. 139–153.

15. This process has been covered by a number of studies. For North Africa, see Diana Davis, *Resurrecting the Granary of Rome: Environmental History and French Colonial Expansion in North Africa* (Athens, OH, 2007); for west Africa, see James Fairhead and Melissa Leach, *Misreading the African Landscape: Society and Ecology in a Forest-Savanna Mosaic* (Cambridge, 1996); for southern Africa, see Kate Showers, *Imperial Gullies: Soil Erosion and Conservation in Lesotho* (Athens, OH, 2005).

16. See the argument of Showers, *Imperial Gullies*.

Part of the desire to plant eucalypts arose simply from a need for timber. The expansion of eucalyptus plantations was fuelled by the desire of foresters and the state to continue a supply of cheap, fast-growing wood for mining, firewood, poles, sleepers, and other industrial products. There was also a strong cultural desire to remake Africa in the image of Europe. To European settlers, South Africa was to be a country of farms, with trees and forests dotting the land.[17] Europeans claimed their farms and cities by embowering them with eucalypts. Throughout the nineteenth and twentieth centuries, the eucalyptus was used as a common motif in literature, scientific discussions, and political prose that equated eucalypts with a Western style of civilization, society, economy, and even nature.[18]

Throughout the nineteenth and early twentieth centuries the search for land pitted white settlers against Africans, with Africans losing out to an expanding frontier of agriculture, ranching, and man-made forests. Foresters in the Cape Colony pioneered the creation of plantations of eucalypts in the late nineteenth and early twentieth centuries.[19] Although in the late 1900s foresters and farmers called for afforestation of white settlements in Natal and lower Zululand with "large plantations of eucalyptus", black wattles (*Acacia mearnsii*) expanded at a faster rate because most species of eucalyptus, except *E. saligna*, did not thrive in KwaZulu-Natal.[20] The trees were popular in Lesotho and Swaziland, with the British government promoting their planting.[21] To fulfill the requirements for the growing white and African populations, eucalyptus plantings expanded across South Africa, especially in the Cape and the Transvaal.[22]

State forestry programs expanded in the wake of the unification of South Africa in 1910. Foresters sought to "wean" Africans from using

17. Beinart, *The Rise of Conservation*, p. 96. For a description of how "noble" eucalypts lined the farms of Natal, see Henry Brooks, *Natal: A History and Description of the Colony* (London, 1876), p. 278.

18. For example, see the romantic discussions of eucalypts and farming in Leonard Flemming, "The Romance of a New South African Farm", *Journal of the Royal African Society*, 21 (1922), pp. 115–128, 123–124. Flemming said that on his farm alone he planted 40,000 trees.

19. See Brett Bennett, "'Fit the Tree to the Climate': Australian-South African Botanical Exchange and the Origins of the Climatic School of Silviculture in South Africa c. 1880–1950", in "Creating an Indian Ocean Rim Ecosystem: Forestry, Science and the British World 1864–1963" (Ph.D., University of Texas at Austin, 2010).

20. Thomas Sim, *Tree Planting in Natal* (Pietermaritzburg, 1905), pp. 139–140. For a discussion of exotics in Natal see Harald Witt, "The Emergence of Privately Grown Industrial Tree Plantations", in Stephen Dovers, Ruth Edgecombe, and Bill Guest (eds), *South Africa's Environmental History: Cases and Comparisons* (Athens, OH, 2002), pp. 90–112, 93.

21. Gertrude Rachel Hance, *The Zulu Yesterday and To-day: Twenty-Nine Years in South Africa* (London, 1916), p. 78. Alice Balfour, *Twelve Hundred Miles in a Wagon* (London, 1895), p. 46.

22. By 1941, around half of all afforestation projects in the Union were in the Transvaal. See *Division of Forestry Annual Report for the Year Ended 31st March, 1941* (Pretoria, 1941), p. 11.

indigenous trees by planting and marketing exotics, such as eucalyptus and pine.[23] Foresters in the Eastern Cape and the Transkei wanted to limit free access to forests and to create a market economy for exotic and indigenous timber. Magistrates and other state officials often rejected this because of a fear of rural protest. A similar management shift occurred in the High Commission Territories. Foresters in Lesotho planted eucalypts to stop soil erosion and to "replant" what the British thought were deforested lands.[24] The Transvaal implemented a large plantation program guided initially by D.E. Hutchins's recommendations of 1903.[25] The efforts represented a larger legal and management shift in government forestry departments encouraged by the Native Land Act (1913) and the Forest Act (1913), which allowed the forced dispossession of Africans for the creation of forest reservations and state plantations.[26]

Of all the British colonies surrounding the Indian Ocean, South Africa took the lead in creating large eucalyptus plantations. These plantations were often planted on native lands formerly grazed by the pastoral animals of Africans. The process of making a plantation itself changed the ecology and thus required economic and social changes. Foresters created plantations by ploughing the soil or burning the existing grasses and then planting seed or transplanting trees grown in a nursery. If the grasses were not uprooted, they crowded out the sun required by young eucalypts and thus retarded the growth of the trees.[27] Foresters in British India and Australia looked with favor upon the plantation techniques in South Africa, where more labor and capital was devoted to their creation than in Australia or India.[28] Leading South African foresters, such as Hutchins, advocated the use of cheap African labor for the creation and maintenance of plantations.[29] Hutchins suggested, using the Cape Colony as his example, that foresters employ minority "races" or "tribes" to guard forest plantations from theft by the majority groups in the area.[30] Laborers made little money. Foresters in the Transkei commonly gave plantation workers only wood or low wages in exchange for their labor.[31]

23. Jacob Tropp, *Natures of Colonial Change: Environmental Relations in the Making of the Transkei* (Athens, OH, 2006).

24. Showers, *Imperial Gullies*, pp. 60–61.

25. D.E. Hutchins, *Transvaal Forestry Report* (Pretoria, 1903).

26. See *Statutes of the Union of South Africa* (Pretoria, 1913).

27. Poynton, *Notes on Exotic Forest Trees in South Africa*, p. 14.

28. R.N. Parker, *Eucalyptus Trials in the Simla Hills* (Calcutta, 1925), p. 1.

29. Hutchins, *Transvaal Forestry Report*, pp. 6–7.

30. *Ibid.*, p. 7.

31. See Jacob Tropp, "Roots and Rights in the Transkei: Colonialism, Natural Resources, and Social Change, 1880–1940" (unpublished Ph.D., University of Minnesota, 2002), pp. 326–328. I would like to thank Jacob Tropp for this citation.

Figure 1. Eleven-year-old *Eucalyptus resinfera* at Klutjes Kraal Plantation, Western Cape, 1910. *Appendix of Report of the Chief Conservator of Forests for the Year Ending 31 December 1911 (Cape Town, 1912).*

Eucalyptus plantations expanded rapidly in the 1940s and after. Private plantations grew much faster than state plantations, although both expanded in size. Large corporations began creating plantations and industrial pulp mills in the interwar years, often with the legal and financial support of the government. By 1960, 73 per cent of forest plantations were owned by private companies and individuals, with 27 per cent owned by the state or union governments.[32] These plantations included 397,961 acres of eucalyptus.[33] Outside South Africa, in the High Commission Territories and independent Swaziland, private corporations developed large plantations of eucalypts.[34]

An interventionist state forestry policy combined with the expansion of white ownership of land – in some areas over 90 per cent of the land – and the forced removal of Africans hastened social change in South Africa.[35] The commodification of land and resources on a local and global scale changed the values of nature and human society in Southern Africa.[36] Africans slowly became integrated into South Africa's wage-labor economy, often with the men remitting monies back home to their families from cities or mines. Forestry laws provided the Nationalist government (elected in 1948) with the legal framework to remove people from lands and replant those lands with exotic species of trees. The forced removal of local communities in the 1950s and 1960s, and the demarcation of state and private forests, meant that an increasing population of Africans had less access to a smaller percentage of South Africa's forests.[37] Whereas before, certain indigenous South African trees provided for African fires and kraals, newer exotic timbers, especially eucalyptus, proved more difficult to utilize through non-industrial techniques.[38]

Eucalypts also had a profound ecological effect on the land. By the early twentieth century eucalypts started to reproduce semi-spontaneously

32. Republic of South Africa Department of Forestry, *Investigation of the Forest and Timber Industry of South Africa: Report on South Africa's Timber Resources, 1960* (Pretoria, 1964), p. 7.
33. *Ibid.*, p. 27.
34. T. Fair and G. Maasdorp, "Swaziland", in Harm de Blij and Esmond Martin (eds), *African Perspectives: An Exchange of Essays on the Economic Geography of Nine African States* (London, 1981), pp. 115–135, 120.
35. See Nancy Jacobs, *Environment, Power, and Injustice: A South African History* (Cambridge, 2003); Timm Hoffman and Ally Ashwell, *Nature Divided: Land Degradation in South Africa* (Cape Town, 2001).
36. There is a vast literature on the commodification of the South African economy and society. See William Beinart and Saul Dubow (eds), *Segregation and Apartheid in Twentieth-Century South Africa* (London, 2003).
37. The numbers of displaced people remain unknown owing to a lack of research. See Jacob Tropp's pioneering study of the forced removal of around 1,900 people in Gqogqora in the Tsolo District in the Transkei during the late 1950s and early 1960s; Jacob Tropp, "Displaced People, Replaced Narratives: Forest Conflicts and Historical Perspectives in the Tsolo District", *Journal of Southern African Studies*, 29 (2003), pp. 207–233.
38. Tropp, *Natures of Colonial Change*, pp. 102–109.

around plantations.³⁹ Animals could not eat the tough, low nutrition leaves of the gum tree, which evolved these characteristics in the low-nutrient Australian environment. One settler near Johannesburg in the late nineteenth century noted that even the locusts would not eat eucalyptus leaves.⁴⁰ Foresters in the Cape tried to use eucalypts to create fire barriers around forest plantations because they "kill out all the grass completely".⁴¹ According to conservationist ideas, trees should encourage rain and promote the flow of streams. Instead, some noted that eucalypts promoted increased aridness of the landscape. One forestry expert on South Africa, T.R. Sim, noted:

> Eucalypts [...] which are quite vigorous while young, dry out the soil, and suffer or die before maturity is reached. [...] Africa as a whole has shown a marked advance of desiccation during the past twenty years [...] the planting of Eucalyptus and Acacias, however useful in other respects, does nothing towards checking this drying out [...].⁴²

A commentator on Basutoland lamented the "great mistake made hitherto in [...] the universal introduction of the eucalyptus, with its known tendency to desiccate – in a country already too dry – and to poison all other vegetable growth in its vicinity".⁴³ Eucalyptus plantations were prone to new pests and diseases, such as the Australian snout beetle, which took root in South Africa and plagued plantations there in the 1930s–1950s.⁴⁴

Twentieth-century criticisms of eucalyptus plantings in South Africa took two main forms: a nationalist critique and an environmentalist critique. Both positions could blend into one another. As ecologists discovered the uniqueness of the Cape and South African flora, nationalists began decrying the use of exotics such as the eucalyptus. Jan Smuts, the international statesman and Prime Minister, hated the planting of exotics such as eucalyptus and pines in the Western Cape because they destroyed the Cape's unique flora.⁴⁵ White farmers also worried about the desiccating effects of eucalypts.

The South African government responded to constant criticisms of the trees from farmers and some foresters. In 1935, at the Empire Forestry Conference, criticisms of eucalypts became so strong that the Minister of Agriculture and Forestry appointed a committee to look into the

39. Joseph Davy, "Transvaal", *South African Association for the Advancement of Science/Suid-Afrikaanse Tydskrif Vir Wetenskap* (Johannesburg, 1904), p. 275.
40. Maryna Fraser (ed.), *Johannesburg Pioneer Journals 1888–1909* (Cape Town, 1986), p. 80.
41. "Eucalyptus Screens as Fire Protection Belts", *Indian Forester*, 31 (1905), p. 297.
42. Sim, *Tree Planting in Natal*, pp. 10–11.
43. R. Crawshay, "Basutoland and the Basuto", *The Geographical Journal*, 21 (1903), pp. 645–655, 651.
44. See National Archives of South Africa Pretoria [hereafter, NASAP], CEN 151, E/5/3/10.
45. W.K. Hancock, *Smuts: The Fields of Force, 1919–1950* (Cambridge, 1968), p. 411.

Figure 2. Botanists and indigenous plant advocates have called for the removal of this old and famous grove of eucalypts at the Pietermaritzburg Botanic Gardens. *Photograph by the author.*

hydrological effects of eucalypts plantations.[46] The South African government opened research stations to test the effects of exotics on water supply. A movement against the tree gained steam in the 1950s–1970s.[47] By the 1950s and 1960s, foresters had quit planting eucalypts in Lesotho. Kirstenbosch Botanical Gardens began leading a national movement against exotics by eradicating eucalypts and other non-native species, starting in the 1960s.[48] Currently, the government of South Africa officially defines a number of species of eucalyptus as being invasive. Remaining stands of eucalypts are increasingly under threat from those who seek a more "native" South African ecology.

Yet even with this criticism and individual decisions not to plant eucalypts, the tree continued to grow in popularity because of an expanding export and domestic economy of pulpwood. By the 1980s, South Africa was

---

46. NASAP, FOR 336, A1054/7/18. See the final publication, Department of Agriculture and Forestry, *Forests in Relation to Climate, Water Conservation and Erosion* (Pretoria, 1935).
47. See, for example, the work of the forest researcher C.L. Wicht during the 1940s–1960s.
48. Sally Argent and Jeanette Loedolff, *Discovering Indigenous Forests at Kirstenbosch* (Cape Town, 1997), p. 8.

exporting 30 million rand of pulpwood per year.[49] This increased the size of ecological disturbances and provided a bridgehead for eucalypts to begin advancing slowly beyond the formal boundaries of plantations. The expansion of private plantations also had consequences for African labor – Africans were often put into single-sex housing and the labor force was distinctly gendered, with women often taking the more difficult and less lucrative jobs such as planting and weeding.[50] Yet with a scarcity of employment in South Africa, working in plantations and pulp mills provided the cash required for a capitalist economy.

The eucalyptus remains a controversial subject in present-day post-apartheid South Africa. Many see the trees as a legacy of European dominance, although some see eucalyptus plantations as a way to increase African employment and economic growth. There is an immense amount of research on eucalypts. South African scientists study the effects of eucalypts on local ecologies, hydrology, and on the lives of Africans who work on and live near plantations. Yet even with this present-day interest, a broader historical examination is required to understand South Africa's eucalypts today.

The present article has suggested that the introduction and effects of eucalypts in South Africa cannot be understood merely in economic terms; the widespread planting of eucalypts should also be understood as the legacy of a desire by European settlers to make a healthy, aesthetically pleasing, and self-sufficient African landscape. Rejections of eucalypts are often an inversion of the same colonial conservation ideology – instead of stressing a cosmopolitan, global ecology, many criticize the eucalyptus from a desire to restore the "natural" ecology to South Africa, a position that can be described as "ecological nationalism". Jan Smuts, who politically differed from modern-day South African critics of eucalypts, would nonetheless have agreed that eucalypts do not belong in most of South Africa. Yet with the existence of powerful timber plantation and pulpwood businesses in South Africa and an economy with high unemployment requiring ever more jobs, it seems unlikely that ecological nationalists will succeed in removing eucalypts from South Africa any time soon.

INDIA 1850–1980

The history of eucalypts in colonial India is one of enthusiasm, failure, and then a steady decline of interest. Eucalypts flourished in India only after independence in 1947. The East India Company slowly gained more

---

49. Robert Rotberg, *Suffer the Future: Policy Choices in Southern Africa* (Cambridge, MA, 1980), p. 124.
50. Ricardo Carrere and Larry Lohmann, *Pulping the South: Industrial Tree Plantations and the World Paper Economy* (London, 1996), p. 145.

power and land in India during the eighteenth and early to mid nineteenth centuries. After the Indian Mutiny of 1857, Britain took over the formal rule of India in 1858. Many officials of the East India Company, and after 1858 the Government of India, hoped that species of eucalyptus could improve the health of Europeans while also providing useful timber required for fuel and the sleepers for railways. Many boosters of eucalypts enthusiastically offered studies showing the efficacy of the *E. globulus* in promoting health and curing diseases such as malaria, the "Sind sore", and the "Delhi boil".[51] Yet, more often than not, these cures worked less effectively than hoped.[52] The *E. globulus* and other eucalypts fell into this category: they smelled nice but could not ward off diseases.

At the same time that the ostensible medical benefits of eucalypts waned, state forestry flourished in the subcontinent. State forestry developed in British India out of a complex set of actors and forces. Many botanists, doctors, and missionaries throughout the tropical world, and especially in India, had witnessed the massive ecological destruction of forests in the early to mid nineteenth century, and they argued that deforestation led to decreased rainfall, increased erosion, and lowered water tables.[53] At the same time, capitalists in London financed a massive railway expansion in India during the 1850s and 1860s.[54] These booming railways needed large trees to create sleepers for the rail tracks. The East India Company and the Government of India also had larger strategic and military interests in protecting a large supply of timber for India's large population and the navies and armies of the British Empire. It was out of this broad milieu that India-wide state forestry developed in the 1850s–1870s.

Foresters and botanists in India during the mid- to late nineteenth century imported and planted many different tree species from around the world. Some of the most hopeful candidates for plantations were Australian eucalypts, especially *E. globulus*. Out of all regions of India,

---

51. Edward Waring, *Pharmacopœia of India: Prepared Under the Authority of Her Majesty's Secretary of State for India in Council* (London, 1868), p. 71. See also the discussion of Lord Kerr's ideas by Surgeon-Major E. Morton in "Arboriculture in its Relation to Climate", *Indian Forester*, 1 (1875), pp. 142–155.

52. See James Sykes Gamble, *A Manual of Indian Timbers: An Account of the Structure, Growth, Distribution, and Qualities of Indian Woods* (Calcutta, 1881), p. 189.

53. See Richard Grove, *Green Imperialism: Colonial Expansion, Tropical Island Edens and the Origins of Environmentalism, 1600–1860* (Cambridge, 1995), for colonial forestry before 1860, and Barton, *Empire Forestry and the Origins of Environmentalism* for 1855 to the present.

54. For an overview of the capitalist policies of the British in India see P.J. Cain and A.G. Hopkins, *British Imperialism 1688–2000* (London, 2001). State forestry, in many ways, arose as a reaction to gentleman capitalists. See Gregory Barton and Brett Bennett, "Environmental Conservation and Deforestation in India 1855–1947: A Reconsideration", *Itinerario: International Journal on the History of European Expansion and Global Interaction*, 38 (2008), pp. 83–104, 83–89.

the Nilgiri Hills, a highlands region in Madras, proved to be the most efficacious site for the growth of *E. globulus*.[55] There, foresters created plantations of "Australian" trees of acacia and eucalyptus. Foresters grew these trees to provide fuel for an expanding European community in the hills. Between the 1860s and 1880s, state foresters planted around 1,000 acres of state eucalyptus plantations.[56]

Plantations were seen as a way of creating a wage-labor and land-revenue system for the indigenous people living in the Nilgiri Hills. Many of these plantations were often on or near "waste lands" claimed near *Badaga* villages in the eastern half of the Nilgiri Hills plateau.[57] In 1871 the *Badagas* had over 13,922 houses in the district.[58] British foresters blamed the *Badagas* for killing trees illegally for timber, and many revenue officials complained that *bhurty*, a form of shifting agriculture, impoverished the soil.[59] There were British foresters and revenue officials who justified *Badaga* practice by arguing that the *Badagas'* shifting lifestyle was a result of low soil fertility and that it encouraged the clearing of swamps.[60] But in the end, anti-shifting cultivation policies won out. During the late nineteenth century Madras foresters and revenue officials sought to use revenue settlements and plantations to encourage the *Badagas* to become sedentary farmers and grazers.[61] The *Badagas* worked as laborers on plantations starting in the 1860s; sometimes they worked

55. Edward Balfour, *The Timber Trees, Timber and Fancy Woods, as also, The Forests of India and of Eastern and Southern Asia* (Madras, 1862), pp. 111, 179; Hugh Cleghorn, *Report upon the Forests of the Punjab and the Western Himalaya* (Roorkee, 1864) p. 125; W. Francis, *The Nilgiris* (Madras, 1908), pp. 201–221. For official discussions of eucalyptus plantings in Madras in the mid to late nineteenth century see *Report of the Conservator of Forests for the Official Year 1860–61* (Madras, 1861), p. 8; *Report of the Conservator of Forests for the Official Year 1862–63* (Madras, 1863), pp. 13, 25, 64–65; *Report of the Conservator of Forests for the Official Year 1865–66* (Madras, 1867), pp. 3, 7–8, 65–68; *Report of the Conservator of Forests for the Official Year 1868–69* (St George, 1870), p. 19; *Annual Administration Report of the Forest Department. Madras Presidency for the 12 Months Ending 30th June 1898* (Madras, 1899), p. 33.
56. W. Francis, *Madras District Gazetteers: The Nilgiris* (Madras, 1908), pp. 215–216. This figure does not include private plantations and plantings, which were also extensive.
57. *Annual Administration Report of the Forest Department 1898*, p. 33. Anthropologists tended to view the growth of eucalypts around the regions where hill tribes lived with approbation. J. Shortt, "An Account of the Tribes on the Neilgherries", *Transactions of the Ethnological Society of London*, 7 (1869), pp. 230–290, 234.
58. Francis, *Madras District Gazetteers: The Nilgiris*, p. 130.
59. Hugh Cleghorn, *The Forests and Gardens of South India* (London, 1861), p. 177; Madhav Gadgil and Ramachandra Guha, *This Fissured Land: An Ecological History of India* (Oxford, 1992), pp. 123–134.
60. Kativa Phillip, *Civilizing Natures: Race, Resources and Modernity in Colonial South India* (New Brunswick, NJ, 2003), pp. 95–96.
61. Deborah Sutton, *Other Landscapes: Colonialism and the Predicament of Authority in Nineteenth-Century South India* (Copenhagen, 2009), pp. 134–135.

without payment because *monigars*, villagers chosen by the British to collect revenue and to find labor, forced them to work without payment.[62]

With a third of the forests on the Nilgiri Hills reserved, an expanding plantation frontier, and new laws in 1863 that required all unclaimed lands to be auctioned, it became more difficult for the demographically expanding *Badagas* to acquire new lands.[63] The landscape of the Nilgiri Hills became a haven for plantations of coffee, tea, cinchona, and eucalyptus, while traditional *Badaga* lifestyles became more difficult to sustain. By the twentieth century, the *Badagas* integrated more effectively into settled, mixed agriculture than most hill tribes in India, although they were forced into this lifestyle by expanding plantations in the Nilgiri Hills. But they succeeded in spite of, not because of, eucalyptus plantations and other forest reserves. They lost many lands that they had formerly claimed and were hemmed in by plantations and state-forest reservations.

Even with the success in the Nilgiri Hills, many foresters complained about the failure of *E. globulus* and other species of eucalyptus in the Himalayas, the hotter climates of the plains of central and north-west India, and in humid Bengal. Active experiments continued throughout the late nineteenth and early twentieth centuries, and many smaller plantations grew throughout India. Except in the Nilgiri Hills, however, most eucalyptus species grew poorly and earned little profit. Even in the most successful areas of Madras, resistance to the eucalyptus arose: the Government of Madras, fearing the tendency of eucalypts to dry out the landscape, issued an order in 1881 stating that eucalypts should not be planted around water springs.[64] Foresters continued to plant eucalypts, but there were worries by British officials about the trees' ecological effects, their aesthetics, and the economic costs of plantations.[65]

The failure of eucalypts in most of India led foresters to research the successes and failures of the genus. One of the problems of early introductions was the failure to recognize the climatic zones in which eucalyptus species could grow. The Government of India forester, R.N. Parker, showed in 1925 that most of the eucalyptus species planted in India came from the cooler parts of Australia, not its tropical north.[66] He noted that the most successful plantings of eucalyptus were in the Nilgiri Hills and parts of South Africa – areas with cooler climates. Eucalyptus species that did grow in these areas failed to thrive; they did not naturally regenerate, remaining only along

---

62. *Ibid.*, pp. 94–96.
63. *Ibid.*, pp. 101–105.
64. Sutton, *Other Landscapes*, pp. 138–139.
65. Part of the criticism of eucalypts was that they "overgrew" in Ootacamund and dominated the landscape. See Edgar Thurston, *The Madras Presidency with Mysore, Coorg and the Associated States* (Cambridge, 1913), p. 266.
66. R.N. Parker, *Eucalyptus in the Plains of North West India* (Calcutta, 1925), pp. 4–5.

the roads or in the plantations where they were planted. Another of his studies on eucalypts in the Himalayas suggested that they would not naturally reproduce and thus could be maintained only through a costly program of continued replanting. Additionally, eucalypts grew well only in the Himalayas on prime agricultural land, little of which was available for plantations. Compared to South Africa, a country that had a more powerful white-settler population and a less populous and prosperous indigenous population, it remained financially and socially infeasible to make eucalypts a successful plantation tree in India. By the end of British rule, eucalypts had helped push certain hill tribes in the Nilgiri Hills off their original lands, although the effect of the genus elsewhere in India remained negligible.

The Indian Forest Service (IFS) continued to manage the state forests of India after the transfer of power in 1947. While the organizational structure of the IFS remained similar to its colonial form, the ethos of the department changed as the new Nehru government sought to industrialize rapidly through Five-Year Plans. The Second Five-Year Plan aimed to bring India into modernity by emphasizing technology to overcome underdevelopment. The National Forest Policy of 1952 strictly defined the protection of forests in terms of the state, not in terms of local communities.[67] As Madhav Gadgil and Ramachandra Guha have noted, this was a turning point in transforming the IFS into a service oriented towards industrial policies.[68]

Silvicultural experiments and enthusiasm for eucalypts in India increased from the 1950s to the 1970s.[69] Foresters sought to fix the "problem" of eucalypts: for a century foresters around the world had sought to plant eucalypts successful in tropical climates. In India, the most promising eucalyptus were the *E. hybrid*, or the Mysore gum, which could grow in subtropical and tropical climates, and the *E. tereticornis*. Plantations of eucalypts, especially *E. hybrid* and *E. tereticornis*, began to be planted more extensively in the 1950s and 1960s. Plantings expanded almost threefold. In Uttar Pradesh there were 31,000 hectares of eucalyptus in 1962, and 82,000 hectares in 1969.[70]

In the Western Ghats, foresters destroyed less economically important rainforests in 1975 and replaced them with eucalypts, many of which died in the high rainfall areas.[71] These failed forests were largely abandoned. Most of the remaining eucalypts (around one-third to one-half of the

67. As cited in Gadgil and Guha, *This Fissured Land*, p. 194.

68. *Ibid.*, pp. 183–189.

69. The most prominent work published by the FAO in the 1950s was André Métro, *Eucalypts for Planting* (Rome, 1955). Australians also played a prominent role in increasing yields of eucalyptus in India. See Doughty, *The Eucalyptus*, pp. 163, 133.

70. *Ibid.*, p. 134.

71. Madhav Gadgil and Ramachandra Guha, *Ecology and Equity: The Use and Abuse of Nature in Contemporary India* (London, 1995), pp. 50–51.

species of trees in forests) created new forests with invading trees that are not of the same diverse types as existing forests.[72] Problems quickly arose with the trees that did succeed in India, as eucalypts colonized farms surrounding plantations, dominated the canopy, and deprived crops of sunlight. The best success rates for the Mysore gums were only 36 per cent of expected yield.[73] Instead of helping to produce cash for farmers, afforesting the landscape, and advancing India's economy, eucalypts proved to be far less successful than hoped.

By the 1980s, the Indian government began promoting a policy of massive afforestation because of the continuing loss of forest cover. Indian foresters also developed strategies of social forestry that encouraged participation in forest management by local communities. Foresters encouraged villagers to plant eucalyptus trees as a fast-growing tree that could be sold for cash and used for firewood. Oftentimes, foresters gave seedlings of eucalypts for free, as in Karnataka in the 1980s.[74] Plantations and small plantings of eucalyptus flourished in the 1980s. Over half a million hectares of man-made eucalyptus plantations stretched across India at the beginning of the decade.

The expansion of eucalyptus plantations and small plantings created a highly politicized debate among scientists, politicians, and activists about the benefits and determents of eucalypts.[75] The "Great Eucalyptus Debate", as it became known, exposed the ecological and social problems caused and exacerbated by eucalyptus planting. Critics argued that eucalypts destroyed local biodiversity, used more water than other crops, crowded out crops that could be consumed locally, and lowered soil fertility. At the social and economic level, eucalypts took longer to grow than traditional agricultural crops, created higher rural unemployment, promoted absentee landlordism, and raised the price of grains.[76] The planting of eucalypts promoted divergent economic and social patterns: the already wealthy farmers gained from planting eucalypts, but the poor,

72. S.J. George, B. Kumar, and G.R. Rajiv, "Nature of Secondary Succession in the Abandoned Eucalyptus Plantations of Neyyar (Kerala) in Peninsular India", *Journal of Tropical Forest Science*, 5 (1993), pp. 372–386, 377.
73. Doughty, *The Eucalyptus*, p. 134.
74. Vandana Shiva, J. Bandyopadhyay, and N.D. Jayal, "Afforestation in India: Problems and Strategies", *Ambio*, 14 (1985), pp. 329–333, 331.
75. In the 1980s, the *Economic and Political Weekly* hosted a number of articles debating the pros and cons of eucalyptus planting. For a sampling of these rich and spirited debates see Mahasveta Devi, "Eucalyptus: Why?", 18 (6 August 1983), pp. 1379–1381; V.J. Patel, "Rational Approach Towards Fuelwood Crisis in Rural India", 20 (10 August 1985), pp. 1366–1368; J. Bandyopadhyay and Vandana Shiva, "Eucalyptus in Rainfed Farm Forestry: Prescription for Desertification", 20 (5 October 1985); pp. 1687–1688; D.M. Chandrashekhar, B.V. Krishna Murti, and S.R. Ramaswamy, "Social Forestry in Karnataka: An Impact Analysis", 22 (13 June 1987), pp. 935–941; and Shyam Sunder and S. Parameswarappa, "Social Forestry and Eucalyptus", 24 (7 January 1989), pp. 51–52.
76. For example, see the works of Jayanta Bandyopadhyay.

subsistence farmers and laborers did not benefit. These criticisms and protests gained national and international attention through media and academic networks.[77] Protests against eucalypts in Thailand and elsewhere in Asia in the late 1980s and early 1990s drew on the rhetoric the scientific and media networks created and used during the Great Eucalyptus Debate.

Today, eucalypts form part of the ecological and economic mosaic of India. Despite popular criticism, scientists, the state, and businesses continue to plant eucalypts. The criticisms raised by environmental activists in the 1980s continue to be heard. The demographic, cultural, and economic realities of modern India portend a continuity of policies. With an expanding urban Indian population demanding higher living standards, it seems unlikely that eucalyptus plantings will decline in the immediate future.

THAILAND 1900–2000

Eucalypts exist today in Thailand because of continued attempts by state foresters, government officials, and private industry to grow them in community forestry programs and as plantations for export earnings. Eucalypts are not a result of Thailand's "colonial" forestry relationship with Britain a century ago, except insofar as eucalypt plantings are a legacy of the entrenched central power given to Bangkok and the Royal Forest Department (RFD) during that period. Thailand's state forestry program started in the late nineteenth century when the Bangkok monarchy and the Ministry of the Interior created the RFD in 1896 to appease British business and Foreign Office officials, stop excessive deforestation in northern Siam, and, more importantly, gain control of the lucrative teak trade dominated by the Chiang Mai chiefs who paid vassalage to Bangkok.[78] Thai forestry laws drew on British Indian and European models that gave the state immense power in the creation and management of state forest reserves.

The French planted the first known eucalyptus trees in Bangkok in 1905.[79] Yet those trees made no noticeable ecological or economic impact for the entire first half of the twentieth century. Teak dominated the

77. See Ramachandra Guha, "Chipko: Social History of an 'Environmental' Movement", in *idem, The Unquiet Woods: Ecological Change and Peasant Resistance in the Himalaya* (Oxford, 1989), pp. 152–184.

78. See Gregory Barton and Brett M. Bennett, "Forestry as Foreign Policy: Anglo-Siamese Relations and the Origins of Britain's Informal Empire in the Teak Forests of Northern Siam, 1883–1925", *Itinerario: International Journal on the History of European Expansion and Global Interaction*, 34 (2010), pp. 65–86. See also Peter Vandergeest and Nancy Peluso, "Empires of Forestry: Professional Forestry and State Power in Southeast Asia, Part 1", *Environment and History*, 12 (2006), pp. 31–64.

79. Doughty, *The Eucalyptus*, p. 190.

forestry economy of Thailand throughout the first three quarters of the twentieth century.[80] Attempts to encourage eucalypts in the early and mid-part of the century failed. Sukhum Thirawat, the forest conservator for the central region of Thailand, noted, "to tropical foresters Eucalyptus is something of an enigma; a genus so versatile and yet despite con-siderable attempts at introductions over long years, not one species can be cited as a success anywhere".[81] More than any person, Thirawat helped to introduce eucalypts into Thailand. He experimented with the different types of eucalypts that could be planted in Thailand, presenting some of his results at the Second World Eucalyptus Conference in 1956 in Rome. From his experiments in Thailand he concluded that the *E. camaldulensis* grew best throughout Thailand. Other experiments with international agencies during the 1960s–1980s encouraged foresters throughout Thailand to continue testing and planting fast-growing eucalypts. Still, teak remained the dominant focus of planting and extraction until the 1980s.

Changes in the political economy of Thailand in the 1950s–1970s ushered in a new phase in Thai forestry that emphasized the nationali-zation of forest leases, increasing timber yields, and expanding the size of state-forest reserves. Starting in the early 1950s, the Thai government began nationalizing many of its forest leases, effectively taking them back from European, especially British, corporations. Government forestry policies did not stop deforestation, which continued at about 10 per cent per year in the late 1970s.[82] Deforestation increased in Thailand from the 1960s onwards, especially in the densely populated north-eastern part of Thailand, where rural landlessness, expanding population, shifting culti-vation, and illegal logging – often allowed secretly by corrupt government officials – chipped away at the remaining forests. With help from the FAO and foreign donors, the RFD and the Thai government tried to persuade shifting cultivators and other villagers in the north and north-east to participate in *taungya*, a program "to reforest areas of the forest estate which have been degraded by over-exploitation or shifting cultivation".[83] These programs provided a model for community eucalyptus plantations in the 1980s.

In the 1980s foresters and government officials began promoting more widely the planting of the fast-growing *E. camaldulensis* in the *taungya* programmes. These trees grew in three to five years, could be turned into

80. See James Ingram, *Economic Change in Thailand* (Stanford, CA, 1971).

81. Sukhum Thirawat, *The Eucalypts for Tropical Climates: Based on Experiences Gained from the FAO Eucalyptus Study Tour in Australia 1952* (Bangkok, 1952), p. 1.

82. Sathit Wacharakitti, Pairote Pinyosorasak, and Prasong Sanguantham, *Report on Forest Inventory of the Pilot Project Area for Development of Reforestation, Northeast Thailand* (Bangkok, 1980), p. 12.

83. *Forestry for Local Community Development*, FAO Paper No. 7 (Rome, 1978), pp. 85–86.

pulpwood for export to Taiwan and Japan, and supported the green rhetoric of the state.[84] In 1985 the government, under General Prem Tinsulanonda, implemented a partial logging ban to protect 15 per cent of the forests for parks and natural preserves. The government also wanted to use 25 per cent of the remaining forests for commercial forestry, including eucalyptus plantations. With the support of the FAO, the Thai government promoted a program of "community forestry" in 1985 that used private and local capital investment to create plantations of trees on "marginal" agricultural lands, for local subsistence, and also for export. On the face of it, this policy sought to increase local timber production while protecting the forests. Yet deforestation continued. In 1989 the RFD announced a logging ban on the forests of Thailand. Thailand would grow the trees they needed for export and domestic consumption.

Yet there were problems with the eucalyptus planting programs of the late 1980s and 1990s. Thai foresters analyzing the planting of eucalypts in north-eastern Thailand during the late 1980s found that rural Thais lacked information about the planting, care, and uses of *E. camaldulensis*, even though it remained by far the most popularly planted tree.[85] Instead of seeing this as a failure, foresters advocated extensive education programs that would then allow the private sector to take over the role of afforestation, leaving the RFD to "concentrate its direct efforts in reforestation in certain erosion sensitive areas, and make it easier for others to contribute to tree growing in other areas (within and outside reserved forests) for cash".[86]

The planting of eucalyptus caused friction among the rural peoples who were supposed to benefit most from them.[87] Tinsulanonda's community forestry policies implemented in 1985 were widely unpopular among rural Thais in the north-east, and protests against the laws broke out because the government forced farmers who had no title off lands that had been claimed for replanting. Forced government removals and protests culminated in the Kho Jo Ko resettlement plan in 1992 when the Thai military forcibly removed villagers out of forests, cut the forests down, and then replanted them with eucalyptus. After the 1991–1992 military junta had been overthrown, villagers and farmers in the north-east protested

84. For a discussion of "green capitalism" see Raymond Bryant and Sinéad Bailey, *Third World Political Ecology* (London, 1997), pp. 61–62.

85. See the report by Narinchai Patanapongsa, *Resources and Constraints of Forestry in Thailand: Guidelines for the Establishment of Forestry Extension in the Royal Forest Department, Thailand* (Bangkok, 1987).

86. *Ibid.*, p. 122.

87. Buddhists often spearheaded movements. See Kamala Tiyavanich, *Forest Recollections: Wandering Monks in Twentieth-Century Thailand* (Honolulu, HI, 1997), pp. 245–247; Amare Tegbaru, "Local Environmentalism in Northeast Thailand", in Arne Kalland and Gerard Persoon (eds), *Environmental Movements in Asia* (Padstow, 1998), pp. 151–178. See also Carrere and Lohmann, *Pulping the South*, pp. 235–238.

this program vigorously, eventually winning concessions from the government that included the stopping of forced removals and the imposition of limits on the size of eucalyptus plantations.[88]

Rural landlessness was (and remains) a serious issue in Thailand, as millions of people who have no land titles live in the northern and north-eastern provinces of the country.[89] While foresters complained about how "landless farmers have converged on the area [north-eastern Thailand] from many parts of the Kingdom", these farmers worried about making enough money and growing enough food to survive.[90] Rural people also complained that well-connected Thai elites and corporations illegally cut down forests that should have been protected under the Reserved Forests Acts and then replanted these areas cut down with fast-growing eucalypts for export.[91] Like in India during the 1980s, those who had the most power and wealth benefited from eucalyptus plantings, while their planting was not as helpful for the economic development of more marginal peoples.

Extension programs did work in expanding medium-size plantations of eucalyptus in the 1990s.[92] Much of the expansion occurred between 1994 and 1997 when the RFD gave out seeds freely. Large pulp exporters also had a hard time growing a sufficient amount of eucalypts because the Reserved Forest Act limited the size of plantations and companies were forced to contract out to private holders. This led to expanding rates of smallholder planting, which caused a glut of supply after the Asian currency crisis of 1997 led to a collapse in the south-east Asian economy. After the crash, private corporations pursued expansive land purchases from farmers who had borrowed money during the boom to grow plantations outside forest reserve areas. One scholar working in Thailand remarked that, "Displacement [...] resembles an ongoing process of poorly regulated land purchases by an industry, facilitated through smallholder debt and the economic imbalances of Thailand's rural sector during the boom."[93] This is an ongoing process.

Unlike in India or South Africa, in Thailand the eucalyptus is not of colonial origin. Thai foresters and elites became interested in the fast-growing tree in the 1950s–1980s. The late 1980s and early 1990s witnessed the peak of

---

88. Carrere and Lohmann, *Pulping the South*, p. 237.

89. M. Patricia Marchak, *Logging the Globe* (Quebec City, 1995), pp. 223–225. See also Andrew Walker's discussion of the relationship between forestry tenure and agricultural tenure in "Seeing Farmers for the Trees: Community Forestry and the Arborealisation of Agriculture in Northern Thailand", *Asia Pacific Viewpoint*, 45 (2004), pp. 311–324.

90. Wacharakitti *et al.*, *Report on Forest Inventory*, p. 12.

91. This criticism is documented by Carrere and Lohmann, *Pulping the South*, pp. 231–235.

92. Keith Barney, "Re-encountering Resistance: Plantation Activism and Smallholder Production in Thailand and Sarawak, Malaysia", *Asia Pacific Viewpoint*, 45 (2004), pp. 325–339, 328–331.

93. *Ibid.*, p. 330.

plans for plantations, while criticism of eucalypt plantings remains popular among rural NGOs and academics. With strong financial incentives for the Thai elite, medium-size farmers and foreign corporations to encourage eucalyptus for export and domestic consumption, and an international network of scientists and activists arguing against the planting of exotic species of trees, eucalypts will likely remain a controversial, though widely grown, tree for the next decade or more.

CONCLUSION

As this article has shown, the creation of eucalyptus plantations in South Africa, India, and Thailand caused socio-economic and ecological change that affected marginal groups who worked as part of plantation schemes or lived on or near plantations. Yet the genus remained popular, despite over 100 years of criticism and the continued failure of tropical eucalypts until the 1960s.

The success of the tree depended upon a number of changing economic, social, and cultural assumptions. Boosters of eucalypts came in many forms: those who believed that the tree could stop malaria, those who saw it as a wonder-wood that would grow quickly and easily in any climate, and those who thought that it might provide villagers with a cash crop. A common institutional framework supported eucalyptus plantings. Eucalyptus species thrived in a scientific framework based on a hybrid of European and imperial forestry models that promoted the creation of single-species forest plantations. Yet the decision by states and businesses to create plantations also resulted in increasing population growth and a culture of consumption, not merely as an imposition of European scientific imperialism.

However similar in its spread, the effects of eucalyptus plantings in specific countries and regions had different trajectories that depended on local social and ecological factors. In Southern Africa, European settlers used eucalypts to build up a self-sustainable nation in Africa. Eucalyptus plantations emphasized and, through the appropriation and demarcation of lands, encouraged ecological and social changes to the land and peoples of Southern Africa. Critics in South Africa today dislike the tree because of its hydrological effects on arid environments and its destruction of local species of flora and fauna. In India, initial attempts to plant eucalypts failed, except in the Nilgiri Hills, where plantations helped to justify the appropriation of lands from local tribes. After independence and continued research into the genus, IFS officials found a variety of eucalyptus species that they believed would grow quickly and provide an excellent cash crop for people living near forests. The same dream of finding a cash crop for rural peoples while reforesting a denuded landscape spurred the imagination of RFD foresters and government officials In Thailand.

Yet the realities of this vision never lived up to the initial desires either in India or Thailand: the perceived and real social and ecological problems caused by social forestry schemes and state afforestation programs have energized international non-governmental organizations into active opposition against the planting of eucalypts. While some small and medium-size farmers have gained, the expansion of plantations has led to continued displacement of farmers and people without land claims.

What can we learn about globalization and the modern world from the history of the eucalyptus? During past centuries humans – in democracies, empires, and dictatorships – sought to create a modern ecological world that reordered nature to fit larger economic and social visions of modernity. These visions of modernity emphasized only certain traits and attributes of plants and animals. Eucalypts are consistent with these visions, although the realities of their diffusion and growth rarely lived up to the initial hopes of their champions. In the desire to create the modern globalized world, humans attempted, often successfully, to create increasingly homogenous ecologies and economies. By the 1960s and 1970s, foresters found ways of manipulating eucalypts to gain higher yields, and industrialists found new processes to utilize the hard woods. The growth of the global economy provided large markets for pulpwood and other wood products.

Yet this reordering came at a socio-ecological cost, especially for groups – such as shifting cultivators and pre-capitalistic societies – who did not fit neatly into the conception of capitalist modernity. Most obviously, this global reordering failed to create a more egalitarian society for all, and instead reinforced divergent developmental trajectories. If they indicate the future, the social and ecological problems that arose when establishing an environment and economy created for global industry should give us pause for thought. The history of eucalypts, like many environmental histories of the modern world, reveals not the complete failure of modernization, but rather that the attempt to create a homogenous ecology and economy has failed to deliver egalitarian economic growth at the same time that the resulting environmental change destroyed much of the ecological and social uniqueness of the world.

IRSH 55 (2010), Supplement, pp. 51–77 doi:10.1017/S0020859010000490
© 2010 Internationaal Instituut voor Sociale Geschiedenis

The Mid-Atlantic Islands: A Theatre of Early Modern Ecocide?

STEFAN HALIKOWSKI SMITH

Department of History, Swansea University

E-mail: S.Halikowski-Smith@swansea.ac.uk

SUMMARY: The Iberian rediscovery of the mid-Atlantic islands in the late Middle Ages was accompanied by all kinds of utopian projections. However, within a hundred years, both human and animal populations were made extinct, and the rich forest cover was rapidly depleted for cash-cropping industries, primarily sugar. Historians view the migration of the international sugar industry from the mid-Atlantic islands to Brazil as an example of expanding economies of scale, but contemporary accounts indicate what now might be called widespread ecocide as a major contributing factor. This essay looks at the environmental ramifications of the sugar industry as well as other cultures, and assesses whether it is indeed appropriate to speak of ecocide in the context of the mid-Atlantic islands in the early modern period.

The neologism "ecocide" can be used to refer to any large-scale destruction of the natural environment, though the context into which the term was born turned on the catastrophic consequences to the environment unleashed by the Vietnam War with its extensive use of napalm.[1] While the war moved Jean-Paul Sartre famously to equate colonialism with genocide, commentators quickly extended his declaration to ecocide.[2] Ecocide became a primary accusation in the ongoing political struggle of the native North American Indians against petrochemical companies since 1978.[3]

While a number of activists today like Patrick Hossay and Peter Ward[4] more generally propound grim prognoses for the human species as

---

1. Barry Weisberg, *Ecocide in Indochina: The Ecology of War* (San Francisco, CA, 1970).
2. Jean-Paul Sartre, "On Genocide", *Ramparts* (February 1968).
3. Ward Churchill, *Struggle for the Land: Native North American Resistance to Genocide, Ecocide and Colonialization* (San Francisco, CA, 2002). See especially the chapter entitled "Last Stand at Lubicon Lake".
4. Patrick Hossay, "Ecocide" and "Toxic Planet", in *idem, Unsustainable: A Primer for Global Environmental and Social Justice* (London, 2006), pp. 22–34; Peter Ward, *The Medea Hypothesis: Is Life on Earth Ultimately Self-Destructive?* (Princeton, NJ, 2009).

enshrined in the "Medea hypothesis", namely that we are on the path to self-destruction, there is room to discuss whether this is as a result of the "characteristics of evolution having as its basic unit the species rather than the biosphere", or if it was specifically the Industrial Revolution that conjured up new threats to the global environment. Here, early modern historians might try to make a case for ecocide occurring at an earlier date on the basis of the strong and sustained social protest that environmental damage provoked.[5] At any rate, Richard Grove is adamant that colonial ecological interventions, especially in deforestation, irrigation, and soil "protection", have exercised a far more profound influence over most people than the more conspicuous and dramatic political aspects of colonial rule that have traditionally preoccupied historians.[6]

Whilst critics of the belief in ecocide usually assert that human impacts are not sufficiently serious as to threaten the Earth's ability to support complex life, and underestimate Nature's capacity to adapt, further problems are created for the ecocide lobby by a necessary distinction between the "murder of the environment" and the "state of nature" itself displaying "universal signs of violence", as Darwin observed.

The case study for ecocide chosen here will employ the looser definition suggested above – any large-scale destruction of the natural environment – and apply it to the mid-Atlantic islands, sometimes referred to in the literature as Macronesia. This comprises the Canary Islands, "rediscovered" during fourteenth-century maritime voyages undertaken from Portugal, Genoa, and Majorca, as well as the uninhabited archipelago of Madeira discovered around 1418, the Azores around 1432, and Cape Verde around 1456. Collectively, this space has been christened the Méditerranée Atlantique by the Portuguese historian Luís Adão da Fonseca, and it emerged from the mists of history as part of the greatest triumph of the fifteenth century, the conquest of the Atlantic.[7]

The previously uninhabited islands of the Atlantic are often drawn attention to as primary examples of ecocide, both in Grove's pioneering and classic work on eco-history, *Green Imperialism*, and by some of the primary influences on Darwin's thinking. Amongst the sixteen major

---

5. Richard Grove, *Green Imperialism: Colonial Expansion, Tropical Island Edens and the Origins of Environmentalism, 1600–1860* (Cambridge, 1995), which concentrates on the late eighteenth and early nineteenth centuries although noting efforts by Caribbean authorities in the seventeenth century to preserve their forests and protect edible sea birds. See p. 5.

6. *Ibid.*

7. Felipe Fernández-Armesto, "Refloating Atlantis: The Making of Atlantic Civilization", in *idem, Civilizations: Culture, Ambition, and the Transformation of Nature* (London, 2000), pp. 403–434; Luís Adão da Fonseca, "La découverte de l'espace Atlantique", *Cadmos*, 53 (1991), pp. 11–25; *idem*, "Le Portugal entre la Méditerranée et l'Atlantique au XVe siècle", *Arquivos do Centro Cultural Português*, 26 (1989), pp. 145–160; and, more generally, *idem, The Discoveries and the Formation of the Atlantic Ocean* (Lisbon, 1999).

Figure 1. Map of the mid-Atlantic archipelagos.

books which Darwin carried with him on *The Beagle* was that by
Alexander Beatson, an Indian army engineer, who published *Tracts
Relative to the Island of St Helena* in 1816. This book includes a listing by
William Roxburgh of the endemic plants of St Helena, commenting on
their rates of extinction.[8] Islands, because of their limited extent and
aspect of confinement, became, Vinita Damodaran argues, "symbolic of
the explored world, and encouraged ideas about limited resources and the
need for conservation or sustainability".[9]

"INSULAMANIA": THE MID-ATLANTIC ISLANDS AS UTOPIAN PROJECTIONS

The pessimistic conclusions drawn by later commentators from the early
modern encounter between humanity and the mid-Atlantic islands stand
cheek by jowl with other, earlier texts bursting with excitement at the
prospect of their rediscovery. The distinguished Florentine historian, Leo
Olschki, built on a platform of literary texts from this period to make a
case for "insulamania", island-mania on the geographical horizons of
early modern humanity, perhaps most easily exemplified by the mon-
strously swollen proportions accorded the islands on Portuguese and
other Mediterranean portolan charts, when compared to the continental
land masses, and seamen queuing up for royal grants of land rights to
islands still to be discovered.[10] We would do well, furthermore, to draw
attention to that genre of atlas – the *isolarium* – that specifically came into
being around the end of the fifteenth century and, as Lestringant argues, is
a fine expression of Renaissance "singularity" (see Figure 2).[11]

   "Insulamania" fused with the Christian search for Eden, which had
traditionally been attributed, as we find on the Hereford *Mappa Mundi* of
1253, to an island somewhere to the east, but also with the search by
humanist philosophers like Thomas More and Mandeville for the ideal

8. Alexander Beatson, "An Alphabetical List of Plants, Seen by Dr Roxburgh Growing on the
Island of St Helena, in 1813–14", in *idem, Tracts Relative to the Island of St Helena* (London,
1816), pp. 295–327.
9. Vinita Damodaran, "Environment and Empire: A Major Theme in World Environmental
History", in Mary N. Harris and Csaba Lévai (eds), *Europe and its Empires* (Pisa, 2008), p. 132.
10. Leo Olschki, *Storia letteraria delle Scoperte geografiche* (Florence, 1937). See, for example, the
grant of 21 June 1473 to Rui Gonçalves da Câmara in reward for his services in Africa of "an island
that shall be found by himself or by his ships", in Manuel Monteiro Velho Arruda, *Colecção de
documentos relativos ao descobrimento e povoamento dos Açores* (Ponta Delgada, 1932), p. 41. For
more about the development of portolan charts, see Konrad Kretschmer, *Die italianischen Por-
tolane des Mittelalters, Ein Beitrag zur Geschichte der Kartographie und Nautik* (Berlin, 1909).
11. Frank Lestringant, "Insulaires de la Renaissance", in *Cartes et figures de la terre* [catalogue
of an exhibition held at the Centre Georges Pompidou] (Paris, 1980), pp. 450–475; George
Tolias, "*Isolarii*, Fifteenth to Seventeenth Centuries", in David Woodward (ed.), *Cartography in
the European Renaissance* (Chicago, IL, 2007), pp. 263ff.

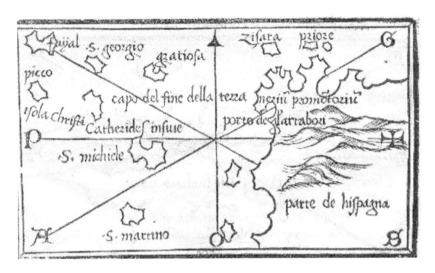

Figure 2. An *isolarium*.
Source: *Isolaria di Benedetto Bordone nel qual si ragiona de tutte le Isole del mondo con li lor nomi antichi & moderni, historie e fauole [...] (Venice, 1547).*
William L. Clements Library, Ann Arbor. Used with permission.

society, which needed a certain degree of isolation to flourish.[12] Finally, there were legendary traditions that attributed gold (a source of great fascination to European society during a century marked by the "bullion famine") to the sands of the Isle of the Seven Cities, from the early fifteenth century equated with the Azores.[13] All of these factors led to a great deal of social expectation being placed on the mid-Atlantic islands in the fifteenth century and first half of the sixteenth century. For our purposes here, the fact that oceanic islands were perceived as highly desirable "Edenic" locations in long-running European cultural traditions serves to emphasize the shock of their manifest and rapid degradation.

Initial reports, then, only emphasize the natural bounty and wealth of these new discoveries. As the royal chronicler Damião de Góis starts out in his description of the Azores:

> These islands are called Açores for their abundant nature [*muita criaçam*] when they were discovered, and that is still the case [...]. They are very temperate in

12. G.R. Crone has argued that the western location of the mid-Atlantic islands rendered them an "anti-paradise", a counterposition to the terrestrial paradise in the east. See Vitorino Magalhães Godinho, *Mito e Mercadoria, utopia e prática de navegar: séculos XIII–XVIII* (Lisbon, 1990), p. 244. Otherwise, Louis-André Vigneras, "La búsqueda del Paraíso y las legendarias islas del Atlántico", *Anuario de Estudos Americanos*, 30 (1973), pp. 809ff.

13. See the map of around 1492 that Charles De La Roncière incorrectly attributed to Columbus: *La carte de Christophe Colomb* (Paris, 1924). For the bullion famine, see John Day, "The Great Bullion Famine of the Fifteenth Century", *Past & Present*, 79 (1978), pp. 3–54.

winter and summer, and very luxuriant [*viçosas*] in springs and streams, with
very good water, and fruits, especially thorny fruit [*d'espinho*] of all kinds.[14]

Study of the royal toponyms (*toponímias reais*) and early names set down in
texts such as the *Libro del Conocimiento* by two anonymous Franciscans
(written in c.1300) and on portolans such as the Zuane Pizzigano map
of 1424 suggests that the rich natural resources of the islands were drawn
upon to support this Edenic projection – Madeira meaning "wood",
Canarias meaning "canaries", "Brasil" from its sappan wood, Columbária
from its doves, Sal in the Cape Verde archipelago from its salt deposits,
Açores meaning "hawks", Corvo for "crow", the Lobos Marinhos or "sea
lion" islands in the proximity of the Canaries, etc.[15] Finally, we must ima-
gine how the natural bounty of the islands, when compared with the empty
sterility of the surrounding ocean surfaces, must have struck worldly mar-
iners and voyagers such as Jan Huyghen van Linschoten and Pyrard de
Laval as the very paradigm of an "earthly paradise".[16]

Somewhat more rarely, we find literary accounts that dismiss the state of
nature of the mid-Atlantic islands, suggesting that nature needed to be
modified so as to render these *ilhas-refúgio* – places for a saving mission for
humanity – habitable and fit for human beings. The Machin or Machim
legend, the adventures of an English nobleman escaping across the English
Channel with his bride-to-be caught up in a storm, is one such. It recounts
how the anti-hero, landing on Madeira by chance, found it a "forlorn place,
both uncultivated and unpeopled". Only with the second, this time intended
visit in 1419 or 1420 – here by the two "noble esquires" Zarco and Vaz – was
the "wilderness converted into a Garden of Pleasure".[17] Similarly, there is no

---

14. Damião de Góis, *Crónica do Príncipe D. João* (Lisbon, 1977), ch. 9. For some context, see
Graça Almeida Rodrigues, "Tres visões históricas da colonização portuguesa no Atlântico:
Góis, Cadornega e Maldonado", in *Os Açores e o Atlântico (séculos XIV–XVII): actas do
colóquio internacional realizado em Angra do Heroísmo de 8 a 13 de agosto de 1983* (Angra do
Heroísmo, 1984), pp. 378–396.
15. Marcos Jiménez de la Espada (ed.), *Libro del conocimiento de todos los reinos, tierras y
señoríos, Boletín de la Sociedade Geográfica de Madrid*, 2 (1877).
16. *The Voyage of John Huyghen van Linschoten to the East Indies* (London, 1885), II, ch. 94,
pp. 254–258; *The Voyage of François Pyrard of Laval to the East Indies, the Maldives, the
Moluccas and Brazil* (London, 1887–1890), II, pp. 296–302.
17. William Ovington, *A Voyage to Suratt in the Year 1689* (London, 1696), p. 5. The Machin
legend was first set down by Valentim Fernandes da Morávia, a German printer living in Lisbon
in the early sixteenth century. See António Baião (ed.), *O Manuscrito "Valentim Fernandes"*
(Lisbon, 1940). A parallel, but seemingly independent record of the story appeared in a tract
written by António Galvão, *Tratado dos descobrimentos antigos e modernos* (Lisbon, 1563),
trans. Richard Hakluyt as *The Discoveries of the World* (London, 1601). A further version in
résumé form appears in Francisco Manuel de Melo, *Epanáforas da vária História Portuguesa*
(Lisbon, 1660), professing to use the original, an account by a squire of Prince Henry who later
accompanied Zarco on that "first" voyage. According to Melo's account, Machin dies after this
first visit, but his story is passed on, via a Sevillian pilot, to Zarco, the first colonizer.

denying the anonymous chronicler of the *Conquista de la isla de Gran Canaria* the satisfaction with which he relates how the first governor, Pedro de Vera, once the island was finally subjugated in 1483, brought from Spain "fruit trees, sugar cane, vegetables and livestock" (*árboles frutales, cañas de azúcar, legumbres y ganados*) and from Madeira "sugar mill technicians and harvesters" (*maestros y cosecheros de azúcar*).[18]

THE FIRST STAGES OF COLONIZATION: FOREST-CLEARING AND SETTLEMENT STRATEGIES

Even the Edenic visions invariably regarded human colonization as the end result of the process of discovery, and it was not long before the forests of Madeira and the Azores were both put to fire to clear the land for agricultural usage and cut down for use as timber. The fires on Madeira, as the chronicler Zurara recounts the tale, became so fearfully hot that the islanders under their Capitão, Zarco, were obliged to take to their boats (*costretto nel mar fuggire*) to escape the flames which, with considerable exaggeration, were reported to have consumed the island for seven years.[19] Traces of the former forest (*matagal*) that covered the island can still be seen on the north shore of the island, now covered predominantly by a kind of scrub pine (*pinus lauris*), and may indeed have deliberately been left to furnish planks from which boxes to hold the export sugar product (*caixas de açúcar*) were made.

In the Azores, where the same deforestation occurred, the trees cut down were principally cedars, but also laurels, dwarf cherry trees (*ginjas*), beeches, and several other species.[20] After the earthquake of 1630, the wooden roof of Vila Franca's Matriz church was built from cypress trees from Furnas; this was probably the last time virgin timber was used for construction on São Miguel. Today, as the historical geographer Soeiro de Brito reports, trees can be found only in "the bottom of some profound depression (*grota*) in the earth, in strips of hardly accessible upland (*arribas*), or on crinkled (*rugosas*) stretches of earth marked by recent lava flows".[21]

The Canaries were similarly forested, despite their inhabitants, particularly the western islands – El Hierro was praised in the Norman chronicle of 1402 *Le Canarien* for its "large groves (*boccages grands*), which are green in all seasons (of) a hundred thousand pine trees, most of

18. B. Bonnet and E. Serra Rajols (eds), *Conquista de la isla de Gran Canaria. Crónica anónima* (La Laguna, 1933), p. 40.
19. Benedetto Bordone, *Libro de tutte l'isole del mondo* (Venice, 1528), p. 15v; cf. Gomes Eannes de Azurara, *Chronicle of the Discovery and Conquest of Guinea* (London, 1896–1899), II, pp. xcix–c.
20. Gaspar Frutuoso, *Saudades da Terra* (Ponta Delgada, 1822–1831), book 4, I.
21. Raquel Soeiro de Brito, *No trilho dos Descobrimentos: estudos geográficos* (Lisbon, 1997), p. 29.

which are so thick that two men can hardly make their arms meet round them".[22] They were similarly subjected to slash-and-burn tactics (*derrubas e queimadas*), to the point that the visitor Thomas Nicols could write, concerning Gran Canaria in the 1560s, that "wood is the thing that is most wanted".[23]

Island councils were quick to broach this issue, concerned that what was both a source of income and a fragile resource was endangered. Every form of exploitation required a licence, and a number of caveats were put in place: the cutting of trees near springs was prohibited; no trees that were large enough for construction were to be taken for fuel wood; ten new trees were to be planted for each pine removed; livestock were prohibited from entering the forest, and fires were outlawed, as was night hunting in the dry season. Certain species, such as *aceviño*, a kind of holly (*ilex canariensis*), were explicitly prohibited, and areas such as the Montañas de Doramas of Gran Canaria were protected. Export was closely controlled and at times prohibited, with severe fines for violation.[24]

This wave of unparalleled legislation (at least from a Portuguese perspective) may have had positive repercussions in the short term, but it was not substantial enough to halt the wave of continued *exterminio* in later centuries, no more so than during the last two world wars. Günther Kunkel estimates that the laurel forest (*laurisilva*) cover currently occupies less than 1 per cent of its original area.[25]

The deforestation of Madeira was taken by many contemporary authors as an example of destruction and turning nature into wilderness. Hakluyt, for example, considered the process in the same light as that which had happened to the English colony of Virginia.[26] Some historians

---

22. *The Canarian: Or, Book of the Conquest and Conversion of the Canarians in the Year 1402*, Messire Jean de Béthencourt, trans. and ed. with notes and an introduction by Richard Henry Major (London, 1872), p. 74.

23. Thomas Nicols, *A Pleasant Description of the Fortunate Ilandes, Called the Islands of Canaria* (London, 1583), p. 6v.

24. José Peraza de Ayala, *Las ordenanzas de Tenerife*, 2nd edn (Madrid, 1976); Leopoldo de la Rosa, *Catálogo del Archivo Municipal de La Laguna* (Sucesor del antiguo cabildo de Tenerife), *Revista de Historia* (Universidade de La Laguna), various issues, 1944–1960; Acuerdos de Cabildo de Tenerife, in Elias Serra Rafols and Leopoldo de la Rosa (eds) *Fontes Rerum Canarium* IV: 1497–1507, 1949; V: 1509–1513, 1952; XI: 1514–1518, 1965; XVI: 1518–1525, 1970 (La Laguna); Francisco Morales Padrón, *Ordenanzas del Consejo de Gran Canaria, 1531* (Seville, 1974); Pedro Cullén del Castillo (ed.) *Libro Rojo de Gran Canaria* (Las Palmas, 1947); Leopoldo de la Rosa, *Evolución del régimen local en las Islas Canarias* (Madrid, 1946). More generally, Alfredo Piqué, "La destrucción de los bosques de Gran Canaria a comienzos del siglo XVI", *Aguayro*, 92 (1977), pp. 7–10.

25. Günther Kunkel, *Die Kanarischen inseln und ihre Pflanzenwelt* (Stuttgart, 1980), pp. 85–86.

26. Richard Hakluyt, "A Notable Historie Containing Foure Voyages made by certain French Captaines into Florida [...]", in *idem*, *The Principal Navigations, Voyages, Traffiques and Discoveries of the English Nation made by Sea or Overland to the Remote & Farthest Distant*

have gone far in assessing the impact of such savage forest depletion, arguing on this basis for the wholesale shift in the regional economy; observers of similar fires, such as the one which raged on Cephalonia in the Ionian sea in 1797, and could be seen as far away as Zante, suggested that consequently the climatic regime of the island became palpably less equable.[27]

But the forest-burning episode perhaps casts too large a shadow over subsequent realities. Fine furniture continued to be produced in Madeira from the local yew and cedar and exported to Portugal in such abundance that "loftier dwellings" (*grandes alturas das casas, que se vão ao ceeo*) started to become the norm back in Portugal and to the point that "almost all Portugal" became adorned with tables and other furniture made from the wood of Madeira.[28] Many of the hard woods – *til* (stinkwood), *barbuzano* (ironwood), *teixo* (yew), and *vinhático* (Brazilian mahogany) – continued to be supplied to the mainland for the purposes of large-ship building, for which it was ideal.[29] The magnificent dragon tree (*Dracacea draco*), which provided red dye for the textile industry, remained.[30]

Otherwise, the ashes contributed to a rich soil that allowed vines and cereal crops to flourish, at least initially before the soil became exhausted and an unnamed nobleman from Brittany was called upon to impart new techniques, namely a kind of fallow regime (*fertilização pelo tremeço enterrado em verde*).[31] Wheat, for example, which did so well on Madeira from the 1430s to the late 1460s, whence it was exported to black Africa, dropped off subsequently and ceased to be exported; indeed, since then the island has been a wheat-deficit area, having to import from the Azores in 1516, where the early harvests "caused astonishment" (*espanto*).[32]

Quarters of the Earth at any Time within the Compasse of these 1600 Years, 8 vols (London, 1926), VI, p. 229.

27. Fernand Braudel, *The Mediterranean and the Mediterranean World in the Age of Philip II* (London, 1972), pp. 141–144; Othon Riemann, *Recherches archéologiques sur les îles ioniennes* (Paris, 1879), p. 4.

28. Thomas Bentley Duncan, *Atlantic Islands: Madeira, the Azores, and the Cape Verdes in Seventeenth-Century Commerce and Navigation* (Chicago, IL, 1972), p. 10; Gomes Eannes de Azurara, *Chrónica do descobrimento e conquista de Guiné* (Paris, 1841), p. 14; Gerald R. Crone (ed.), *The Voyages of Cadamosto and Other Documents on Western Africa in the Second Half of the Fifteenth Century* (London, 1937), p. 9.

29. Jerónimo Dias Leite et al., *Descobrimento da Ilha da Madeira e Discurso da Vida e Feitos dos Capitães da dita Ilha. Tratado composto em 1579 e agora publicado* (Coimbra, 1947).

30. *The Voyages of Cadamosto*, op. 7. Ca' da Mosto is usually cited from the corrupt but more accessible text in Giovanni Battista Ramusio's *Navigationi et viaggi* (Venice, 1550–1558); a better one, first published in Francanzano da Montalboddo's *Paesi nouamenti retrouati* (Vicenza, 1507), is reproduced in António Brásio, *Monumenta missionaria Africana: Africa Ocidental*, 3 vols, ser. II (Lisbon, 1963–), I, pp. 287–374.

31. Ernesto do Canto (ed.), *Archivo dos Açores*, IV (Ponta Delgada, 1882), p. 169.

32. Raquel Soeiro de Brito, *A Ilha de São Miguel. Estudo Geográfico* (Lisbon, 1955), p. 68.

"Massive" soil erosion was another problem that occurred in the wake of forest clearance, as was true in Barbados and Jamaica after 1560.[33]

And yet enough farmland remained for Madeira to win the epithet "Queen of the Islands" for its abundance in comestibles, quickly becoming an indispensable base or stopping-off point safeguarding the extension of Portuguese trade routes around Africa and towards the Orient. The Portuguese explorer of West Africa, Antão Gonçalves, for instance, made repeated stops at Madeira during his expeditions in 1441 and 1442 "because of the great supplies (mantiimentos) that there were".[34] Writing in 1455, the knowledgeable Venetian Alvise Ca' da Mosto marvelled at the "vines the Infante had planted [...] brought from Candia at his orders", and which Ca' da Mosto described as "the finest sight in the world".[35] Wines, alongside wheat, salt and sugar, were the chief international export goods from the Canaries, as interesting analysis of inquisitorial interrogations of ninety-one foreign sailors between 1558 and 1598 reveals.[36]

Forest was not the only foundation stone of mid-Atlantic nature to be sacrificed on the Europeans' arrival. We might mention the "sea wolves" (lobos marinhos) or sea lions, slaughtered by Gonçalves Baldaia and his crew from amongst a colony estimated at around 5,000 animals, "with abandon [...] because they were easy to kill";[37] Vasco da Gama did much the same on a colony of seals he came across, firing at them with the ship's cannon and killing penguins too "as was our [sic] will".[38] But before them, the arrival of the Guanche aboriginals too had led to the extinction of certain large reptiles and insular mammals, including the giant lizard, Lacerta goliath (which attained one metre in length), and Canariomys bravoi, the giant rat of Tenerife.

While ecologists acknowledge that extinction is a complement to evolution in order to make room for new species to evolve, and thus a positive factor, they have struggled to determine an appropriate "natural" pace for what they would like to call "background levels of extinction". One scientist, David Jablonski, a palaeontologist, has estimated background levels at "perhaps a few species per million years for most kinds of organism".[39] European intrusion invariably heightened this pace, although not to the full extent of deep pessimists such as Alfred Russell

33. David Watts, The West Indies: Patterns of Development, Culture and Environmental Change since 1492 (Cambridge, 1987).
34. Azurara, Chrónica do descobrimento, p. 164.
35. The Voyages of Cadamosto, p. 10.
36. Maria Berenice and Moreno Florido, "Rutas comerciales atlánticas: una aproximación inquisitorial", Jahrbuch für Geschichte Lateinamerikas, 41 (2004), pp. 39–63.
37. Azurara, Chrónica do descobrimento, p. 64.
38. Alváro Velho, Diário da Viagem de Vasco da Gama: facsimile do códice original transcrição e versão em grafia actualizada (Oporto, 1945), I, p. 10.
39. David Jablonski, "Background and Mass Extinctions: The Alternation of Macroevolutionary Regimes", Science, 231 (1986), pp. 129–133.

Wallace, who feared that the arrival of "civilized man" to the "virgin forests" of the Malay archipelago would "disturb the nicely-balanced relations of organic and inorganic nature" to the point of thorough extinction.[40] Then there are the consequences of newly arrived fauna brought to the islands, particularly rabbits. A single, pregnant rabbit was set loose by the first captain of the Madeiran island of Porto Santo, Bartolomeu Perestrello. The descendants of the rabbit flourished and multiplied so exceedingly that within a few years they had infested the whole island, decimating the crops "as if a punishment (*amoestação*) from God", as the chronicler João de Barros writes.[41] All attempts to eradicate them failed, and the settlers became unable to sow anything (*nom podyam semear nhũa cousa*) and were forced to take to Madeira, fifty kilometres to the south-west. When they returned, they abandoned agriculture in favour of rearing cattle.[42] Other rabbits were brought to La Palma by Don Pedro Fernández de Lugo, the second *Adelantado*, or Lieutenant-Governor, of Tenerife. After the persistent drought of 1545, they apparently grazed all the tree shoots and herbs at the top of the Caldera de Taburiente, after which the upper part of the island remained "quite bare and desolate".[43]

Generally speaking, and in comparison to the ease with which Madeira was settled and colonized within two generations, or the high and balanced productive output which was attained on the two large islands of the Canaries, Tenerife and Gran Canaria, the settlement process of the nine islands of the Azores was a "lengthy, intermittent and hesitant process".[44] Here, the clearing met with mixed success. André Thevet explains how

> [...] of these islands, some are inhabited that before were deserted, and many are forsaken that in times past were inhabited and peopled, as we see hath happened to many cities and towns of the Empire of *Greece*, *Trapezande* and *Egipt*, such is the ordinance of God, that things héere in earth shall not be perdurable, but subiect to changing.[45]

On some of the islands, Flemish landowners like Joz de Utra (van Huerter), together with their serfs and companions, were attracted by

---

40. Alfred Russel Wallace, *The Malay Archipelago* (New York, 2007) (first publ. 1869), p. 340.
41. João de Barros, *Da Ásia*, Década 1, livro 1, f. 6–8 (Lisbon, 1552).
42. Azurara, *Chrónica do descobrimento*, p. 387.
43. George Glas (trans. and ed.), *The History of the Discovery and Conquest of the Canary Islands* (London, 1764), p. 266.
44. Duncan, *Atlantic Islands*, p. 11.
45. André Thevet, *The new found vvorlde, or Antarctike wherin is contained wo[n]derful and strange things, as well of humaine creatures, as beastes, fishes, foules, and serpents, trées, plants, mines of golde and siluer: garnished with many learned aucthorities, trauailed and written in the French tong, by that excellent learned man, master Andrevve Theuet. And now newly translated into Englishe, wherein is reformed the errours of the auncient cosmographers*, trans. Henrie Bynneman (London, 1568), ch. 83, 136v.

generous land grants and tax concessions, in the words of one privilege on tithe and portage for products exported from the islands "so that the islands may be well populated".[46] In 1468 Utra founded the town of Horta, on Faial. One landowner, Wilhelm van der Haegen, an erstwhile merchant of Bruges, was granted the island of São Jorge, but had to abandon it for lack of profit.[47] In others, colonization had to be supplemented by the forced exile of criminals, though official deportation orders appear to have been rescinded. In 1453, for example, a sentence of life exile to São Miguel was commuted to exile in Ceuta.[48] Historians have analysed this turnaround in different ways. Timothy Coates thinks that the islands were ultimately able to attract a sufficient number of free colonizers, and could thus dispense with *degredados*, while more scrupulous research suggests that the revocation of the order was made on the basis that life itself was so tenuous there that this decision was simply considered too harsh.[49] One group of Flemish colonists were so bitterly disappointed (*denojados*) that they wanted nothing less than to kill their captain.[50]

ECONOMIES OF EXPLOITATION

As we shall see later on, much of the initial economic exploitation was the harvesting of indigenous rock dyes and *conchas marinas* (marine shells, including cowries), sent on to the coasts of Guinea where they were used as a form of currency. A lot of the land was simply left for pasture. Sending out cattle, for example, was the initial development strategy of the Captain Donatory of Porto Santo, Perestrello, with regard

46. King Afonso's charter to Dom Pedro for the Azorean island of São Miguel is in Arruda, *Colecção de documentos relativos ao descobrimento*. For more on the Flemish in the Azores, see J. Mees, *Histoire de la découverte des îles Açores et de l'origine de leur dénomination d'îles flamandes* (Ghent, 1901). The charter of the island of Terceira to Prince Henry's "servant" (*servidor*) Jacome de Bruges stipulated rights for colonists "of his [Jacome's] choice", provided that they were Catholics. See the charter of 2 March 1450 in João Martins da Silva Marques (ed.), *Descobrimentos portugueses: documentos para a sua história* (Lisbon, 1944), I, 401, no. 315.

47. António dos Santos Pereira, *A Ilha de S. Jorge (séculos XV–XVII)* (Ponta Delgada, 1987).

48. Document dated 12 March 1453 in João Martins da Silva Marques, *Descobrimentos portugueses; documentos para a sua história*, 2nd edn (Lisbon, 1988), II, 344, no. 223.

49. Timothy Coates, *Convicts and Orphans: Forced and State-Sponsored Colonizers in the Portuguese Empire, 1550–1755* (Stanford, CA, 2001), p. 61; Peter Russell, *Prince Henry "The Navigator": A Life* (New Haven, CT, 2000), p. 103, based on *Monumenta Henricina* (Coimbra, 1960–1975), IX, no. 242. The wording of the 1453 commutation explains: "because the said islands were not such that men could sustain life".

50. See the cartouche for "Ylha do Fayal e Pico" on the Behaim globe, as transcribed by E.G. Ravenstein, *Martin Behaim: His Life and His Globe* (London, 1909), which explains the revolt as provoked from disappointment that neither silver nor tin deposits were found (*denojados que nom acharom o que lhes foy promettido*).

to the Desertas islands, "intending to have them peopled like the other [island of Porto Santo]".[51] The first note we have regarding the colonization of the Azores is a royal instruction (*carta régia*) of D. Alfonso V of 1439 to send sheep to the seven islands.[52] Large grazers (*gado grosso*) and pigs tended to be introduced after goats and sheep, hardier and more independent, and with them slowly developed tanning industries (*curtumes*).

Cereals such as wheat, barley, and rye – considered by historical geographers to constitute "more complex agriculture" – were grown from early on in the Azores, reflected in mundane commercial charters concerning the building of windmills and the baking of bread. Góis relates the abundance with which the farmers were rewarded: "oft times the peasants harvested from one *alqueire* of seed twenty or thirty".[53] As a consequence, the best land on the islands tended to be given over to this activity. However, while early reports suggested that there was "so much wheat produced on São Miguel that each year a number of boats arrive in order to load wheat to send to Portugal", and that some was sent to relieve famines in the Portuguese *presídios* in North Africa, such as Azemmour in 1488, on other islands we find petitions from concerned citizens requesting the prohibition of grain exports, as happened in the town of Velas on the island of São Jorge in 1591, which suggests that even self-sufficiency was a struggle to attain.[54]

More often than not, however, the export of Azorean grain was "independent" of the requirements of local needs and supply, and attuned rather to prices that it could command on international markets.[55] Price series confirm both a general upward trend and decades marked by astonishing rises; one finds, for example, a 171.4 per cent appreciation between 1584 and 1594.[56] Not all of this, however, was straightforward outside demand. As a Madeiran petition of 1563 explains, the problem lay

---

51. Azurara, *Chrónica do descobrimento*, p. 391.

52. Gaspar Frutuoso ascribes the same strategy to an anonymous Greek colonist of São Miguel in the Azores around the year 1370, although the story is almost certainly fanciful in its historical veracity if not in the idea or intention. See Gaspar Frutuoso, *Saudades da Terra* (Ponta Delgada, 2005), livro IV, p. 5.

53. Góis, *Crónica do Príncipe D. João*, p. 28. In *Mito e Mercadoria*, pp. 245–246, Godinho estimates that production was 5,000 *moios*, which later rose to 15,000 *moios* (sufficient to feed between 75,000 and 200,000 mouths). In the 1580s, this figure rose beyond 20,000 *moios*, and hovered around 40,000 *moios* at the beginning of the eighteenth century.

54. Joel Serrão, "Le Blé des Îles Atlantiques. Madère et Açores aux XVe et XVIe siècles", *Annales. ESC*, 9 (1954), pp. 337–341; Pereira, *A Ilha de S. Jorge*, p. 152.

55. M. de Assis Tavares, "A Pobreza na Ribeira Grande durante a Segunda metade do século XVI", *Arquipélago* (1983), Numéro Especial, p. 51.

56. A.H. de Oliveira Marques, "O preço do trigo em S. Miguel no século XVI", *Revista de Economia*, 14:4 (1962), pp. 213–266; Vitorino Magalhães Godinho, "A 'revolução dos preços' e as flutuações económicas no século XVI", in *idem*, *Ensaios*, 2nd edn (Lisbon, 1978), II, pp. 223–245.

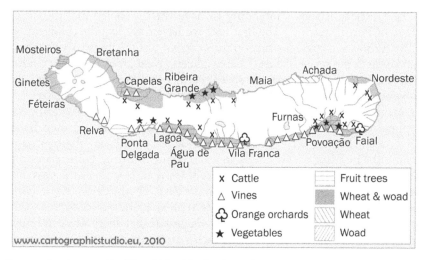

Figure 3. Land use on São Miguel island in the sixteenth century.

with those who owned the grain, for "the greater part of those who, on the said Azores islands, possess bread are judges and aldermen (*vereadores*) and landowners, who order the gates (*portas*) of the said islands to be closed by municipal order (*por suas posturas*) whenever they want", so as to keep the price of their stocks buoyant.[57]

It is worth looking at the following map (see Figure 3) showing generalized land use on the island of São Miguel.[58] We can consequently judge for ourselves how limited human invasive agriculture was, despite the *sesmaria* laws by which grants of land would be rescinded if the land were not cultivated; we can estimate the proportion of land exhibiting invasive agriculture at around one-fifth.

At this point, I would like to investigate a little more closely the impact of subsequent sugar cultivation on the mid-Atlantic island ecosystems. The transplanted sugar industries from southern Spain and Sicily were an instant success in the mid-Atlantic, where they spread from Madeira (c.1425) and the Canary Islands to the Azores and Cape Verdes.[59] Ca' da Mosto, who visited Madeira in 1455, then estimated production at about 400 pitchers or *cantaros* — about 60,000 lbs. He correctly foresaw the rapid development of the industry on the island, aided by the balmy and

57. Cited in Godinho, *Mito e Mercadoria*, p. 246.
58. Soeiro de Brito, *No trilho dos Descobrimentos*.
59. María Luisa Fabrellas, "La producción de azúcar en Tenerife", *Revista de Historia*, 18 (1952), p. 471; G. Camacho y Pérez Galdós, "El cultivo de la caña de azúcar y la industria azucarera en Gran Canaria (1510–1535)", *Anuario de Estudos Átlanticos*, 7 (1961), pp. 11–70.

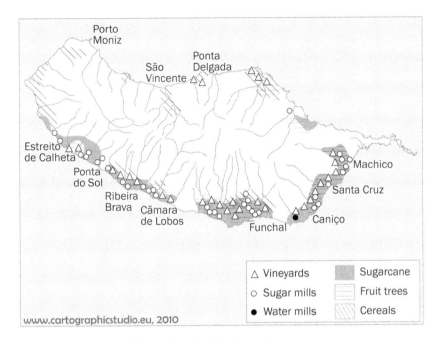

Figure 4. Land use on Madeira at the end of the sixteenth century.

moist climate (see Figure 4). Madeiran sugar became a global commodity, to be found in the markets of Bristol and Flanders in the late 1460s, later sent as far afield as Pera on the Black Sea, Chios, and Constantinople. The deputies of the Portuguese Cortes of 1481–1482 extolled the economic success of the Madeiran islands, enumerating the "twenty forecastle ships and forty or fifty others which loaded cargoes chiefly of sugar, without counting other goods and other ships which went to the said islands [...] for the nobility and richness of the merchandize of great value which they have and harvest in the said islands".[60]

By 1500, Madeira was the world's leading producer and consequently attracted investments from the two most developed regions of the world, northern Italy and Flanders. An account book of 1494 of the Superintendency for Sugar in the *capitania* of Funchal entitled *Livro do Almoxarifado Açuquarres das Partes do Funchal* stipulates a booming supply of 100,000 *arrobas* (3.2 million lbs), halcyon days before disease and imposed export ceilings struck the industry in the early sixteenth century. It also sheds light on the scale of production, which was in the hands of small- and medium-sized producers and was not large-scale

60. *Monumenta Henricina*, XV, p. 88.

production, as had been previously supposed.[61] Documents from the Câmara de Funchal dated 1493 and included in Frutuoso's chronicle, *Saudades da Terra*, suggest an output of 80,000 *arrobas* in the hands of 80 *mestres de fabrico* on the island, suggesting that there were about this number of mills (*engenhos*).[62]

Sugar-cane plantations prospered in only some of the mid-Atlantic islands. After about 1450 Madeira was the leading supplier, but over the course of the sixteenth century it was overtaken by São Tomé, where an anonymous Portuguese pilot estimated production of as much as 150,000 *arrobas* by 50 *engenhos* in c.1554.[63] By the 1500s the Canary Islands had also become important, with 12 sugar mills on both Tenerife and Gran Canaria in the 1560s (perhaps substantially more earlier), 4 on La Palma, and 1 on Gomera.[64] If sugar showed signs of prosperity on São Miguel in the Azores around 1560, it never really took off – Gaspar Frutuoso in 1589 stated that the climate was too humid for the mills, but there was already by this time strong competition from Brazil, lack of wood for production, and the appearance of a parasite (*bicho*) which destroyed crops.[65] Tobacco did better here. But the production techniques the Iberians mastered here with respect to sugar saw the islands being used as "stepping stones" to implanting sugar monocultures in Brazil.[66] Both Spain and Portugal experienced a growth of demand for their sugar, evident in the plummeting European prices for the product, which halved over the second half of the fifteenth century, but which did not affect the island's strong growth in exports.[67]

61. *Almoxarifado do açúcar do Funchal* (1494), Arquivos Nacionais da Torre do Tombo, Lisbon, Núcleo Antigo, no. 571, published in Fernando Jasmins Pereira *et al.*, *Livros de Contas da Ilha da Madeira*, 2 vols (Coimbra, 1985–1989). For the myth of "large properties", see S. Greenfield, "Madeira and the Beginnings of New World Sugar Cane Cultivation and Plantation Slavery: A Study in Institution Building", *Annals of the New York Academy of Sciences*, 292 (1977), p. 544.

62. Álvaro Rodrigues de Azevedo (ed.), *Saudades da Terra* (Funchal, 1873).

63. "Navigatione da Lisbona all'isola di San Thomé, posta sotto la linea dell' equinoziale, scritte per me, pilotto portoghese e mandata al magnifico conte Rimundo della Torre, gentiluomo Veronese, e tradotta di lingua portoghese in italiano", in Giovanni Battista Ramusio, *Navigazioni e viaggi* (Turin, 1978–1988), I, p. 306.

64. Camacho y Pérez Galdós, "El cultivo de caña de azúcar", pp. 11–60; see also Fabrellas, "La producción de azúcar en Tenerife", pp. 455–475.

65. Soeiro de Brito, *A ilha de São Miguel. Estudo Geográfico*, p. 73.

66. Frédéric Mauro, *Le Portugal et l'Atlantique, au XVIIe Siecle (1570–1670): étude economique* (Paris, 1960).

67. For a comparison of European sugar prices, see "O Império do Açúcar", in João Lúcio de Azevedo, *Epocas de Portugal Económico*, 3rd edn (Lisbon, 1973), pp. 222–223. We can admire the island's growth in sugar exports from the Saragossa decree of 21 August 1498, published in *Arquivo Histórico da Maadeira. Boletim do Arquivo Distrital do Funchal*, série documental III, XVII (1973), doc. no. 22; Henrique da Gama Barros, *História da Administração*, X (Lisbon, 1945–1954), p. 156.

What effects did growing sugar intensively have on the soil of the islands? This is a question entirely absent from the otherwise classic summaries of the industry, such as that by João Lúcio de Azevedo. In the Recôncavo da Bahía local environmental damage was considerable, especially in terms of defor-estation for crop planting.[68] There is also the question of forest-clearing for wood to heat the enormous copper cauldrons which were needed to boil the cane for six months of the year. Although forest clearing for the *engenhos* had a large impact on the mid-slopes of Tenerife and Gran Canaria, the mills in Madeiran sugar production were powered via complex irrigation systems known as *levadas*, which channelled water across steep and difficult terrain to the mills. The Madeiran *levadas* formed a technical response to the desiccation that occurred particularly in the Canary Islands.[69]

In terms of soil effect, each plantation was continued for between five and ten, sometimes even twelve, years, with a fallow period (*pousio*) between each plantation of between two and three years sufficient to rejuvenate the earth.[70] We would do well to remember that sugar production was merely a cycle in the islands' history, one that readily gave into a third cycle of international trade for Madeira that we have hinted at earlier, also true for the Canaries and Pico and Fayal in the Azores, namely the production of wines. This, once it had got going from the mid-sixteenth century, represented the staple export to the English plantations in North America and the West Indies, while Portuguese fleets took Canarian wines to Angola and Brazil.[71] Meanwhile, on Madeira, sugar production dropped from a peak of 144,000 *arrobas* annually in 1506 to around 45,000 *arrobas* at the end of the sixteenth century as if to accommodate this spread of viticulture.[72]

Some of the "crops" hardly impinged on the local ecosystems. Orchil (aka archil or *urzela*) is a reddish dye (but blue in alkaline pH areas) extracted from indigenous lichens of the *Roccella* and *Lecanora genera*, growing naturally on rocks and cliff-sides on all of the nine main islands of the Azores and on its various offshore islets. Orchil figured in Prince Henry's will, and continued to be exploited for centuries. Gathering it, however, was a difficult and dangerous occupation on account of the

---

68. Peregrine Horden and Nicholas Purcell, *The Corrupting Sea: A Study of Mediterranean History* (Oxford, 2000), p. 334.

69. Fernando Augusto da Silva and Carlos Azevedo de Menezes, "Levadas", in *idem* (eds), *Elucidário Madeirense*, 3rd edn (Funchal, 1965), II; Elof A. Ostman Norrl, "On Irrigation in Madeira", n.d., Manuscript in the Arquivo da Câmara Municipal do Funchal. The first document referring specifically to irrigation on the island is dated 1461.

70. Soeiro de Brito, *No trilho dos Descobrimentos*, p. 41.

71. Duncan, *Atlantic Islands*.

72. Estimates taken from Vitorino Magalhães Godinho, *Os descobrimentos e a economia mundial* (Lisbon, 1963–1968), III, pp. 419–456. Compare this with sugar production in Gran Canaria: the same author estimates the production of the 24 *engenhos* at around 120,000–140,000 *arrobas*. See *Mito e Mercadoria*, pp. 245–246.

rocks and cliffs on which *Roccella* grew, with gatherers suspended on ropes over ledges.[73] However, substantial quantities of this dyeing agent were collected. In a few days, eight Spanish orchil-gatherers brought to the Cape Verde islands in 1731 collected a cargo of 500 *quintals* (29,375 kg).[74]

Some scholars have argued that attempts to cultivate orchil elsewhere in the Canary Islands as an alternative, like woad, to eastern supplies of indigo, failed, both due to a harsher, drier climate and due to the continued difficulties in subduing the *Guanche* populations.[75] Their findings are contradicted by sources like Ludovico Guicciardini, in his description of the trade of Antwerp in 1567, where he specifies that Spain supplied "Orcille of *Canaria*, which is an herbe to die with, called of the Florentines *Raspe*".[76] It was exported via Antwerp to manufacturers in England and Flanders. Portugal, too, supplied *orcille* "from their own country" to Antwerp. Orchil cultivation in the Canary Islands, then, was probably just a singular failure of Prince Henry's expeditions in the mid-1450s. Later, rich beds of orchil were discovered in the Cape Verdes, and even in Angola, where it grew on trees.[77]

Another introduced dye-plant was woad (*pastel*), of which production, like other raw materials in proto-industrializing areas of northern Europe, especially in England, Normandy, Brabant, but also bustling Lombardy, was declining at the end of the Middle Ages.[78] Seeds (*sementes*) were imported from France, and techniques of its cultivation were passed on from Flanders via a certain Govarte Luiz.[79] It was a valuable crop on

73. Maria Olímpia da Rocha Gil, "A economia dos Açores nos séculos XV e XVI", in Luís de Albuquerque (ed.), *Portugal no Mundo* (Lisbon, 1989), I, p. 226; Annette Kok, "A Short History of the Orchil Dyes", *The Lichenologist*, 3 (1966), pp. 248–272. The Florentine noble family the Rucellai had originally discovered the plant's qualities in the thirteenth century on business ventures into the Levant. See Leandro Maria Bartoli and Gabriella Contorni, *Gli Orti Oricellari a Firenze: un giardino, una città* (Florence, 1990), p. 4.

74. Jean P. Hellot, *L'Art de la teinture des laines et des étoffes de laine en grand et petit teint* (Paris, 1750); see also Edward Bancroft, *Experimental Researches Concerning the Philosophy of Permanent Colours*, 2nd edn (London, 1813), p. 294.

75. Peter Russell, "Prince Henry and the Necessary End", in *idem*, *Portugal, Spain and the African Atlantic, 1343–1490: Chivalry and Crusade from John of Gaunt to Henry the Navigator and Beyond* (Aldershot, 1995), p. 10; David Abulafia, "L'Economia italiana e le economie mediterranee ed atlantiche", in Francesco Salvestrini (ed.), *L'Italia alla fine del Medioevo: i caratteri originali nel quadro europeo* (Florence, 2006), pp. 355–380.

76. Lodovico Guicciardini, *The Description of the Low Countreys* (London, 1593), p. 38.

77. Anon., "Orseille", in *Encyclopédie du Dix-Neuvième Siècle* (Paris, 1853), XVIII, pp. 138–139.

78. Elizabeth M. Carus-Wilson, "La Guède française en Angleterre: un grand commerce du Moyen Âge", *Revue du Nord*, 35 (1953), pp. 89–105.

79. Francisco de Faria e Maia, *Capitães dos Donatários (1439–1766). Subsídios para a História de S Miguel* (Ponta Delgada, 1949), p. 26.

which foreign businessmen like Lucas de Cacena made their fortunes. Initially in Sevillian Genoese (an area of important woad production), Cacena moved to Angra on the island of Terceira. Although hard data on the production of woad in the Azores are hard to come by, Cacena's evident success was rewarded by him being made a *fidalgo da casa del rei* by King João III.[80] Cacena's business partners in Antwerp, the Affaitati, could sell 16,000 bales of Azorean woad on the European marketplace in 1543.[81] It competed vigorously with wheat for available agricultural land, especially on the island of São Miguel, where Captain Donatory Gonçalo Vaz Coutinho lobbied for restricting its cultivation to one-third of the island's cultivated area.[82] It contributed to the periodic grain shortages of the sixteenth century, although by the end of the century *pastel* was being replaced in most European markets by cheaper and higher quality dyes from the New World.[83]

"NATURAL" DISASTERS, OR SUPERNATURAL RETRIBUTION?

The forest-clearing in the Azores was met by ominous portents, which were understood by the human population as protests of Nature. According to the islands' chroniclers, volcanoes erupted and the earth trembled underneath the settlers (*abalos de terra*). Explosive and effusive eruptions, as well as tectonic earthquakes (*sismos*), hit São Miguel at seemingly regular intervals thereafter.[84]

What is interesting for our purposes is not the physical causes or even consequences of these tectonic movements, which ecological historians have suggested, even in the case of the largest eruption in human history on the Aegean island of Thera/Santorini c.1628 BCE, do not seem to provide

---

80. Pierluigi Bragaglia, *Lucas e os Cacenas: mercadores e navegadores de Génova na Terceira (sécs. XV–XVI)* (Angra do Heroísmo, 1994). More generally, Francisco Carreiro da Costa, *A cultura do pastel nos Açores – subsídios para a sua história* (Ponta Delgada, 1946).

81. Lodovico Guicciardini, *Belgium Universum, Seu omnium inferioris Germaniae regionum accurata descriptio* (Amsterdam, 1646), p. 101, cols 1–2. This sales figure is confirmed by independent estimates supplied by the Provedor das Armadas, Pêro Andes do Canto.

82. Faria e Maia, *Capitães dos Donatários*, p. 262.

83. For an estimate of production on São Miguel, see do Canto, *Archivo dos Açores*, II, p. 155; Hilario Casado Alonso, "El Comercio del Pastel. Datos para una geografía de la industria pañera española en el siglo XVI", *Revista de historia económica*, 8 (1990), pp. 523–548; and Fritz Lauterbach, *Der Kampf des Waides mit dem Indigo* (Leipzig, 1905).

84. Primary accounts of these disasters can be found in do Canto, *Archivo dos Açores*, series "Vulcanismo nos Açores desde a época da descoberta até ao presente", I–VI; J.H. van Linschoten, *Navigatio ac Itinerarium Iohannis Hugonis Linscotani in Orientalem sive Lusitanorum Indiam* (The Hague, 1599), trans. and reprinted in *Boletim do Instituto Histórico da Ilha Terceira*, I (1943), pp. 161–162; in Padre A. Cordeiro, *História Insulana das Ilhas a Portugal sugeitas no Oceano Occidental* (Lisbon, 1866), I, p. 202; and in Frutuoso, *Saudades da Terra*, livro IV, pp. 84–87.

evidence "for widespread environmental transformation".[85] Although causing substantial fatalities (around 200 deaths following the Furnas eruption of 1630, according to the account of Padre Manuel Gonçalves, a Jesuit from the College of Ponta Delgada), these disasters pale when set next to the 5,000 who perished in the "dreadful earthquake at Lima and Callao" in 1746, from which only 200 were saved.[86] Rather, I would like to gauge the human response, which here was predominantly one of guilt for the human intrusion on the islands. The human response to this earthquake was much the same as in Lisbon during the famous earthquake of 1755, when the axiom "Whatever Is, Is Right" was adhered to, and which provoked for the first few days following the later Lisbon earthquake contrition and repentance, as if God had punished not only the traditional sins of the ordinary man, but Portugal itself, a land which had been specially chosen by God for His work and which had fallen by the wayside.[87]

We have a good record of the human response to earthquakes in the Azores thanks to a *Romance* penned in verse form by the chronicler Gaspar Frutuoso, who wrote down the events of 1522 later in the century from hearsay and conversations with elderly people on the islands during his appointment as vicar (*vigário*) at Ribeira Grande.[88] Skating over the causes, the tragic event unfolds amidst fine, calm weather, with the dislodging of rocks and earth and landslides, burying the town. The deaths caused provoked lamentations and popular clamour. Frei Afonso de Tolêdo, as a man of the cloth, heard confessions and offered comfort to the survivors. Voices from the earth were heard, but they were illusory,

85. Horden and Purcell, *The Corrupting Sea*, p. 306; cf. W.F. Jashemski, "Pompeii and Mount Vesuvius, AD 79", in Payson D. Sheets and Donald K. Grayson, *Volcanic Activity and Human Ecology* (New York, 1979), pp. 587–622.

86. *A True and Particular Relation of the Dreadful Earthquake which happen'd at Lima, the Capital of Peru, and the Neighbouring Port of Callao* (London, 1750).

87. Cf. Judite Nozes (ed.), *The Lisbon Earthquake of 1755: Some British Eye-Witness Accounts* (Lisbon, 1987), and Jelle Zeilinga de Boer and Donald Theodore Sanders, "Earthquakes in England: Echoes in Religion and Literature", in *idem, Earthquakes in Human History: The Far-Reaching Effects of Seismic Disruptions* (Princeton, NJ, 2005). Jean Delumeau has suggested that the Church in the Counter-Reformation deliberately manipulated typologies of natural disaster so as to replace chronic anxiety over survival with fear of divine retribution for sin. See his *La Peur en Occident (XIVe–XVIIIe siècles): une cité assiégée* (Paris, 1978).

88. The 360-verse *romance* forms cap. LXXIII of Livro IV of Gaspar Frutuoso's *Saudades da Terra: história das ilhas do Porto-Sancto, Madeira, Desertas e Selvagens*, A.R. de Azevedo (ed.) (Funchal, 1873), ch. 12. The *romance* is accompanied by a prose version: "Do grande e furioso tremor ou terramoto da terra que houve na ilha de S. Miguel em tempo de Rui Gonçalves da Camara, quinto Capitão dela e Segundo o nome, con que se subverteu Vila Franca do Campo, a mais nobre e principal das vilas que nele havia"; *ibid.*, cap. LXX. For some literary criticism, see Luís da Silva Ribeiro, *O Romance de algumas mágoas do terramoto de Vila Franca em 1522* (Angra do Heroísmo, 1951). *Romance* verse was a popular way to record *relaciones de sucesos*, or news, across the iberian world. In his *Romancero popular del siglo XVIII* (Madrid, 1972) Francisco Aguilar Piñal has collected thousands of such *romances* published in Andalusia.

Figure 5. Photograph of Garachico, rebuilt on the lava delta formed by the eruption of 1706. *Terra Publishing, London. Used with permission.*

for what was recovered were only corpses and goods. Further other-worldly signals were heard: in the sky, for instance, and new tremors followed. In 1591, inhabitants aware of these portents, quickly took to the fields and abandoned their houses, which were filled with "grief-filled lament" (*lastimoso pranto*). Meanwhile, rather than a tsunami or fires which burned for weeks, as occurred in Lisbon in 1755, in the Azores a plague attack quickly followed, lasting eight years. Thus, as is common in such circumstances, it was the consequences of the earthquake rather than the earthquake itself which caused the greater environmental impact in the case of São Miguel. A substantial population exodus to Brazil followed this sorry chapter in the island's history.

The Canary Islands, and here specifically Tenerife and Gran Canaria, also bore the brunt of repeated volcanic eruptions, an estimated twelve since the sixteenth century.[89] Here again, reports tend to downplay the immediate damage, though in the case of an eruption on 5 May 1706 on Tenerife an entire town (Garachico) subsequently disappeared under the molten basalt, which then spread in a fuming lobe into the sea (see Figure 5).

89. See Table 1 "Volcanismo reciente en el Archipielago Canario", in J. Fuster *et al.*, *Geología y Volcanología de las Islas Canarias* (Madrid, 1968) (volumes on Tenerife and Gran Canaria).

Although nobody was killed on this occasion, as the community had time to flee with their possessions to the neighbouring town of Icod, the entire town had to be rebuilt, the plan retraced over the surface of the new lava flows rather than being recommenced elsewhere, as was the case with a number of towns relocated after flooding in the Paraná valley, such as Corrientes (1598) and Santiago del Estero (1630).[90] While accounts of this natural disaster focus less on humanity's responsibility for this calamity, *religiosos* nevertheless had an important role to play in sustaining morale and God was invoked for succour rather than attributing blame. In many ways, the inhabitants of the Canaries took events as they unfolded in their stride, as if it were part of the original scheme of colonization: their predecessors, the *Guanches*, had long savoured a healthy respect for the power of the volcano, Teide, towering over them, and which they had called Echeide, the inferno.[91]

To conclude, while earthquakes and the ensuing plague outbreak in the case of São Miguel have been accorded by some historians the responsibility for an early end to the Azorean sugar industry,[92] it is equally interesting to assess the impact on the human inhabitants, who in their eyes bore the responsibility for the natural cataclysm, and which they explained in terms of their forest clearances and disturbances of the natural equilibrium.

THE POPULATION DYNAMICS OF MID-ATLANTIC COLONIZATION

In all of this, the strikingly polarized fates of the different islands in the mid-Atlantic need to be emphasized. We can demonstrate this point best in terms of populations. Initially, there was nothing to distinguish the demographic strategies from one island to the next. Free labour in Madeira – principally the emigration during the 1420s of farmers from lands belonging to Prince Henry or to the Order of Christ, the majority coming from the Algarve – was supplemented by the importation of slave labour from Africa, estimated at around 3,000 souls in 1522.[93] In the Azores, at first the Crown planned to transport convicts (*degredados*) to populate the island of São Miguel in 1453, a policy which was put into

---

90. María del Rosario Prieto, "The Paraná River Floods during the Spanish Colonial Period: Impact and Responses", in C. Mauch and C. Pfister (eds), *Natural Disasters, Cultural Responses: Case Studies Toward a Global Environmental History* (Lanham, MD, 2009), p. 296.

91. Carmen Romero Ruiz, *Las Manifestaciones volcánicas históricas del Archipiélago Canario*, 2 vols (Sta Cruz de Tenerife, 1991); cf. J.C. Carracedo *et al.*, "The 1677 Eruption of La Palma, Canary Islands", *Estudios Geológicos*, 52 (1996), pp. 103–114.

92. Andrzej Dziubiński, "La Fabrication et le Commerce du Sucre au Maroc aux 16 et 17 siècles", *Acta Poloniae Historica*, 54 (1987), pp. 5–37.

93. Mauro, *Le Portugal et l'Atlantique*, p. 150; see also António H. de Oliveira Marques, *História de Portugal* (Lisbon, 1973), I, p. 218.

force the following year.[94] Numbers were supplemented by blacks and Moorish slaves.[95] It was their combined labour that cleared the forests on islands such as São Miguel prior to the earthquake.

But overpopulation (*superpovoamento*), rather than underpopulation, rapidly became the chronic problem of these islands. On some, such as Madeira and São Miguel, the population outstripped even those islands' very rich agricultural resources, and emigrants were found from the Micaelenses by the Governor General and founder of the Captaincy of Bahía, Tomé de Sousa; they moved on to Brazil in return for food and transport aboard as well as "lands for cultivation and to exploit freely other than the payment of the tenth to God" (*terras para plantarem e aproveitarem livremente sem delas pagarem mais do que a dízimo a Deus*).[96] In the seventeenth and eighteenth centuries, the surplus population of Madeira and the Azores found employment in the King of Portugal's armies and navies and were an important element in the settlement and colonization of Brazil, particularly the southern province of Santa Catalina.[97]

This situation needs to be contrasted with that, say, in the poorly watered Cape Verdes. Here there has never been enough arable land to sustain more than a few people, although rather than persisting with the traditional cereals (rye, barley, wheat) instead experiments were made with *milho miúdo*, or pearl millet, which was grown on the African mainland opposite the islands, to moderate success.[98] As the Portuguese historical geographer Orlando Ribeiro succinctly put it: "In such a land so unfavourable to agriculture, the type of colonization which was characteristic of the Azores and Madeira was not possible."[99]

The imported European human population suffered terribly from malaria, diagnosed by European physicians at the time as "remittent" or "intermittent" fevers, that burgeoned during the rainy season (*tempo das águas*)

---

94. Da Silva Marques, *Descobrimentos Portugueses*, I, p. 517, II, p. 344.

95. Gaspar Frutuoso, *Saudades da Terra* (Ponta Delgada, 1998), livro IV, p. 10.

96. Do Canto, *Archivo dos Açores*, XII, p. 414 (Carta de El-Rei D. João III, 11 September 1550).

97. Maria da Conceição Vilhena, "Viagens no século XVIII. Dos Açores ao Brasil", *Studia*, 51 (1992), pp. 5–15; Raquel Soeiro de Brito, "Aspectos da emigração na ilha de S. Miguel", *Estudos de História de Portugal: homenagem a A.H. de Oliveira Marques*, II (Lisbon, 1983), pp. 533–546; José Damião Rodrigues, "Das ilhas ao Atlântico Sul. A Política Ultramarina e a emigração Açoriana para o Brasil no reinado de D. João V", *Anais de História de Além-Mar*, 8 (2007), pp. 57–67.

98. This was almost certainly *Pennisetum glaucum* (L.) R. Br. and not *Panicum miliaceum* Lin., a *milho miúdo* grown in northern Portugal. For a discussion of the problems associated with the early modern usage of the Portuguese term *milho* see Paul E.H. Hair, "*Milho, Meixoeira* and Other Foodstuffs of the Sofala Garrison, 1505–1525", *Cahiers d'Études Africaines*, 17:66–67 (1977), pp. 353–363.

99. Orlando Ribeiro, *Aspectos e Problemas da Expansão Portuguesa* (Lisbon, 1962), pp. 156–158.

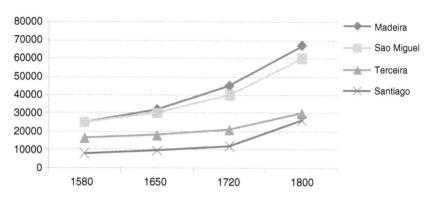

Figure 6. Island population growth, 1580–1800. [Madeira, São Miguel, Terceira, Santiago] *Statistics taken from Duncan, Atlantic Islands, appendix II.*

between July and October rendering the islands a "white man's grave" and which seriously threatened colonization. The Florentine merchant Francesco Carletti, who visited Santiago in 1593, wrote that Europeans were never healthy on that island and that the few Portuguese he saw there were weak and pallid, seeming more dead than alive.[100] Six Cape Verdean governors died before the completion of their triennial terms of office during the seventeenth century, and three bishops also died after brief terms of service. Of seven Jesuits who arrived in 1604 and 1606, four died within a few weeks and the mission had to be closed.[101] Consequently, generous tax concessions and other *regálias* needed to be offered to induce colonists to move there.[102] This policy was supplemented by *degredo*, the judicial commutation of lengthy prison sentences to banishment and exile, which proved particularly successful as a method for peopling the islands of S. Tomé and Principe to the south.[103]

100. Francesco Carletti, *Ragionamenti del mio viaggio intorno al mondo* (Milan, 1941), p. 7.
101. *Cabo Verde, Guiné, S. Thomé e Príncipe: curso de extensão universitaria – ano lectivo 1965–66* (Lisbon, 1965), pp. 515–525. For the tribulations of the Jesuit mission, see Nuno da Silva Gonçalves, SJ, *Os Jesuitas e a missão de Cabo Verde (1604–1642)* (Lisbon, 1996).
102. "A ylha de sam tome priuillegio aos moradores della pera poderem resgatar e trautar todallas mercadorías e cousas nadas e criadas na dita ylha, na terra firme dello rio Real ilha de fernam de poò Atee toda a terra de mani comgo e outras liverdades qui feitas na dita carta"; 26 March 1500, Arquivos Nacionais da Torre do Tombo, Lisbon, *Livro das Ilhas*, f. 81.
103. The number of convicts exiled in the Cape Verdes was actually low: only 14 individuals between 1466 and 1513, if we go by the documents published in Luís de Albuquerque (ed.), *História Geral de Cabo Verde: Corpo Documental*, 2 vols (Lisbon, 1988–1990). A substantial number of Jewish children who ended up in Portugal after the official Spanish expulsion order of 1492 were sent to S. Tomé with Álvaro da Caminha, appointed second Captain-General over the islands in the same year. See *Chronica del Rey D. João II*, M. Lopes de Almeida (ed.) (Porto, 1977), ch. 68.

The European arrival in the Canary Islands, however, heralded the full-scale population collapse of its light-skinned native *Guanches* peoples, whom both genetic (ABO allele frequencies) and linguistic evidence (base-10 counting systems, Libyco-Berber and Punic inscriptions in rock carvings) relate to the pre-Islamic Berbers of North Africa, and who had little more than Neolithic technology and reared goats and pigs.[104] Archaeological evidence suggests they possessed no nautical skills and had been out of touch with the African mainland since migrating there at some time between 1000 and 100 BCE.[105] The expedition of 1402 undertaken by Jean de Béthencourt and Gadifer de la Salle in the name of the King of Castile landed in Lanzarote, built a fortress, captured the ruler of one of the smaller outlying islands, and forced a military surrender, followed by Christian baptism for the subjugated population. Thereafter, it took the colonists over ninety years to conquer all seven islands – despite the Portuguese Prince Henry's repeated expeditions to make conquests and plant settlements – for although armed only with javelins and rocks, the *Guanches'* knowledge of the mountainous terrain and determination to hang on to their land and way of life made them formidable opponents (see Figure 7).

Eventually, plague achieved what horses, cannons, and armour and muskets could not; on Christmas Day 1495 the last *Guanches* surrendered in Tenerife. Remaining insurgents were hunted down from the hills, their traditional dress was outlawed and they were sold as slaves and put to work on the new sugar plantations, just as their brethren had been enslaved over the previous 100 years. Others were taken to Valencia, Andalusia, the Algarve, and Madeira.[106]

The extinction of the *Guanches* as a race from around this time tends in historical scholarship to be overshadowed by the debate over Easter Island and the fate of its population, doomed by deforestation and overfishing, perhaps spurred on by the immense, eerie statues (*moai*) left behind as testimony to their erstwhile presence.[107] In truth, the two are not commensurable phenomena, for the *Guanches* were a victim of genocide from without and the Easter Islanders of extermination from within. But accusations of genocide, so easily presented from standard

104. N. Maca-Meyer *et al.*, "Ancient mtDNA Analysis and the Origin of the Guanches", *European Journal of Human Genetics*, 12:2 (2004), pp. 155–162; J. Bynon, "The Contribution of Linguistics to History in the Field of Berber Studies", in David Dalby (ed.), *Language and History in Africa* (New York, 1970), pp. 64–77. The *Guanches* in fact comprised a number of linguistically and perhaps ethnically quite distinct peoples.
105. Felipe Fernández-Armesto, *The Canary Islands After the Conquest* (Oxford, 1982), pp. 5–12.
106. Alberto Artur Sarmento, *Os escravos na Madeira* (Funchal, 1938).
107. Jared Diamond, *Collapse: How Societies Choose to Fail or Succeed* (New York, 2005).

Figure 7. A rare illustration of Canary Island *Guanches* from the island of El Hierro, c.1590. *Leonardo Torriani, "Descrittione et historia del regno de l'isole Canarie". University Library of Coimbra, Portugal. Used with permission.*

historical narratives of the conquest of the Canaries, run into obstacles when confronted with the findings of modern science, which has shown how aboriginal *Guanche* mitochondrial DNA (collected from Canarian archaeological sites) has been passed on to today's Canarians in considerable proportions.

According to the recent findings of Nicole Maca-Meyer and her research partners, "despite the continuous changes suffered by the population (Spanish colonization, slave trade), aboriginal mtDNA (direct maternal) lineages constitute a considerable proportion (42–73 per cent) of the Canarian gene pool". She goes on: "since the end of the 16th century, at least two-thirds of the Canarian population had an indigenous substrate".[108] Y-DNA, or Y-chromosomal (direct paternal) lineages, were not analysed in this study. However, the researchers cite an earlier study giving the aboriginal Y-DNA contribution at 6 per cent,[109] although these results have been critiqued as possibly flawed. Regardless, Maca-Meyer *et al.* state that historical evidence does support the explanation of "strong sexual asymmetry [...] as a result of a strong bias favouring matings between European males and aboriginal females, and to the important aboriginal male mortality during the Conquest".[110] So, there are two sides

108. Identified as mtDNA haplogroup U subclade U6b1.
109. C. Flores *et al.*, "A Predominant European Ancestry of Paternal Lineages from Canary Islanders", *Annals of Human Genetics*, 67 (2003), pp. 138–152.
110. Maca-Meyer, "Ancient mtDNA Analysis and the Origin of the Guanches", p. 155.

to the coin: while the European conquest of the Canaries saw the extermination of *Guanche* males, females were selected as mating partners and, through them, *Guanche* genes were passed on.

CONCLUSIONS

Ecocide is, more than anything, a call today to raise world attention on environmental issues and as such is a political programme, rather than a historically verifiable state of affairs. Historians of the mid-Atlantic islands would do better to heed the notion of economic cycles, different productive phases in the islands' history, and bear witness to the social tensions arising from competing notions of land use: between cereal cultures and the sugar industry, between silviculture and agriculture, between cash-cropping exporters and those who sought to attract population, between mobile, pastoralist populations (initially the *Guanches*, later the poorer elements of society) and sedentary ones (both town-builders and *fazendistas* keen to cadastralize land and establish clear boundaries of possession).

The islands may have lost a large part of their forest cover, to the point that trees like the Madeiran *til* are now registered on the IUCN Red List of Endangered Species, and even their original human population, but rather than becoming redundant wastelands, instead became beacons for international trade and expanding, successful agricultures, whether sugar, cereals, or wine. Rather than preach catastrophism, which is generally unconvincing,[111] we would do better to see the relationship between human life and nature as interactive and embedded within a kaleidoscopic environment in which little or nothing is permanent, and in which there are winners as well as losers.

---

111. Tim Flannery, "A Great Jump to Disaster", *New York Review of Books*, 56:18 (19 November 2009).

IRSH 55 (2010), Supplement, pp. 79–101 doi:10.1017/S0020859010000507
© 2010 Internationaal Instituut voor Sociale Geschiedenis

Environmental Change and Globalization in Seventeenth-Century France: Dutch Traders and the Draining of French Wetlands (Arles, Petit Poitou)*

RAPHAËL MORERA

Centre d'Histoire des Techniques et de L'Environnement, Paris

E-mail: morera.raphael@gmail.com

SUMMARY: Between 1599 and the end of the 1650s, the French Crown sustained a policy of land reclamation at a large scale. It was led by the French aristocracy who were helped by representatives of the merchant elites of Amsterdam, such as Hieronimus van Uffelen and Jean Hoeufft. The works in both Arles (Provence) and Petit Poitou (Poitou) show that land reclamation involved a radical change in society, reinforced the authority of the Crown in the areas concerned, and disrupted the former social balances built around the marshes. Thus, land reclamation aroused several conflicts which revealed its deep impact on the environment. So, this article demonstrates how the making of the modern state, backed by the development of European trade and banking, caused ecological and social changes by connecting the political and financial powers on a European scale.

In the long-term history of wetlands, the sixteenth century represents a turning point as at that time very large funds were injected into a new system of drainage.[1] In the Low Countries and in northern Italy more than anywhere else, the conquest of the wetlands turned into an extensive business.[2]

The change was particularly marked in Holland, where people were obliged to manage the consequences of the intensive mining of peat which had occurred during the Middle Ages.[3] To drain the lakes created by the

---

* I should like to thank Alice Arnould, Daniel Dessert, Christelle Rabier, Géraldine Vaughan, and Marjolein 't Hart, who helped me put this essay into good order.

1. John F. Richards, *The Unending Frontier: An Environmental History of the Early Modern World* (Berkeley, CA [etc.], 2003).
2. Salvatore Ciriacono, *Acque e agricoltura. Venezia, l'Olanda e la bonifica europea in Età Moderna* (Milan, 1994), pp. 208–242.
3. Karel Leenders, *Verdwenen venen. Een onderzoek naar de ligging en exploitatie van thans verdwenen venen in het gebied tussen Antwerpen, Turnhout, Geertruidenberg en Willemstad,*

resulting subsidence, the Dutch employed new techniques, using wind-mills to divert water into canals and rivers. The spread of this model, called the *boezem* system, enabled the extension of agricultural land and the growth and urbanization of the population. It marked the beginning of a new relationship between human societies and marshes, as the drai-nage work was supported by the central political authorities and financed by capitalist groups.[4] That development was enhanced in the last twenty years of the sixteenth century when refugees from Flanders and Brabant put their money into drainage projects in the northern Netherlands.[5]

As early as the 1580s, the water-management skills of the Dutch had become a model throughout Europe. The role of Dutchmen in the draining of wetlands could be documented in such very different regions as Britain, Germany, Russia, Italy, and France.[6] In England, Humphrey Bradley, a Dutch engineer and a native of Bergen op Zoom in Brabant, came to drain the Fens in the 1580s.[7] Soon after, Bradley was called to France, where he launched a wave of land reclamation. From 1599 to the end of the 1650s, the intervention of foreign engineers and financiers was continuous. At least 12 swamps were drained and no fewer than 150 and perhaps as many as 260 square kilometres of wetlands were converted to arable lands or meadows. That surface area can be compared to the 1,115 square kilometres which the Dutch, who in contrast to the French were short of arable land, drained in the meantime for themselves.[8]

The draining of French wetlands was thus a major event, and can usefully be analysed in its European context. Indeed, the alliance between the French monarchy and foreign merchants and bankers who were interested in international trade was the only means to carry out drainage projects in France, so the draining of French marshes was strongly embedded in the internationalization of the seventeenth-century economy.

1250–1750 (Brussels, 1989); Gerardus van de Ven, *Man-Made Lowlands: History of Water Management and Land Reclamation in the Netherlands* (Utrecht, 1993); Milja van Tielhof and Petra van Dam, *Waterstaat in stedenland. Het hoogheemraadschap van Rijnland voor 1857* (Utrecht, 2006), pp. 52–86.

4. Van Tielhof and van Dam, *Waterstaat in stedenland*, pp. 152–179; Siger Zeischka, *Minerva in de polder. Waterstaat en techniek in het hoogheemraadschap van Rijnland, 1500–1865* (Hil-versum, 2008), pp. 198–239.

5. See for instance *Extract uyt het octroy van de Beemster met de cavel-conditien en de caerten van dien. 't Register van de participanten. Ende verscheyden keuren tot welstand van de dijckage. Bij de Hooft–inghelanden, dickgraef ende heemraden gemaeckt* (Amsterdam, 1613).

6. Ciriacono, *Acque e agricoltura*, pp. 243–310.

7. H.C. Darby, *The Draining of the Fens* (Cambridge, 1956); L.E. Harris, *The Two Nether-landers: Humphrey Bradley and Cornelis Drebbel* (Leiden, 1961); idem, *Vermuyden and the Fens: A Study of Sir Cornelius Vermuyden and the Great Level* (London, 1953).

8. Jan de Vries and Ad van der Woude, *The First Modern Economy: Success, Failure and Perseverance of the Dutch Economy, 1500–1815* (Cambridge, 1997), p. 32.

Although the French had money to invest, Dutch bankers were more readily able to provide funds, resources, and skills. As the main investors were not natives of the regions where the land reclamation had taken place, the drainage operations caused conflicts which reveal the socio-political significance of land reclamation. Moreover, as both the cases of Arles (Provence) and Petit Poitou (Poitou) show, such projects launched by Henri IV had a far-reaching environmental impact.[9]

LAND RECLAMATION IN SEVENTEENTH-CENTURY FRANCE AND THE ECONOMIC DEVELOPMENT OF AMSTERDAM

In 1583, Henri III granted an entitlement to drain the lake of Pujaut (Gard, Languedoc) in southern France.[10] In 1599, Henri IV continued the policy and changed the scale of its application by promulgating an edict which promoted land reclamation throughout the kingdom.[11] He gave Humphrey Bradley the power to drain all of France's lakes and marshes. That same year, Bradley joined Conrad Gaussen, a Dutch merchant who had settled in Bordeaux, in order to drain the marshes there and those of Lesparre, located in the low estuary of the Gironde (Guyenne).[12] In 1600, Bradley attempted to extend his activities to the French Atlantic coast and started to drain the Tonnay-Charente marshes (Charente-Maritime). Despite the support of the monarchy and the creation of a very favourable legal framework, Bradley could not cope alone with the opposition he had to face.[13] He had to contend with former users of swamps, and he barely managed to raise enough money to finance his projects.

In 1605, therefore, he set up an association with the Comans brothers and François de la Planche, or van der Planken.[14] Even though the first

9. Even though these works began in Bordeaux (Guyenne), after the publication of a *privilège* in 1599, I will highlight two cases, Arles (Provence) and Petit Poitou (Poitou), completed in the 1640s.

10. A. Coulondres, "Notices sur le dessèchement des étangs de Rochefort et de Pujaut", *Mémoires et comptes-rendus de la société scientifique et littéraire d'Alais* (1876), pp. 15–54.

11. *Edit pour le dessèchement des marais portant commission à cet effet à un etranger* (Fontainebleau, 1599).

12. Edouard de Dienne, *Histoire du desséchement des lacs et marais en France avant 1789* (Paris, 1891), pp. 117ff.; R. Morera, "Les assèchements de marais en France au XVIIe siècle (1599–1661). Technique, économie, environnement" (Ph.D., University of Paris 1 Panthéon-Sorbonne, 2008), [hereafter, "Les assèchements de marais XVIIe siècle"].

13. *Edict du roy pour le dessèchement des Marais* (Paris, 1607); *Arrest et reglement fait par le roy en son conseil sur le dessèchement des marais de France* (Paris, 1611); *Declaration du roy, faite sur l'interprétation & modification de l'Edict fait en faveur du dessèchement des marais en France* (Paris, 1613).

14. Archives Nationales, Paris [hereafter, AN], Minutier central [hereafter, MC], LIV 464, 19 janvier 1605.

contract does not mention him, Hieronimus van Uffelen was also involved in this company.[15] The Comans and de la Planche were natives of Brabant, and ultra Catholic. They had been called by Sully, then prime minister and Surintendant des finances, to develop tapestry manufacturing in Paris in the hope that it would limit textile imports from the Low Countries.[16] Settled in Paris in the early seventeenth century, they quickly extended their activities to include the leather and grain trades.[17] In the Parisian notaries' archives, it appears that they were associated with Van Uffelen, who came from Antwerp, in various businesses.[18]

In 1585, his family had moved to Amsterdam, where they traded in copper and lead as well as in drapery. Their Russian trade flourished and two family members established themselves in Venice, where they acted as agents. Van Uffelen also participated in overseas trade by buying shares in the Dutch East India Company.[19] The family's integration into Amsterdam's merchant elite was strengthened when Jacomo van Uffelen married Maria van Erp in 1616. She was the daughter of a famous copper trader, Arent van Erp,[20] and the sister-in-law of Pieter Cornelisz Hooft, a major trader in herring, oil, and grains. Hooft was one of the first shareholders of the VOC and was many times mayor of Amsterdam.[21] Thus, from the beginning, the French land reclamations launched by Henri IV had involved members of the commercial elite of Amsterdam who had come originally from the Brabant region.

Those Flemish and Brabant capitalists were backed by the French aristocracy as early as 1605, thus providing a strong political network. Jean de Fourcy was the Surintendant des bâtiments du roi, in charge of the administration of the royal buildings, and a member of the Conseil d'État, an increasingly powerful instrument of central government.[22] Originally close to Sully, he became a "creature" of Richelieu as early as the 1610s. Antoine Ruzé d'Effiat was Jean de Fourcy's brother-in-law and became

---

15. *Edict du roy pour le dessèchement des Marais.*

16. Jules Guiffrey, *Histoire de la tapisserie depuis le Moyen Age jusqu'à nos jours* (Tours, 1886), pp. 294ff.

17. AN, MC, LI 21, 30 août 1608 (for the leather trade); MC, XVII 161, 28 avril 1615 (for Levant trade).

18. Eric Henk Wijnroks, *Handel tussen Rusland en de Nederlanden, 1560–1640* (Hilversum, 2003), pp. 244–260.

19. Johannes Gerard van Dillen, *Het oudste aandeelhoudersregister van de Kamer Amsterdam der Oost-Indische Compagnie* (The Hague, 1958), p. 211.

20. Johan Engelbert Elias, *De vroedschap van Amsterdam, 1578–1795*, 2 vols (Haarlem, 1903), I, p. 60.

21. *Ibid.*; Van Dillen, *Het oudste aandeelhoudersregister*, pp. 71 and 200.

22. Louis Battiffol, "Les travaux du Louvre sous Henri IV d'après de nouveaux documents", *Gazette des Beaux-Arts* (1912), p. 178; Bernard Barbiche, "Henri IV et la surintendance des bâtiments", *Bulletin monumental*, 142 (1984), pp. 19–39.

Surintendant des finances in 1625.[23] Nicolas de Harlay was a former Intendant des bâtiments du roi and a former ambassador of Henri III and Henri IV. Until 1639, the association remained stable, despite the deaths of Jean de Fourcy in 1625 and Antoine Ruzé d'Effiat in 1631. For instance, in 1634, Henry de Fourcy, son of Jean, and Luca van Uffelen, son of Hieronimus, were still involved in a joint business to export grain to Malta.[24] Furthermore, the owners of French-drained lands used the network of Dutch merchants to sell the produce from their new properties at favourable prices.

For more than thirty years, the draining of the French marshes relied on the association of three different groups: French aristocrats and financiers, foreign capitalists, and the engineer Humphrey Bradley. The scheme worked effectively because of the shared interests of French financiers and capitalists and merchants from the southern Netherlands. In that context, no fewer than eight different sites were drained: Bordeaux and Lesparre in Guyenne, Tonnay-Charente in Saintonge, Sarliève in Auvergne, Capestang in Languedoc, the Marais Vernier in the Seine estuary, and the swamps of Sacy-le-Grand in Picardy.

The organization of the drainage work was continued at the end of the 1630s, even though by then several of the main investors had died. As early as 1640, Johan Hoeufft (1578–1651) and Barthélémy Hervart (1606–1676) began their participation in these projects. Hervart was a German banker from Augsburg,[25] where his family had been established for a long time, ever since his grandfather had joined Jacob Fugger.[26] Hervart started his career at the court of Weimar, taking charge of the treasury. During the 1630s, he played the role of go-between with France. Richelieu chose him as middle-man to pay the mercenaries of the Duke of Weimar.[27] During the 1640s, he served Mazarin with the same loyalty as he had served Richelieu. He was also one of the main partners of Thomas Cantarini, Pierre Serantoni, and Vincent Cenami, who were bankers and associates of Mazarin.[28] Thanks to his loyalty, Hervart became a key figure in French finances and was made Surintendant des

---

23. Françoise Bayard, Joël Félix, and Philippe Hamon, *Dictionnaire des surintendants et contrôleurs généraux des finances: du XVIe siècle à la Révolution française de 1789* (Paris, 2000), pp. 60–63.

24. AN, MC, XIX 406, 19 mars 1634; MC XIX 407, 30 avril 1634.

25. Claude Dulong, *Mazarin et l'argent. Banquiers et prête-noms* (Paris, 2002), pp. 263–335; Georges Depping, "Un banquier protestant en France au XVIIe siècle, Barthélémy Herwarth, contrôleur général des finances (1606–1676)", *Revue historique*, 10 (1879), pp. 285–338, and 11 (1879), pp. 63–80.

26. Léon Schick, *Un grand homme d'affaires au début du XVIe siècle. Jacob Fugger* (Paris, 1957), pp. 60–63.

27. Claude Badalo-Dulong, *Banquier du roi, Barthélémy Hervart 1606–1676* (Paris, 1951).

28. Dulong, *Mazarin et l'argent*, pp. 12ff., 149–212.

finances in 1655.[29] He must have met Johan Hoeufft in Weimar, where Hoeufft was also employed by Richelieu to supply the army.

Hoeufft was a merchant from Roermond, or Guelders, in the modern-day Dutch province of Limburg.[30] After travelling with his family, he moved to France and settled in Rouen (Normandy) in 1600, and received a *lettre de naturalité* the following year.[31] Whereas the Comans brothers came to Paris as Catholics, Hoeufft was a Protestant and so was an example of a Protestant migrant from the Low Countries. Hoeufft had experienced a steady rise in international trade ever since his arrival in France. During the first two decades of the century, he developed his business mainly by means of Atlantic trade.[32] Based in Rouen, he acted as an intermediary between the United Provinces and Spain. After 1609, in a peaceful period, he began to trade directly with Spain. The notaries' archives of Rouen reveal that Hoeufft was an active shipowner exporting French grains to Italy.[33] He quickly became used to working with the Dutch East India Company, to which he supplied ships and sold materials to construct them,[34] and built strong links with Protestant merchants in the Atlantic region.

Until 1630, his main speciality was the trading of metal goods, weapons, and vessels.[35] Probably, he was close to Van Uffelen, and was thus informed about land reclamation. While continuing his former business, he took great interest in the development of the French financial system. Since 1624 the French monarchy had been fighting the Spanish Crown by financing the troops of Bernard of Saxe-Weimar, among others. Thanks to his family in Amsterdam, Hoeufft was placed in charge of building a link between France and the Weimar court. In compensation for his services, Hoeufft was granted a number of tax farms,[36] which meant that he could collect different taxes to reimburse his advances to the French monarchy.

---

29. Daniel Dessert, *Argent, pouvoir et société au Grand Siècle* (Paris, 1984).

30. Jacques Bottin and Pierre Jeannin, "Entre conviction et réalisme: deux hommes d'affaires protestants du premier XVIIe siècle", in Guy Martinière, Didier Poton, and François Souty (eds), *D'un rivage à l'autre, ville et protestantisme dans l'aire atlantique (XVIe–XVIIe siècles)* (Paris, 1999), pp. 157–171.

31. Archives Départementales, Seine-Maritime, C 1260.

32. Bottin and Jeannin, "Entre conviction et réalisme", pp. 160–161.

33. Jacques Bottin, "Négoce et crises frumentaires: Rouen et ses marchands dans le commerce international des blés, milieu XVIe – début XVIIe siècle", *Revue d'histoire moderne et contemporaine*, 45 (1998), p. 579. At the beginning of the seventeenth century Hoeufft possessed, in his own name, two ships of 160 and 200 tons.

34. Bottin and Jeannin, "Entre conviction et réalisme", pp. 160–161.

35. AN, MC, LXXIII 295; AN, MC, LXXIII 296, 25 janvier 1621.

36. To pay his debts, the King of France used to give his creditors the right to collect and keep the revenues of taxes, so that they could recover their money from taxpayers' contributions; AN, E 96 A, fo. 275; E 140 B, fo. 327; E 167, fo. 268; E 199 A, fo. 367. On this point see Françoise Bayard, *Le monde des financiers au XVIIe siècle* (Paris, 1988).

Hoeufft thus became an agent of Richelieu, who used Hoeufft's connections in Holland to raise funds on the Dutch money market.[37] In the next decade, Mazarin employed him in a similar way.[38] In the first half of the seventeenth century Hoeufft progressively became indispensable to the French monarchy.

In view of the enormous funds involved, it is clear that Hoeufft could not have succeeded alone. He belonged to one of the most powerful bourgeois families of the United Provinces. Hoeufft was a bachelor and had no children, but his nephews followed very successful careers. Two of them require some special attention. Johan Hoeufft junior was canon of the Utrecht diocese, and as a shareholder in the drainage work of Petit Poitou, he took the title of Lord of Fontaine-le-Comte and Choisival.[39] But that was not his main business, for he was also a director of the Dutch East India Company and closely involved in its overseas trade.[40] In 1638 he married Isabella Deutz, the daughter of Hans Deutz and Elisabeth Coijmans.[41] The marriage was the best proof of the perfect integration of the Hoeufft family into the world of international trade. Isabella Deutz was the granddaughter of Balthasar Coijmans, who had built his fortune in international trade and who was, in 1630, the second wealthiest man in Amsterdam.[42] Furthermore, Isabella's brother, Johan Deutz (1618–1673), made a brilliant career in Amsterdam, becoming in 1654 the director of trade with the Levant and obtaining in 1659 a monopoly of the mercury trade in northern Europe.[43]

The second nephew of Johan Hoeufft who participated in the construction of his social network was Diderick junior (1610–1688). He spent all his life in Dordrecht and died as Lord of Fontaine-Peureuse, a tribute to his involvement in the draining of the marshes of Sacy-le-Grand, near Compiègne, in Picardy.[44] Like that of his cousin, the social integration of Diderick can be established from his marriage. In 1641 he married Maria de Witt.[45] She was Jacob de Witt's daughter and sister of Johan de Witt, the political leader of the United Provinces from the 1650s until the 1670s.[46]

---

37. Archives des affaires étrangères, Paris, Correspondance politique, Hollande 17, no. 97.
38. "Abrégé du compte de la recepte faite sous le nom de Monseigneur le Cardinal de Mazarin depuis 1641 jusques en l'année 1648", in Dulong, *Mazarin et l'argent*, pp. 241–243.
39. Elias, *De vroedschap*, II p. 633.
40. *Ibid.*
41. *Ibid.*
42. J.G. Frederiks and P.J. Frederiks, *Kohier van den tweehonderdsten penning voor Amsterdam en onderhoorige plaatsen over 1631* (Amsterdam, 1890), p. 69.
43. Elias, *De vroedschap*, II, p. 633.
44. *Ibid.*, p. 634.
45. Herbert H. Rowen, *John de Witt, Grand Pensionary of Holland, 1625–1672* (Princeton, NJ, 1978), p. 108.
46. *Idem*, *John de Witt: Statesman of the "True Freedom"* (Cambridge, 1986).

This then was the history of the drainage entrepreneurs of the Petit Poitou and Arles marshes. Furthermore, Johan Hoeufft participated in an international business network. His family and their business links with the greatest Dutch capitalist families gave him a solid financial base. Several of his relatives and allies were involved in overseas trade, one of the major pillars of Dutch economic growth in the seventeenth century.[47]

The drainage projects undertaken in France between 1599 and the middle of the seventeenth century were based on a collaboration between the French central government and a small group of capitalists and financiers whose main business was based in Amsterdam. Their economic and political powers reinforced each other in a social construction that continued for almost sixty years and resulted in a strong politico-economic network.

THE DRAINAGE WORKS: A SOCIO-POLITICAL ISSUE

Between 1599 and the 1640s, most of the French drainage projects were undertaken with the help of foreign investors. Thanks to the edicts of 1599 and 1607, they could easily expropriate property from its owners and simply throw out former users of the swamps who did not want to sell their lands or cooperate in the drainage work. Admittedly, they also imported new ways of growing wheat and raising cattle. In that way, the globalization of the economy had consequences on a local scale, even though the drained swamps were very far from the economic core. The cases of Arles and Petit Poitou will clarify the nature of the social disruption caused by the drainage.

The most famous marshes drained in France during the seventeenth century were those of Petit Poitou.[48] During the twelfth and thirteenth centuries, the Cistercian monks of the area had already conducted an important drainage operation and had constructed the hydraulic infrastructures of the swamps.[49] Progressively, that equipment fell into disrepair, especially during the Wars of Religion, when Poitou became a region much disputed between Catholics and Protestants.[50] As a consequence, between the middle of the sixteenth century and the 1640s the swamps were left derelict. The marshes had started to lure investors at the

---

47. De Vries and Van der Woude, *The First Modern Economy*, pp. 377–408; J.L. van Zanden, *The Rise and Decline of Holland's Economy: Merchant Capitalism and the Labour Market* (Manchester, 1993), pp. 35–41.
48. Yannis Suire, *Le Marais poitevin. Une écohistoire du XVIe à l'aube du XXe siècle* (La Roche-sur-Yon, 2006).
49. Jean-Luc Sarrazin, "Les Cisterciens et la genèse du marais poitevin (France), (vers 1180–vers 1250)", in Léon Pressouyre and Paul Benoit (eds), *L'hydraulique monastique. Milieux, réseaux, usages* (Grâne, 1996), pp. 111–117.
50. Suire, *Le Marais poitevin*, pp. 23–28.

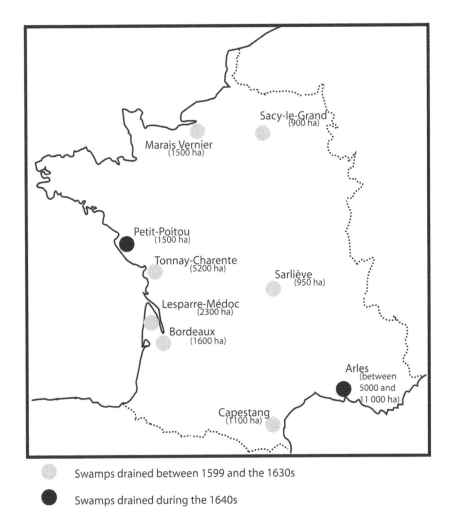

Figure 1. Land reclamation in France between 1599 and the 1650s.

beginning of the 1640s, by which time the drainage programme of Tonnay-Charente, located in Saintonge, a few kilometres to the south of Petit Poitou and near the city of La Rochelle, had begun to prove its profitability (see Figure 2).[51]

The merit of that work has been attributed to the Dutch for a long time, but the manner of their intervention was unclear. Recently, Yannis Suire tried to show that the draining of Petit Poitou had been the work of local

51. Morera, "Les assèchements de marais XVIIe siècle", pp. 301–302.

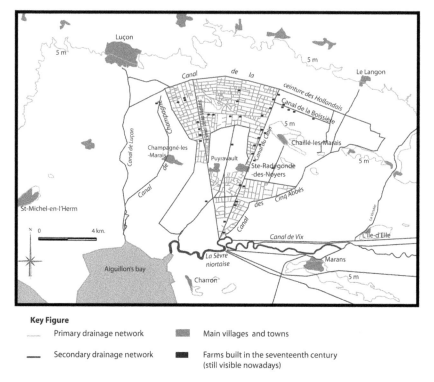

Key Figure

— Primary drainage network   � Main villages and towns

— Secondary drainage network   ■ Farms built in the seventeenth century
(still visible nowadays)

Figure 2. The drained swamps of Petit-Poitou.
Sources: Cartes IGN au 1/50 000 1327, 1328, 1427 et 1428 and Pierre Siette, Plan et description particulière des marais desseichés du Petit Poitou *(1648).*

investors only.[52] It is probable that the local aristocracy did play a key role. In 1641, an entitlement to drain the Petit Poitou swamp was granted to Pierre Siette, an engineer and cartographer to the king, and a representative of the Duke Antoine de Gramont and the Prince de Condé.[53] Alongside those two investors, it is also useful to mention Julius de Loynes, Richelieu's personal secretary.[54] So, to that extent, the reclamation of the Petit Poitou marshland was under aristocratic control, and certainly Richelieu and then Mazarin guided operations.

52. Suire, *Le Marais poitevin*, pp. 56ff.
53. *Declaration du roy, contenant la continuation des privilèges accordez pour le dessechement des marais des provinces de Poictou, Xaintonge & Aulnis* (Paris, 1641); Pierre Siette was actually a frontman for Antoine de Gramont: *Privileges pour les maraiz des paroisses de Parampuire, Ludon et Blanquefort en Guyenne* (Paris, 1649), p. 5; *Arrêt du conseil privé … portant que la dixme des fruicts qui se levent sur le sterres cy-devant en marais, à présent desseichées et mises en culture dans l'estendue de la paroisse de Saint Bonnet sera payée à raison de vingt gerbes l'une* (Paris, 1651), p. 1.
54. Joseph Bergin, *Pouvoir et fortune de Richelieu* (Paris, 1987), pp. 59ff.; originally published as *Cardinal Richelieu: Power and the Pursuit of Wealth* (London, 1985).

Nevertheless, the archives, kept in Utrecht, of the Society for the Draining of Petit Poitou show that these local contractors depended on Dutch investors.[55] Octavio de Strada, who monitored the work for Hoeufft, wrote two notebooks which list the expenditure of Johan Hoeufft in Petit Poitou between 1642 and 1651, the year of his death. During that decade Hoeufft invested 168,135 livres tournois (lt.) in his own name in Petit Poitou. In the meantime, he also lent 622,000 lt. to the main associates in the drainage work, and 200,146 lt. to his own representative in the region, Octavio de Strada.[56] The Utrecht books show that Johan Hoeufft provided all the money required, enabling the local aristocracy to take control of the region by granting them generous loans and indirectly strengthening support for the monarchy in the region. The land reclamation work therefore affected the agrarian balance and the structure of land ownership.

Almost nothing is known about the exploitation of the Petit Poitou swamps just before their reclamation, and even demographic and economic studies are lacking. Nevertheless, some information can be drawn from de Strada's notebooks. First, it is important to note that the land reclamation was a very hierarchical enterprise.[57] De Strada settled two farmers in the *polder* in order to conduct and survey the work. During the 1640s the work faced no judicial opposition nor were there riots against their installation. On the one hand, such a silence can be explained by political support for the operation, as the main aristocrats of the region were themselves involved in the land reclamation. Furthermore, the monasteries of the area were too weak to take any action.

On the other hand, there were the demographics of the region. Indeed, it is striking that de Strada's notebooks mention – several times – workers coming from Auvergne or Holland.[58] That indicates that the drainage entrepreneurs could not find the labour force they needed in Poitou alone and that they had to import them from more remote regions. In other words, the lack of opposition could certainly be explained by the demographic weakness of Poitou and the consequent abandonment of the swamps, which allowed for a reinforcement of the aristocracy's economic dominance. It is all the more interesting to compare the case of Poitou with the project at Arles in lower Provence, where the demographic trend was the opposite.

In association with Barthélémy Hervart, Johan Hoeufft also superintended important works in the Rhone delta.[59] Operations began there in 1642, the same year as in Petit Poitou, and the pattern of the enterprise

---

55. Rijksarchief Utrecht, Huis Zuilen [hereafter, RUHZ], 691 and 692.
56. RUHZ, 692, fo. 187v.
57. Morera, "Les assèchements de marais XVIIe siècle", pp. 338–366.
58. RUHZ, 692 fo. 684r.
59. Dienne, *Histoire du desséchement*, p. 289; Morera, "Les assèchements de marais XVIIe siècle", pp. 353–356.

was the same.[60] Hoeufft did not settle in Provence, so he had to entrust an employee with overseeing the business. He chose Jan van Ens, whose uncle was involved both in land reclamation in Picardy, and in French finances.[61] Van Ens managed the work from 1642 until his death in 1653. Because of the conflicts he had to face, Octavio de Strada joined him in 1648.[62]

Like the swamps of Petit Poitou, the marshes of Arles had been drained since the Middle Ages,[63] and their infrastructure too suffered similarly from the social disruption at the end of the sixteenth century, which lasted – in Provence – until 1629.[64] Despite the similarities, however, the social context in which the work took place was deeply different. First, Hoeufft, Hervart, and their associates did not finance aristocratic support and so intervened in their own names. So, in accordance with the Edict of 1599, after draining the swamp they jointly owned two-thirds of the land as soon as the work was completed, between 1645 and 1646.[65] As a consequence, they controlled a huge part of the territory of Arles and thus caused a local agrarian revolution by dispossessing members of the local elite.[66]

To carry on this land allocation, all the Arlesian countryside was surveyed in order to ascertain which parcels of land would be given to Van Ens. That work was entrusted to Jean Pellissier, an Arlesian surveyor, and Johan Voortcamp, a Dutch cartographer who had come especially to assist in the drainage work.[67] Their mission was concluded by the publication of two reports giving the names and titles of all the former landowners of the swamps, including the quantity and quality of the lands they possessed. Thanks to that document, it is still possible to understand how Hoeufft's investments completely changed the relationship between Arles and its countryside.[68]

60. Bibliothèque Municipale d'Arles [hereafter, BMA], Fonds Véran, no. 493.

61. Archives Départementales, Oise, H 1698, pièce nos 11 and 12.

62. AN, MC, CXXII 445, 5 juillet 1648.

63. Louis Stouff, "La lutte contre les eaux dans les pays du bas Rhône, XIIe–XVe siècles. L'exemple du pays d'Arles", *Méditerranée*, 3-4, (1993), pp. 57–68; Emeline Roucaute, "Gestion et exploitation du marais arlésien au Moyen Âge", in Joëlle Burnouf and Philippe Leveau (eds), *Fleuves et marais, une histoire au croisement de la nature et de la culture* (Paris, 2004), pp. 245–251.

64. Jean-Maurice Rouquette *et al.*, *Arles, histoire, territoires et cultures* (Paris, 2008), pp. 479–494.

65. To pay the investors for the land reclamation, the Edict of 1599 required two-thirds of the drained lands be given to the entrepreneurs at the end of the reclamation work, with the other third being for the former landowners.

66. Archives municipales d'Arles [hereafter, AMA], DD 85, fo. 39 and ff.

67. Archives Départementales des Bouches-du-Rhône, B 3344.

68. "Rapports de désemparation des terreins desséchés pour prix du contrat du 16 juillet 1642, des 14 août 1645 et 30 avril 1646", *Délibération de l'association du desséchement des marais d'Arles qui adopte le projet tendant à rendre le canal d'Arles à Bouc utile au desséchement du 5 mars 1827* [hereafter, DAD], (Arles, 1827), pp. 62–88.

First, the two surveyors clearly distinguished two kinds of land. The *coustières* were the most elevated and the driest lands. Even though they were improved by the work, that part of the country was not involved in the redistribution. The *coustières* comprised 840 hectares over a total surface of 5,824 hectares. In contrast, the *paluds* were the lowest and the wettest part of the country. The entire property switch allowed by Van Ens's work has been calculated for this part of the territory at 4,978 hectares.

The survey reports by Voortcamp and Pellissier allow comparison of the re-apportionment of property before and after the drainage work, and thus enable us to understand the significance of the social consequences of the work. Concerning the situation before the land was drained, two types of information should be taken into account. The surveying of the *paluds* clearly shows that the area was highly fragmented, since the 4,973 hectares were split into 114 parcels. The division was so thorough that 56 parcels were smaller than 10 hectares. On the other hand, it is relevant to underline that almost half of the *paluds* were divided into only 9 parcels.

Such an extreme division might explain why the reclamation could have been led only by a foreigner supported by the Crown. Indeed, the ownership of the land surrounding Arles was so split up that it was too difficult to reach any agreeable compromise among the landowners. Furthermore, the survey demonstrates that a large part of the Arlesian population was interested in exploiting the marshes, as 46 per cent of the land and 23 per cent of the parcels belonged to nobles, whereas a large part was in the hands of unidentified individuals – probably commoners of some sort (see Tables 1 and 2). Thus the Arlesian aristocracy was by far the strongest landowner in the marshes.

In accordance with the Edict of 1599, two-thirds of the total land reclaimed was given to Van Ens; he therefore took possession of 3,316 hectares of land. The reclamation thus caused a huge change in the character of land ownership, involving all groups and classes. Nevertheless, the small landowners may have been the main victims of his work since their parts of the marshes were reduced to tiny parcels.

Van Ens could thus dominate the entire Arlesian countryside. He took his two-thirds share in each parcel, so that his property was divided into 114 different parts. This seemed to be a weakness at first sight, but it actually reinforced his work, none of the landowners being effective enough to propose alternative ways of managing the water. So, four years after his arrival in Provence, Hoeufft and his associates became the most important landowners in the Arlesian area and transformed the traditional partition of landed property.

The new ownership of the territory drastically changed the social balance of the town.[69] On the one hand, supporters of the growth of royal

---

69. Morera, "Les assèchements de marais XVIIe siècle", pp. 371ff.

Table 1. *Property distribution before drainage work carried out by Van Ens (1645–1646)*

Types of landlord	Size of parcels (in hectares)								
	A	B	C	D	E	F	G	H	Total
Nobles	4		53	44	114	804	375	886	2280
Bourgeois	11	4	60			88	401	540	1104
Church	2	5	9		126	80		469	691
Undefined individuals	44	27	32	90	68	180			441
King's lieutenant								349	349
Lawyers	7	17		54	30				108
Total	68	53	154	188	338	1152	776	2244	4973

Types of landlord	Number of parcels								
	A	B	C	D	E	F	G	H	Total
Undefined individuals	27	7	4	5	2	2			47
Nobles	3		6	3	3	7	2	2	26
Bourgeois	8	1	7			1	2	1	20
Lawyers	4	4		3	1				12
Church	1	1	1		3	1		1	8
King's lieutenant								1	1
Total	43	13	18	11	9	11	4	5	114

Key: A < 5 hectares; 5 ≤ B < 10 hectares; 10 ≤ C < 20 hectares; 20 ≤ D < 50 hectares; 50 ≤ E < 100 hectares; 100 ≤ F < 300 hectares; 300 ≤ G < 500 hectares; 500 hectares ≤ H.
Source: "Rapports de désemparation des terreins desséchés pour prix du contrat du 16 juillet 1642, des 14 août 1645 et 30 avril 1646", DAD, pp. 62–88.

power in Provence backed the operations, while adherents of the parliament of Provence, an institution that had traditionally rallied opposition to the king, launched a long-lasting struggle against the drainage entrepreneurs.[70] Attitudes to land reclamation were therefore determined by political divisions.[71] The main social consequences of the draining operations were connected to the political evolution of Provence.

The opposition to Van Ens's work strengthened ancient divisions. The struggle between the two parties took two different forms. First Hoeufft's

70. During the seventeenth century the process of extending the power of the central administration never ceased, and the king of France and his councils were constantly challenging various provincial and local rights and liberties. As representative and defender of the liberties of Provence, the parliament of Aix-en-Provence thus tried to undermine the growth of the king's power. This opposition culminated in the Fronde at the end of the 1640s and the beginning of the 1650s.
71. René Pillorget, *Les mouvements insurrectionnels en Provence entre 1596 et 1715* (Paris, 1975), pp. 528ff.; Rouquette *et al.*, *Arles, histoire, territoires et cultures*, pp. 495–504.

Table 2. *Property distribution after drainage work carried out by Van Ens (1645–1646)*

Types of landlord	Size of parcels (in hectares)								
	A	B	C	D	E	F	G	H	Total
Van Ens	59	54	117	238	206	1613		1029	3316
Nobles	6	28	10	72	225	421			762
Bourgeois	26	13			29	314			382
Church	2	3	11	58		157			231
Undefined individuals	55	11	35	13	60				174
King's lieutenant						116			116
Lawyers	8	4	24						36
Total	156	113	197	381	520	2621		1029	5017

Types of landlord	Number of parcels								
	A	B	C	D	E	F	G	H	Total
Van Ens	49	14	16	13	5	14		3	114
Undefined individuals	35	3	5	1	2				46
Nobles	5	7	1	4	5	4			26
Bourgeois	12	4			1	3			20
Lawyers	8	1	3						12
Church	2	1	1	3		1			8
King's lieutenant						1			1
Total	111	30	26	21	13	23		3	227

Key: A = 5 hectares; 5 ≤ B < 10 hectares; 10 ≤ C < 20 hectares; 20 ≤ D < 50 hectares; 50 ≤ E < 100 hectares; 100 ≤ F < 300 hectares; 300 ≤ G < 500 hectares; 500 hectares ≤ H.
Source: Table 1.

enterprise was undermined by riots and the destruction of the new infrastructure. Arlesian archives provide proof of outbreaks of violence, which also involved inhabitants of the nearby town of Tarascon (see Figure 3 overleaf). Located a few kilometres to the north of Arles, Tarascon could only release its flood waters onto Arles's territory. If the water flow were to be stopped, Tarascon's countryside would be condemned to remain under water. That is the reason why Arles's neighbours were so angry when, in 1647, a boat was sunk in a freshly dredged canal in order to make it flood into some recently seeded land owned by Van Ens and destroy the future harvest.[72] His opponents thus forced Van Ens to choose between his lands and those of Tarascon's inhabitants, and in the end the Tarascon mobilization compelled Van Ens to flood his own lands.

For its part, the chapter of Saint-Trophime, in the episcopal see of Arles, chose a different way to undermine Van Ens. The draining of a

72. AMA, DD 85, fos 134v–135r.

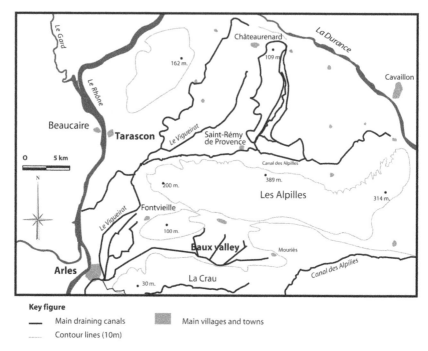

Key figure

— Main draining canals ▨ Main villages and towns
---- Contour lines (10m)

Figure 3. Tarascon's plain, the north of Arles territory and the Baux Valley.
Source: Carte IGN TOP 100 066.

large part of the Arles territories had actually involved a population move.
The peasants of the Crau, a dry and infertile region located in the south-
east of Arles's territory, came to settle in the new land. This shift had a
heavy impact on the chapter's budget, which suddenly lost the revenues of
the tithe usually paid by the peasants. Indeed, the drained lands were
exempted from this clerical tax during the first twenty years of their
exploitation.[73] In response to the change involved in land reclamation, the
chapter launched legal proceedings to restore its right to the tithe on the
new land.[74] After being heard in an ecclesiastical court, the dispute was
finally settled by the Intendant of Provence, the representative of the king
in the region, who imposed a compromise between the contractors and
the chapter, and obliged Van Ens to pay a part of the tithe.[75]

To overcome those two kinds of opposition, the entrepreneurs had to
seek the permanent backing of the central government, and without the
intervention of the Queen Regent and her prime minister, Mazarin, they

73. BMA, no. 873 vol. XI, fos 403v–404v.
74. BMA, no. 873 vol. XI, fo. 351.
75. AMA, DD 85, fos 160r–160v.

would not have been able to defeat their opponents.[76] It is thus all the more significant to note that Hoeufft and his associates succeeded. Despite the difficulties, he managed to make a lot of money from his exploitation of the new land. In fact, the major social consequence of the land reclamation concerned the social structure of the city of Arles.

Intrinsically bound to the growth of centralized power, the success of the drainage work went hand in hand with the marginalization of the supporters of the Provencal parliament's authority. In short, Hoeufft's investment was used by the monarchy as a means to transform the social structure of Arles. From that point of view, the cases of Petit Poitou and Arles are very different. Indeed, in Poitou the monarchy's authority faced no opposition. Another difference lay in the impact on the local populations.

From north to south, the economic trend of the seventeenth century in France was very different. Since the work of René Baehrel, it has been firmly established that southern France was marked by both economic and demographic growth, while the situation of northern France was less favourable.[77] Before its draining in the 1640s, Arles's swamps were used intensively, as is revealed in the several trials launched against the entrepreneurs. A summons addressed to Van Ens by Antoine Garnon, an Arlesian fisherman, revealed that the Dutch engineer had filled in his canal in order to modify the hydraulic network.[78] Thus, the land reclamation deprived this fisherman of his main source of revenue.

The initial contract signed in 1642 gave Van Ens ownership of the whole hydraulic structure so that he could take possession of all the fisheries settled in the swamps, including the ownership of the new levées and plantings. Thanks to those rights he was able to exploit the trees and mustard that grew on the dykes. Indeed, mustard plants contributed to consolidate the dykes and offered a convenient income to the landowner. In 1647 Truchenu, an Arlesian noble who had been accustomed to exploit it before Van Ens's work, launched an action against him because Van Ens had confiscated the mustard harvest.[79] As the new owner of the whole hydraulic network, Van Ens also collected taxes on the navigation on his canals. The quarries of Fontvieille, which used to sell their stones in Arles, were thus among the firm opponents of the drainage work.[80] These examples illustrate the fact that the land reclamation had a deep impact in all layers of Arlesian society.

76. "Lettre close de la Reine mère sur les canaux creusés par J. van Ens, du 6 octobre 1648", DAD, p. 116.

77. René Baehrel, *Une croissance: la Basse-Provence rurale de la fin du seizième siècle à 1789* (Paris, 1961).

78. AMA, DD 85, fos 57ff.

79. AMA, DD 85, fos 180ff.

80. AMA, DD 87, fo. 165r.

Thus, both Petit Poitou and Arles demonstrate its strong societal impact. In Poitou, as in Provence, the drainage work was used to strengthen the power of the French monarchy and the local implantation of its loyal aristocracy. The Crown employed the funds, the skills, and the commercial networks of the Dutch traders to extend its power throughout the whole kingdom, while its aristocracy used them to exploit their wetlands. At the same time, land reclamation was linked to the dispossession of the local peasantry. And, as we shall see, the policy also had a deep impact on the environment of the wetlands.

ENVIRONMENTAL CONSEQUENCES OF LAND RECLAMATION IN ARLES AND PETIT POITOU

To measure the environmental impact of the work undertaken in the seventeenth century, historians need a long-term analysis. The modern draining of Arles and Petit Poitou affected areas equipped and exploited since the Middle Ages and gave them the shape they have today. In both regions, capitalist operations led by Johan Hoeufft caused lasting environmental changes. Nevertheless, those changes progressed differently in Poitou and Provence.

The swamp of Petit Poitou is located in the bay of the Aiguillon and is the result of tidal sediment.[81] Despite its geological origins it had not been subject to flooding from the sea for a long time, but it was regularly flooded by the waters of the Lay and Vendée, coastal rivers flowing into the Aiguillon bay. The main purpose of the drainage projects was therefore to divert that water into the sea as quickly as possible. The modern entrepreneur was helped by the intensive work completed in the area by Cistercian monks, who had already begun to drain the area during the twelfth and thirteenth centuries.[82]

When he arrived in Poitou to manage the land reclamation, de Strada found former canals still visible in the landscape, even though they were filled in with sediment. The task then was to renew the old infrastructure. He dredged the pre-existing canals and built new sluices, using local and foreign labour to do so. Thus, de Strada used workers from Auvergne, where he had settled, and imported Dutch cows and materials, including timber and bricks from Amsterdam and Hamburg.[83] Within a few years, he had succeeded in converting an unexploited swamp into arable and grazing land from which grain was exported to Amsterdam.[84]

The draining of the Petit Poitou swamp provided Hoeufft and his associates with a good return on their investment, thanks to the sale of grain and interest paid by associates. Nevertheless, the operation was not

81. Fernand Verger, *Marais maritimes et estuaires du littoral français* (Paris, 2005), p. 158.
82. Sarrazin, "Les Cisterciens".
83. RUHZ, 691, p. 40.
84. RUHZ, 691, p. 129.

solely a short-term business. Indeed, at the beginning of the 1670s Johan Hoeufft's heirs still owned several farms in Petit Poitou. A notebook written between late 1670 and early 1671 shows that more than 20 years after the work had been completed Petit Poitou still provided an annual income of more than 7,264 lt.[85] Two-thirds of that income was derived from oats and one-third from the sale of horses and cows. In return, the owners had to invest 370 lt. a year for the maintenance of the *polder*, to clear the canals, and to maintain the buildings of the area.

So, in a normal year, the land of Petit Poitou could offer landowners an income of almost 7,000 lt. Later, during the eighteenth century, Hoeufft's heirs still possessed their farms in Petit Poitou and chose to sell them at a good profit.[86] Between 1734 and 1741 the 23 farms owned by Hoeufft's heirs were sold and the proceeds of 254,000 lt. were divided among the different branches of the family. This amount clearly shows that the lands drained in the middle of the seventeenth century were still valuable in the following century, indicating that they had been steadily maintained and could still provide good revenues. The drainage works undertaken by Hoeufft and his associates are, even today, characteristic features of the area: all the farms built by Hoeufft still exist, and the toponymy has remained the same (see Figure 1).[87] Moreover, the draining of Petit Poitou prompted a sort of drainage fever, with projects multiplying in nearby regions.[88] Entrepreneurs increasingly turned their attention to the sea, launching a continuous wave of land reclamation that completely altered the environment of Aiguillon's cove within 200 years.

That evolution must be compared with the case of Arles. Settled by the Romans in the first century CE, the city of Arles always had to deal with water problems.[89] It was actually impossible to develop agriculture without draining the territory and protecting it from the Rhone flood. Medieval Arlesians built contrivances specifically to achieve that aim, but by the beginning of the seventeenth century the mechanisms had become inadequate.[90] At that time, they had to face the little Ice Age too and the consequences of social disruption caused by the Wars of Religion.[91]

---

85. RUHZ, 698.
86. Rijksarchief Utrecht, familie Des Tombe, 1117.
87. This continuity clearly appears in a comparison between a map drawn in 1648 by Pierre Siette, a royal cartographer, and the current maps held by the Institut Géographique Nationale; Pierre Siette, *Plan et description particuliere des marais desseichés du petit Poictou avecq le partaige sur icelluy* (1648).
88. Suire, *Le Marais poitevin*, pp. 154–159 and 188–203.
89. Philippe Leveau, "Drainages et colonisation militaire en basse Provence rhodanienne", G. Fabre (ed.), *Organisation des espaces antiques: entre nature et histoire* (Biarritz, 2000), pp. 167–188.
90. Stouff, "La lutte contre les eaux".
91. Emmanuel Le Roy Ladurie, *Histoire humaine et comparée du climat. Canicules et glaciers XIIIe–XVIIIe siècles* (Paris, 2004), pp. 254–263 and 293–315.

Figure 4. Farms of Choisival in the Petit Poitou's swamps. The two barns on the right were built in the 1640s, though they have been restored. The main part of the farms built by Hoeufft has similar barns.
Photograph by the author.

As in Petit Poitou, Hoeufft and his associates dealt with a damaged, but previously developed countryside. Despite the need for new land, Arlesians had neither been able to build a consensus to drain their area, nor to negotiate with other towns of the region to regulate floodwater. Against that background, the mission of Van Ens appears in a different light. He had to change the way the water was managed and renew the old infrastructures. That became feasible as he concentrated all the canals and two-thirds of the land into his own hands.[92] By becoming the most important landowner in the region, he could easily lead the restoration of the former drainage system, and then complete it by digging new canals. Along with his restoration work, Van Ens also constructed a complex system to separate waters according to their origins.[93] Thanks to this system, water from the Baux valley was separated from that coming from Tarascon, and its management was simplified.

As in Poitou, Hoeufft's enterprise led to a crucial environmental change in the Arlesian countryside which still strongly marks the area. Whereas the

---

92. Morera, "Les assèchements de marais XVIIe siècle", pp. 520–523.
93. *Ibid.*, pp. 504–520; BMA, Fonds Véran, no. 493, "Rapport du sieur Bernardy ingenieur, du 29 avril 1733".

draining of Petit Poitou was small-scale compared to all the regional wetlands, the work of Van Ens directly involved the whole left bank of the Rhone from the northern limit of Arles's territory to the Mediterranean Sea (an area of 110 square kilometres). The land reclamation of the 1640s covered all the arable land in the area.

Despite some floods, notably in the 1670s, Van Ens's constructions seem to have remained effective until the mid-eighteenth century.[94] In 1706, a catastrophic flood severely damaged the area, but in 1707 an agreement between Arles and Tarascon allowed for repairs.[95] A few years later, in 1718, Maître Pierre Lenice, the director of the *polder*, a lawyer and member of the Paris parliament, and representative of Hoeufft's heirs, was forced to pay his share of the maintenance charges. The sum of 75,809 lt. had to be paid to the *corps des vidanges*,[96] money which was spent on necessary work to keep the swamps of Arles drained.[97] In 1734 and 1736, two rulings obliged entrepreneurs to dredge canals and renew bridges built within the land drained.[98] Again, Hoeufft's family interests were defended by Maître Pierre Lenice, representative of Hoeufft's heirs, and also by François Devese, Seigneur de Lalo des Pluches, who, as one of Hoeufft's heirs, took a personal interest in the land reclamation.[99]

It seems that reclamation in the Arles region suffered at the end of the eighteenth century, although as soon as the French Revolution began several projects sprang up to continue the work of Van Ens. In 1791, 1795, and in 1802, Arlesian citizens gathered to talk about the need to drain the marshes again.[100] They finally received the support of the French government, which agreed to supervise the work in 1807.[101] The work was then led by an engineer who continued to work in the vein of Van

---

94. Bibliothèque municipales d'Avignon, Ms. 2852.

95. "Transaction entre la ville d'Arles et celle de Tarascon sur les chaussées, le 2 mars 1707", DAD, pp. 219–236.

96. The *corps des vidanges* is an Arlesian institution tasked with maintaining the water infrastructure around Arles. Created in the middle of the sixteenth century, it never managed to do so.

97. "Transaction portant arrêté de compte entre les syndics de l'association des vidanges et les associés au desséchement", DAD, pp. 241–250.

98. "Dispositif du jugement souverain de nosseigneurs les commissaires délégués par l'arrêt du conseil d'Etat du 8 juillet 1732, le 10 février 1734", DAD, pp. 280–290; "Transaction passée entre le corps des vidanges, les sieurs intéressés au desséchement d'Arles et noble Jean-Baptiste Prosper Le Blanc, syndic de robe de la noblesse de Provence, le 6 août 1736", DAD, pp. 296–312.

99. "Transaction passée entre le corps des vidanges", p. 308.

100. "Assemblée juridique du 6 février 1791", DAD, pp. 328–332; "Assemblée juridique du 27 fructidor an 3", DAD, pp. 332–337; "Assemblée juridique du X floréal an X", DAD, pp. 347–356.

101. "Arrêté du préfet qui approuve la délibération du 15 mai 1806, le 24 février 1807", DAD, pp. 448–450.

Ens's projects.[102] For example, the engineers of the Ponts et Chaussées used the network and installations that had been renewed two centuries earlier. Their task was eased by the regular upkeep of the Van Ens installations, which remain the basic framework of modern water management in the low Rhone area.

In short, from technical and environmental viewpoints, both the Arles and Petit Poitou land reclamations were very similar. On the one hand, they both enjoyed a medieval inheritance of former drainage works so that the entrepreneurs could build upon former infrastructures, and each used similar means to reach their ends. Furthermore, the environmental impact of both projects was far-reaching. The infrastructure is still quite effective even today.

CONCLUSION

Focusing on the two cases of Petit Poitou and Arles, I have argued that the whole process of land reclamation undertaken in France between 1599 and the 1650s relied on the involvement of foreign agents, who were employed by the French aristocracy. Most of the foreign agents came from the southern Low Countries and had established their business in Holland. The drainage works of seventeenth-century France benefited from the Dutch Revolt and the beginning of the Eighty Years' War. The role of the Comans brothers, Van Uffelen, and Hoeufft was decisive in the success of Henri IV's policy. They were allowed to invest directly in the land drained and to lend money to other investors. In fact they were used as agents of French royal power. For instance, Hoeufft provided Mazarin with people who were able to manage large drainage projects and market the produce of the new land created. In relation to their commercial connections in Amsterdam, Hoeufft, like Van Uffelen before him, relied on a strong business network.

That organization was the reason why the French monarchy gave its crucial backing to land reclamation. Senior French state officials were directly interested in the successful outcome of the drainage work. As a consequence of their interest, they used their official positions to suppress legal disputes that could have endangered it. Conversely, the drainage entrepreneurs helped the Crown, and the prime minister, to affirm their authority in the areas concerned. The draining of the Arlesian marshes thus accompanied the growth of royal power in Provence. The French monarchy used the economic power of Amsterdam to strengthen its own power over its provinces, while Dutch capitalists benefited financially from the adventure.

---

102. "Explication de la carte chorographique des ouvrages du desséchement des marais d'Arles", DAD, pp. 450–470.

Such collusion between the economic and political powers upset the social balance built by the communities surrounding the different wetlands. Indeed, the draining of the marshes meant appropriation of land by the investors and thus expulsion of former users. In Arles, some fisheries were destroyed, while Hoeufft and his associates took possession of others. Moreover, land drainage involved different kinds of migration. In Arles, Van Ens had to ease the movements of peasants coming from the Crau, which was a small-scale migration. But in Petit Poitou the drainage work was made possible thanks to workers coming from the Auvergne. To sum up, the draining of the French wetlands weakened the local population by curtailing their rights whereas it reinforced the local bourgeoisie and aristocracy, who accepted the growth of royal power.

In that sense, it is interesting to consider the social conditions of their success. In both cases, Hoeufft built hierarchical companies which dealt with the territory as a whole. Van Ens succeeded because he was the sole owner of the canals and because he possessed two-thirds of the area. De Strada and Hoeufft employed exactly the same method in Petit Poitou. The similarity between the statutes of the Arles swamp and those of Petit Poitou supports these findings.[103] The social changes were all the more striking as they left deep marks on the environment. The infrastructure they built, or rebuilt, is still in use today. More than technical skills, the Dutch imported a certain way of exploiting the swamps, which remained undisputed until the end of the twentieth century, when the rise of a new "green consciousness" started to question their achievements again.

103. "Les statuts du petit poitou du 19 octobre 1646", *Recueil de reglements concernant les dessechement des marais* (Paris, 1703), pp. 62–67; BMA, no. 393, "Reglemens et statuts faicts entre Messieurs les Associez au dessechement des Paluds & Marais du Terroir de la Ville d'Arles & les Baux" (Arles, 1653).

IRSH 55 (2010), Supplement, pp. 103–121 doi:10.1017/S0020859010000519
© 2010 Internationaal Instituut voor Sociale Geschiedenis

The Colonial Famine Plot: Slavery, Free Trade, and Empire in the French Atlantic, 1763–1791[*]

JOSEPH HORAN

Department of History, Florida State University

E-mail: jwho4h@fsu.edu

SUMMARY: This essay examines the use of famine-plot rhetoric in the course of disputes over free trade in the French Atlantic during the late eighteenth century. Seeking to discredit officially sanctioned trade monopolies, French plantation owners frequently suggested that the control exercised by metropolitan merchants over transatlantic commerce was responsible for food shortages among the enslaved population of the colonies. In reality, the planters themselves bore primary responsibility for malnutrition in the French Caribbean, thanks to their reliance on the slave trade and support for the expansion of plantation agriculture. While proponents of the colonial famine plot accepted that plantation slavery had made it impossible for the resources available in the colonies to sustain the growing enslaved population, they remained committed to the plantation system. In advocating expanded free trade as the best means to ensure the continued growth of the colonies, French planters anticipated a response to the environmental problems caused by colonial expansion that became increasingly prevalent among proponents of European imperialism during the nineteenth century.

On 29 August 1789 Nicholas-Robert de Cocherel warned his fellow deputies in the French National Assembly that the Caribbean colony of Saint-Domingue, which he represented in the Assembly by virtue of his ownership of several lucrative sugar plantations, "is currently devastated by the most cruel of plagues, that of FAMINE". According to Cocherel, the root cause of this famine was not the encouragement that he and his fellow planters had given to the Atlantic slave trade, which had transported more than a million enslaved Africans to the French colonies over the course of the eighteenth century. Nor could the famine be attributed to their reliance on plantation monoculture, which had seriously weakened the ability of the colonies to sustain their population through local

* The author would like to thank Darrin M. McMahon and Frederick Davis for reading and commenting on earlier drafts of this article.

food production.[1] Drawing on a brand of rhetoric that Caribbean planters had been developing for several decades, Cocherel instead asserted that the ultimate cause of famine in the colonies was deliberate manipulation of the colonial trade by French merchants.[2]

Since the 1760s, wealthy planters such as Cocherel had been using their political influence to spread similar accusations as part of their campaign to bring an end to the exclusive trading privileges enjoyed by the leading merchants of France's major port cities. In order to encourage a relaxation of commercial restrictions, they suggested that the trade monopolies allowed metropolitan merchants deliberately to starve the colonies of basic necessities in order to drive up prices and increase their own profits. This assertion also conveniently offered the planters an opportunity of denying their own basic responsibility for starvation in the colonies.

The rhetoric adopted by Cocherel and his fellow planters during the late eighteenth century closely mirrors the "famine-plot" phenomenon described by historian Steven L. Kaplan. Examining popular reactions to the numerous food shortages and famines that affected metropolitan France over the course of the eighteenth century, Kaplan identified a widespread tendency to blame deliberate manipulation by greedy merchants, speculators, and officials. As Kaplan has demonstrated, the famine-plot phenomenon was a natural product of conditions in eighteenth-century France. For a population that was dependent on the cereal economy, secretive conspiracies seemed to be a logical explanation for periodic food shortages, a tendency that was encouraged by the general lack of transparency in the political system of the *ancien régime*.[3]

1. The history of slavery in the French Caribbean is the subject of an extensive and growing body of research. For some useful general overviews, see Gabriel Debien, *Les Esclaves aux Antilles françaises, XVII–XVIII siècles* (Basse-Terre, 1974); Robert Louis Stein, *The French Slave Trade in the Eighteenth Century: An Old Regime Business* (Madison, WI, 1979); Pierre Pluchon, "L'Économie d'habitation a Saint-Domingue", *Revue d'Histoire Maritime*, 1 (1997), pp. 198–241; David Geggus, "The French Slave Trade: An Overview", *William and Mary Quarterly*, 58 (2001), pp. 119–138; and Frédéric Régent, *La France et ses esclaves: De la colonisation aux abolitions (1620–1848)* (Paris, 2007).
2. Nicholas-Robert de Cocherel, *Motion de M. de Cocherel, député de S.Domingue, à la séance du samedi 29 août 1789, au soir* (Versailles, 1789), p. 1. All translations are by the author unless otherwise noted.
3. Steven L. Kaplan, "The Famine Plot Persuasion in Eighteenth-Century France", *Transactions of the American Philosophical Society*, 72:3 (1982), pp. 1–79. Historians of early modern France have agreed with Kaplan on the extent to which conspiracy theories permeated political culture. See particularly Arlette Farge and Jacques Revel, *The Vanishing Children of Paris*, Claudia Milleville (trans.) (Cambridge, 1991); and Peter R. Campbell, "Perceptions of Conspiracy on the Eve of the French Revolution", in Peter R. Campbell, Thomas E. Kaiser, and Marisa Linton (eds), *Conspiracy in the French Revolution* (Manchester [etc.], 2007). It is also important to recognize that conspiracy rhetoric was by no means a monopoly of the political

Similar conditions encouraged the use of famine-plot rhetoric in the context of France's Atlantic empire, in which the dissemination of accurate information was further handicapped by the vast distance between France and the colonies.[4] While traces of famine-plot rhetoric can be found in travel accounts and government correspondence throughout the history of French colonization during the *ancien régime*, the most explicit version of the "colonial famine plot" revolved around the efforts of leading planters to end the trade restrictions that had been imposed on the colonies. In order to achieve this goal, planters cynically used the suffering of their enslaved laborers as a means of discrediting the commercial privileges enjoyed by metropolitan merchants.

While proponents of the colonial famine-plot persuasion asserted that the immediate cause of starvation in the colonies was the deliberate manipulation of transatlantic commerce by metropolitan merchants, their rhetoric also addressed the broader issues of commercial policy, colonial expansion, and environmental degradation. In this sense, the planters were reacting to a common trend in the history of European imperialism.

As new colonies were incorporated into a global economy that was dominated by European powers, traditional methods of preventing food shortages in these regions were put under increasing strain. The impacts of this trend were particularly devastating in the late nineteenth century, as the incorporation of large parts of Asia and Africa into the European empires produced a series of horrific famines. Supporters of the imperial project, however, viewed these famines not as a product of the policies that they had adopted, but rather as an excuse to further advance the process of incorporating these regions into imperial markets.[5] The rhetoric of the colonial famine-plot provides an early example of this phenomenon. While the planters asserted that it was impossible to nourish the enslaved population of the colonies without foreign commerce, they did not question the plantation system which was responsible for this development. Indeed, their primary goal in advocating free trade was to ensure the continued expansion of the plantation regime.

---

left. See Darrin M. McMahon, *Enemies of the Enlightenment: The French Counter-Enlightenment and the Making of Modernity* (Oxford [etc.], 2001), pp. 57–65.

4. Kenneth Banks, *Chasing Empire Across the Sea: Communications and the State in the French Atlantic, 1713–1763* (Montreal [etc.], 2006).

5. For treatments of famine in the historical context of European imperialism, see Amartya Sen, *Poverty and Famines: An Essay on Entitlement and Deprivation* (Oxford, 1981), pp. 52–85; David Arnold, *Famine: Social Crisis and Historical Change* (Oxford [etc.], 1988), pp. 119–142; William Crossgrove *et al.*, "Colonialism, International Trade, and the Nation-State", in Lucile F. Newman *et al.* (eds), *Hunger in History: Food Shortage, Poverty, and Deprivation* (Cambridge [etc.], 1990), pp. 215–240; Mike Davis, *Late Victorian Holocausts: El Niño Famines and the Making of the Third World* (London [etc.], 2001).

COMMERCIAL REFORM AND THE COLONIAL FAMINE PLOT, 1763–1789

During the eighteenth century, the French plantation colonies were supplied through an extensive transatlantic commerce, which provided a wide range of commodities to the Caribbean, including flour from France, cod from the Atlantic fisheries, and even salted beef from Ireland.[6] Although these products were a significant source of nutrition for both European colonists and enslaved Africans, a mercantilist policy, known as the *exclusif*, strictly limited their commerce to the merchants of France's major port cities. As the plantation regime expanded over the course of the eighteenth century, these prohibitions became increasingly problematic.

Many planters felt that their needs would be better fulfilled by opening the colonies to foreign commerce, thus legalizing the profitable illicit trade with British and Dutch merchants in which they were already engaged. In the aftermath of the Seven Years' War (1756–1763), the Ministry of the Navy, which was responsible for colonial affairs under the *ancien régime*, initiated a program designed to reform the *exclusif*. Under the influence of Jean-Baptiste Dubuc, a wealthy absentee sugar planter from Martinique, in 1767 a policy known as *exclusif mitigé* was introduced, permitting a restricted foreign trade in certain subsidiary goods such as lumber and live animals. In order to prevent a more general breakdown of trade restrictions, this commerce was limited to two secondary ports, Carénage in the colony of Saint Lucia and Môle Saint-Nicholas in Saint-Domingue.[7]

Wealthy plantation owners in France and the Caribbean were unsatisfied with this limited reform. During the war, planters in the Caribbean had gained a new voice in colonial politics with the creation of special Chambers of Agriculture in the main colonies of Martinique, Guadeloupe, and Saint-Domingue. Initially created to rally colonial support for the war effort, these institutions quickly became a vehicle through which the most influential planters sought to shape colonial policy in their favor. During the 1760s planters in the Chambers consistently called for a further relaxation of the *exclusif*, demanding that all the major ports be opened to foreign commerce in more vital goods such as flour, cod, and salted beef.

---

6. Bertie Mandelblatt, "A Transatlantic Commodity: Irish Salt Beef in the French Atlantic World", *The History Workshop Journal*, 63 (2007), pp. 18–47.
7. The most comprehensive study of the debates over colonial trade reform in late eighteenth-century France remains Jean Tarrade, *Le commerce colonial de la France à la fin de l'Ancien Régime: l'évolution du régime de "l'Exclusif" de 1763 à 1789*, 2 vols (Paris, 1972). This summary is drawn from vol. I, pp. 223–338. For the two central decrees of the *exclusif* system, which dated from 1717 and 1727, see *Recueils de Règlements, Édits, Déclarations et Arrêts Concernant le Commerce, l'Administration de la Justice, & la Police des Colonies Françaises de l'Amérique, & les Engagés avec le Code Noir et l'Addition audit Code* (Paris, 1765), pp. 46–61, 221–238.

It was during this period that the Chambers of Agriculture began to attack French merchants, whom they accused of deliberately manipulating commercial policy in order to maintain their exclusive privileges. In 1784, sensitive to this pressure and hoping to encourage closer commercial ties with the newly independent United States, the administration issued a decree permitting the importation of an expanded number of foreign goods, including cod and salted beef, into the leading ports of the French colonies. This decree provoked an intense reaction from French merchants, who launched a propaganda campaign arguing that reform of the *exclusif* would throw the French economy into a crisis. In a series of pamphlets, the planter lobbyist Dubuc engaged in a heated polemic with the merchants, defending the reforms and calling for a further relaxation of the *exclusif*.[8]

The dispute over the *exclusif* reached a peak during the first year of the French Revolution. Absentee sugar planters in Paris had managed to obtain representation in the newly created National Assembly, and they used this platform to campaign for further commercial reform. In the heated political atmosphere of 1789, the planters significantly expanded on their version of the famine plot, a tendency that was further encouraged by fears that the bad harvest in France would affect food supplies in the French colonies.[9] In the late summer, reports from the governor of Saint-Domingue, the largest and most populated colony in the Caribbean, suggested that the island was on the verge of famine. When the Minister of the Navy refused their demands for an extended suspension of the *exclusif* in order to permit the importation of foodstuffs from the United States, the colonial representatives brought the issue to the Assembly, explicitly accusing the merchants of corrupting the political process.[10] These accusations became even more heated when a special committee appointed to examine the matter determined that the claims of famine were greatly exaggerated.

By early 1790, the debates over colonial trade policy had reached a stalemate. While the merchants had successfully blocked the demands of the colonial deputies for a definitive end to the official trade monopolies, the increasing weakness of the administration made it impossible for the

8. Tarrade, *Le commerce colonial de la France*, II, pp. 493–589.
9. On conspiracy rhetoric during the early years of the Revolution, see Timothy Tackett, "Conspiracy Obsession in a Time of Revolution: French Elites and the Origins of the Terror, 1789–1792", *The American Historical Review*, 105 (2000), pp. 691–713.
10. For the reports of the Saint-Domingue administrators concerning the food supply, see Marie-Charles, marquis de Chilleau *et al.*, *Correspondance de M. le Marquis du Chilleau, Gouverneur-Général de Saint-Domingue, avec M. le Comte de la Luzerne, Ministre de la Marine, & M. de Marbois, Intendant de Saint-Domingue, relativement à l'introduction des farines étrangères dans cette colonie* (Paris, 1789). On the efforts of the deputies to draw attention to the crisis, see Louis-Marthe de Gouy d'Arsy, *Première dénonciation solennelle d'un ministre, faite à l'Assemblée nationale, en la personne du Comte de La Luzerne, ministre d'état, de la marine, et des colonies; Extrait des pièces justificatives à l'appui de la dénonciation* (Paris, 1790).

French state to exercise even the limited control of the colonial economy associated with the *ancien régime*. This left the colonists free to ignore trade restrictions more or less. In the years that followed, the issue of colonial trade reform was overshadowed by the more pressing concerns of foreign war and slave insurrection in the colonies.[11]

The extensive use of famine-plot rhetoric in the French debates over colonial trade was not mirrored in the histories of the other European powers with plantation colonies in the Caribbean. Although the British colonies experienced shortages comparable to their French counterparts in the late eighteenth century, British planters managed to exercise a strong influence on colonial policy.[12] French colonial politics, on the other hand, reflected the general lack of transparency that encouraged the famine-plot persuasion during the *ancien régime*.

While wealthy absentee planters such as Dubuc enjoyed some influence on major decisions affecting the colonies, in the final analysis colonial affairs were the sole responsibility of the Minister of the Navy. Although the policy of the *exclusif mitigé* reflected the efforts of the successive ministers to balance the interests of the various merchants and planters, the end result satisfied neither party and produced the polemics in which the colonial famine plot was given its fullest expression. While the political culture of the *ancien régime* influenced the use of famine-plot rhetoric by French planters, their efforts to reform colonial trade policy can be understood only in the context of conditions particular to the colonies. In order to explain fully the development of the colonial famine-plot persuasion, it is necessary to examine the interaction between plantation monoculture, malnutrition, and transatlantic commerce in the French Caribbean.

MALNUTRITION AND THE PLANTATION SYSTEM IN THE FRENCH CARIBBEAN

The expansion of plantation agriculture in the European colonies of the Caribbean during the seventeenth and eighteenth centuries had a significant

11. Jean Tarrade, "Le Révolution et le Commerce Colonial: le Régime de l'Exclusif de 1789 à 1800", in CHEFF (eds), *Etat, Finances et Economie Pendant la Révolution Française* (Paris, 1991). For a concise assessment of the crisis in the French Caribbean during the revolutionary and Napoleonic eras, see David Patrick Geggus, "Slavery, War, and Revolution in the Greater Caribbean, 1789–1815", in David Barry Gaspar and David Patrick Geggus (eds), *A Turbulent Time: The French Revolution and the Greater Caribbean* (Bloomington, IN, 1997), pp. 1–50.
12. On the more permissive trade policies in the Dutch Caribbean, which served as an inspiration for the reforms of the *exclusif mitigé*, see Wim Klooster, *Illicit Riches: Dutch Trade in the Caribbean, 1648–1795* (Leiden, 1998). On the subsistence crisis in the British colonies, see Richard B. Sheridan, "The Crisis of Slave Subsistence in the British West Indies during and after the American Revolution", *The William and Mary Quarterly*, 33 (1976), pp. 615–641. On the political influence of the British planters, see David Beck Ryden, *West Indian Slavery and British Abolition, 1783–1807* (Cambridge [etc.], 2009), pp. 40–82.

impact on local environments. Prior to the arrival of European colonists, the fertile soils and biological diversity of these islands supported an agricultural system that generally provided an adequate and balanced diet for the indigenous populations.

Following the initial colonization of the islands during the seventeenth century, the introduction of sugar cane, coffee, and other luxury crops destined for European consumers encouraged a system of intensive settlement and plantation monoculture that exhausted soils and depleted local flora and fauna throughout much of the region. This ecological transformation played a direct role in the problems of food supply experienced in the colonies during the colonial era.[13] While food production did not cease altogether, it was increasingly inadequate to support the growing population of enslaved laborers transported to the colonies through the Atlantic slave trade. Historians have shown that malnutrition and the wide range of health problems associated with it were endemic among plantation slaves in the Caribbean, and were a leading cause of high rates of slave mortality in the colonies.[14] Although the famine-plot rhetoric articulated by French planters was part of a self-serving political strategy, there is no denying that starvation was a very real problem for their enslaved laborers.

The environmental degradation caused by plantation monoculture was not lost on contemporary observers. In 1790, the French doctor and agronomist Jacques-François Dutrône de la Couture surveyed the state of agriculture in Saint-Domingue. In virtually every part of the colony, he found signs that the expansion of plantation agriculture, and particularly the rapid extension of coffee planting in recent decades, had seriously damaged the ecosystem. Describing the northern plains of the colony, which were by many accounts the richest and most productive area in the French plantation colonies, Dutrône lamented that, "it is to the activity of the cultivator that we owe the stunning prosperity of the region [...] and it is unfortunate that the cause of this stunning prosperity must also necessarily be that of its wastage and ruin".[15] Nonetheless, Dutrône was revealingly focused only on the production of luxury crops, and showed

---

13. David Watts, "Cycles of Famine in Islands of Plenty: The Case of the Colonial West Indies in the Pre-Emancipation Period", in Bruce Currey and Graeme Hugo (eds), *Famine as a Geographical Phenomenon* (Dordrecht [etc.], 1984), pp. 49–70.

14. Frantz Tardo-Dino calculates that, at the very best, the average caloric value of slave diets was sufficient for four days of the week. See his *Le Collier de Servitude: La condition sanitaire des esclaves aux Antilles Françaises du XVIIe au XIXe siècle* (Paris, 1985), pp. 129–142. For a detailed assessment of slave malnutrition in the Caribbean as a whole, see Kenneth F. Kiple, *The Caribbean Slave: A Biological History* (Cambridge [etc.], 1984).

15. Jacques-François Dutrône de la Couture, *Précis sur la canne et sur les moyens d'en extraire le sel essential* (Paris, 1790), p. 343. On contemporary attitudes to environmental degradation in a colonial context, see Richard H. Grove, *Green Imperialism: Colonial Expansion, Tropical Island Edens and the Origins of Environmentalism, 1600–1860* (Cambridge, MA, 1996), pp. 168–308.

little concern for the problems of food production. Indeed, he finished his
survey by advocating commercial reform as the most effective means of
ensuring that more enslaved laborers could be transported to the areas of
the colony that remained productive. Dutrône's account illustrates both
the extent of the environmental problems caused by plantation agriculture
in the Caribbean, and the general neglect of sustainability shown by
proponents of the plantation regime.

Significantly, however, contemporary observers who did pay attention
to food production described a wide range of provisions that were not
only available in the colonies, but were cultivated on the plantations
themselves. Perhaps the best such description was provided by S-J.
Ducoeurjoly, who had extensive experience managing a plantation in
Saint-Domingue at the end of the eighteenth century. In a manual for
prospective planters written in 1802, Ducoeurjoly noted that the Caribbean provided a wide range of potentially nourishing products which
were easy to cultivate alongside the more lucrative export crops. If a
planter wanted to cultivate sweet potatoes, for example, "in two days one
can plant more than enough to last for four months".

Ducoeurjoly's account of plantation provisions also emphasized the existence of multiple safeguards against famine. Yams, for example, "can be
conserved from one year to another in the granary: thus when other
[foodstuffs] are lacking, one does not fear famine so long as one is well-
provided with these". Manioc (also known as cassava), regarded by both
contemporaries and historians as one of the most important sources of
nutrition for Caribbean slaves, offered similar advantages (see Figure 1).
"This is a foodstuff that must not be neglected", he advised, "because once it
is first raised, it will continue to grow, require little effort, accommodate itself
to the initial terrain, and conserve for three or four years in the ground". Nor,
Ducoeurjoly suggested, was it difficult for a planter to raise livestock.
Planting corn, he noted, "will nourish the poultry, and fatten the pigs".[16] This
account of the abundance of provisions available on the plantations of the
French Caribbean contrasts sharply with the claims advanced by proponents
of the colonial famine plot, who suggested that foreign trade was the only
effective way to provide adequate nourishment for the colonies.

Ducoeurjoly's account suggested that responsible planters would have little
trouble securing adequate rations for their slaves, even during the late eighteenth century when the extension of plantation monoculture had already
caused significant damage to local ecosystems. If this was indeed the case,
why was malnutrition such a persistent problem in the French Caribbean?

16. S-J Ducoeurjoly, *Manuel des habitants de Saint-Domingue*, 2 vols (Paris, 1802), II, pp.
70–77. For an assessment of the nature of slave provisioning in the French Caribbean, see
Gabriel Debien, "La question des vivres pour les esclaves aux Antilles Françaises", *Anuario*, 148
(1972), pp. 131–172.

Figure 1. Enslaved Africans preparing manioc flour in the French Caribbean during the eighteenth century.
Source: Nouveau Voyage aux isles de l'Amerique, *Volume 1*.
FSU Libraries, Special Collections Department. Used with permission.

There are some suggestions that the provisions described by Ducoeurjoly were neither as abundant nor as adequate as his account suggests. The Dominican friar Jean-Baptiste Labat, who visited the Caribbean at the turn of the eighteenth century, suggested that manioc flour was "very expensive, very rare, and very difficult to find". A doctor who visited the island of Saint-Lucia during the 1780s contended that local crops were "poorly suited to reviving the energy of the organs", and concluded that widespread malnutrition and disease among the slaves were the results of this deficiency.[17]

17. Jean-Baptiste Labat, *Nouveau voyage aux isles de l'Amérique: Contenant l'histoire naturelle de ces pays, l'origine, les moeurs la religion et le gouvernement des habitans anciens et modernes. Les guerres et les événements singuliers qui y sont arrivez pendant le séjour que*

Another problem was posed by periodic natural disasters such as hurricanes, earthquakes, and droughts, which could cause significant damage to food crops, creating the conditions necessary for famine. In 1776, for example, the Chamber of Agriculture on Martinique issued an urgent plea for help following a series of hurricanes that struck the island. The hurricanes uprooted much of the island's manioc harvest, provoking the inhabitants to engage in a "precipitous consumption" which only exacerbated the shortage. The Chamber lamented the breakdown of social order that followed in the wake of famine, as the population of the colony was driven by hunger to "the most cruel and shameful extremities".[18]

These accounts illustrate some of the difficulties of ensuring adequate food supply that were invoked by proponents of the colonial famine plot as a justification for the introduction of foreign commerce. The most candid observers, however, recognized the real cause of slave malnutrition.

Even proponents of slavery were willing to admit that starvation in the colonies was not caused by a lack of adequate provisions, nor by the restrictions on foreign commerce, but by the plantation system itself. In 1802, Ducoeurjoly lamented the "condemnable indolence" of many planters, who had neglected to provide proper nourishment to their slaves because they were "dominated by the greed of increasing their profits". This explanation directly contradicted the claims advanced by proponents of the colonial famine plot, who suggested that metropolitan merchants were responsible for starvation in the colonies. As Ducoeurjoly recognized, planters themselves bore the final responsibility for providing adequate nourishment to their slaves, and slave malnutrition could be the result only of planter negligence. Nor were such assessments confined to the period when the development of plantation monoculture was most extensive. Even in the late seventeenth century, when the enslaved population of the colonies was still relatively small, the missionary Jean-Baptiste du Tertre observed that, "as the nutrition of the Blacks depends on their masters, it is very different in every case [...] but to tell the truth, they are all nourished in an entirely pitiful manner".[19]

These admissions reveal the full cynicism of the colonial famine plot. While proponents of free trade in the late eighteenth century suggested

l'auteur y a fait, 8 vols (Paris, 1742), III, p. 438; Cassan, "Mémoire sur les cultures de l'isle de Saint-Lucie", in *Mémoires d'agriculture, d'économie rurale et domestique* (Paris, 1789), pp. 60–66.

18. Chambre d'Agriculture de la Martinique, "Mémoire sur la disette actuelle des vivres dans la colonie" (17 June 1776), Archives Nationales d'Outre Mer, Aix-en Provence [hereafter, ANOM], Series F–3, no. 125. On the impact of hurricanes in other parts of the Caribbean, see Louis A. Pérez, Jr, *Winds of Change: Hurricanes and the Transformation of Nineteenth-Century Cuba* (Durham, 2001); Matthew Mulcahy, *Hurricanes and Society in the British Greater Caribbean, 1624–1783* (Baltimore, MD, 2006).

19. Ducoeurjoly, *Manuel des habitants*, pp. 76–77; Jean-Baptiste du Tertre, *Histoire générale des Antilles habitées par les Français*, 6 vols (Paris, 1667), II, p. 513.

that plantation owners were powerless to provide proper nourishment to their enslaved laborers, the reality was that the authority enjoyed by the master in the plantation system was the primary cause of slave malnutrition.

Further insight into the ultimate responsibility of planters for starvation in the colonies is provided by Labat, whose memoirs described his own experiences as the manager of a sugar plantation in Martinique at the turn of the eighteenth century. According to Labat's calculations, the profits from a well-run sugar plantation were more than sufficient to provide adequate nourishment for the enslaved workers. However, he also emphasized the problems that inevitably arose, problems that were exacerbated by the negligence of many planters. Labat described the various means by which planters sought to minimize the expense of feeding their slaves, such as the distribution of "a certain quantity of rum [*eau-de-vie*] every week, which takes the place of flour and meat". Labat also denounced planters who, instead of taking direct responsibility for providing adequate rations to their slaves, allowed them one free day per week (typically a Saturday) to cultivate their own gardens. "If the slaves are sick on that day", Labat asked, "or if bad weather prevents them from working, or being lazy and libertine they pass the Saturday without working, what will they eat for the following week?" Planters, Labat emphasized, had an obligation "to furnish to their slaves, whom they should regard as children, everything necessary for their subsistence".[20]

Like many proponents of slavery, Labat viewed the provision of adequate rations as a powerful justification for the authority of the master. However, he was also aware that, in reality, many planters fell well short of this ideal. As observers such as Ducoeurjoly, du Tertre, and Labat recognized, the authority of Caribbean planters over their enslaved workforces, far from providing a solution to issue of food supply, was actually a significant part of the problem.

The Code Noir of 1685, which theoretically governed the treatment of slaves in the French Caribbean, set a minimum weekly ration, requiring the planters to furnish manioc flour or other Caribbean products, as well as at least two pounds of salted beef or three pounds of salted fish. Given the notoriously widespread disregard of the Code Noir by planters, however, it is likely that even these minimum provisions were rarely provided. Frequent official proclamations calling for more food production in the colonies support contemporary accusations that planters paid little regard to the adequate provisioning of their workforces. In 1776, for example, the royal administrators of Saint-Domingue issued an ordinance lamenting that "the great majority of Planters in this Colony neglect the plantation and cultivation of manioc, bananas, sweet potatoes, yams, rice,

20. Labat, *Nouveau voyage*, III, pp. 438–448.

and maize, so necessary for the nutrition of many people, and generally for all the Slaves". Such neglect, the administrators noted, contradicted a long list of previous regulations, and could easily cause a catastrophic famine.[21]

The frequency of ordinances like this suggests that the lack of adequate provisions was a persistent problem in the French plantation colonies, in spite of official efforts to encourage local food production. In the final analysis, plantation owners bore the ultimate responsibility for the malnutrition of their enslaved workers. The true "famine plot" in the French colonies was a product of the planters' reliance on the Atlantic slave trade, their encouragement of plantation agriculture, and their negligence of the proper nourishment of the enslaved population.

FAMINE PLOT, FREE TRADE, AND COLONIAL EXPANSION IN THE FRENCH ATLANTIC

The wealthy planters lobbying for a reform of the *exclusif* in the late eighteenth century were determined to deny what the most candid observers of slavery in the French Caribbean were willing to admit, that the plantation system was the main cause of starvation in the colonies. In adopting famine-plot rhetoric in the disputes over commercial reform, French planters sought first and foremost to reject their own responsibility for the suffering of their enslaved laborers. To this end, proponents of the colonial famine plot emphasized the lengths to which planters went to provide sustenance for the enslaved population. "Our blacks languish without strength on our plantations, lacking subsistence which we cannot provide to them", the planters sitting in the Guadeloupe Chamber of Agriculture lamented in 1767. In order to feed their slaves, the planters asserted, the colonists had made "exact searches in all the magazines, and even in the ships in the harbor, without finding a single barrel of beef".[22]

This emphasis on the concern shown by planters for the health of their slaves formed the basis of the colonial famine plot. The conclusion advanced by the planters was that if their efforts to provide for their slaves left nothing to be desired, the only possible explanation for malnutrition was the existence of a deliberate effort on the part of French merchants to starve the colonies of basic necessities.

As criticism of plantation slavery began slowly to penetrate French public opinion at the end of the eighteenth century, plantation owners increasingly used famine-plot rhetoric to defend themselves against

21. Méderic-Louis-Élie Moreau de Saint-Méry, *Loix et Constitutions des colonies françoises de l'Amérique sous le Vent*, 6 vols (Paris, 1784–1790), V, p. 729.
22. "Très Humbles Représentations de la Chambre d'Agriculture établie à la Guadeloupe, sur l'arrêt du Conseil d'Etat du Roi du 29 Juillet 1767" (24 November 1767), ANOM, Series F-3, no. 126.

accusations of cruelty. By blaming food shortages on metropolitan merchants, planters emphasized their own impotence to provide better conditions for their enslaved laborers. According to the colonial lobbyist Dubuc, during times of hardship the conditions of the *exclusif* made it impossible for planters to feed their slaves, and "the majority of these unfortunates [...] died of hunger, invoking in vain the charity of the Colonists, who had difficulty supplying their own needs".[23] This assessment was supported by the Chamber of Agriculture of Cap Français, the leading port city of Saint-Domingue, which asserted that in efforts to provide provisions for the enslaved population, "the activity of the planters leaves nothing to be desired". The planters sitting in the Chamber concluded that it was only the influence of French merchants that prevented adequate provisioning.

Critics of slavery, the planters maintained, should direct their complaints against the merchants, "because the enormous depopulation of which they complain, proves the lack of rations that the Colony does not produce, that the Colonist has demanded for sixty years, and that Commerce has had the cruelty to not import".[24] In 1789, the planter representatives to the National Assembly insisted that in seeking a relaxation of trade restrictions, they were above all concerned to ensure the happiness of their enslaved workers, insisting that their demands were motivated "more by *humanity* than by interest".[25]

The planters offered several explanations as to why the merchants were not supplying the provisions that were so badly needed in the colonies. The most benign interpretation was that French commerce was simply unable to provide the necessary supplies. As early as 1761, the newly created Chamber of Agriculture in Port au Prince lamented the "sterility of national commerce, and the oppositions formed by merchants to neutral commerce".[26] In 1767, the planters of Guadeloupe emphasized the

---

23. [Jean-Baptiste Dubuc and Pierre-Ulrich Dubuisson], *Lettres Critiques et Politiques sur les colonies et le commerce des villes maritimes de France, adressées à G-T Raynal* (Geneva, 1785), pp. 101–108. Dubuc advanced similar accusations in another anonymous pamphlet, *Le pour et le contre sur un objet de grande discorde et d'importance majeure. Convient-il à l'administration de céder part, ou de ne rien céder aux étrangers dans le commerce de la métropole avec ses colonies?* (London, 1784).

24. *Mémoire sur le commerce étranger avec les colonies françaises de l'Amérique présenté à la Chambre d'Agriculture du Cap, le 17 février 1784* (Paris, 1785), pp. 7–17. Although this memoir is officially dated 17 February 1784, the explicit reference to the August decree makes it clear that it was composed later.

25. *Réponse succincte des Députés de S. Domingue au mémoire des commerçants des ports de mer* (Versailles, 1789), p. 6, emphasis in original.

26. "Mémoire présenté par les membres de l'Agriculture de la Chambre de Commerce établie au Port-au-Prince, pour exposer au Ministre, ayant le département de la Marine, l'état de cette partie de la colonie de St Domingue" (15 June 1761), ANOM, Series F-3, no. 126.

inability of French merchants to fulfill their responsibilities to the colonies. "The powerlessness of French commerce in this regard is well-known", they asserted; and "we do not doubt the boldness of their promises, but we have long waited for the effects".[27]

In this view, the main fault of the merchants was clinging to their monopoly over colonial commerce when they were unable to provision the colonies sufficiently. From this basis, however, planters seeking a reform of the *exclusif* quickly passed to conspiracy theories. By 1769, the planters of Guadeloupe had much more specific accusations to make against the merchants of France. The planters complained that in the debates over commercial reform, "several speculators have raised misleading questions, totally foreign to the issue at hand". Even as they demanded expanded permission to trade with foreign merchants, the planters predicted that French merchants would "rise against the propositions that we are advancing, because the private interest that guides them calculates nothing for the group, and accords everything to self-interest".[28]

As the debates over the *exclusif* intensified in the 1780s, planter lobbyists began to advance more explicit descriptions of the conspiracy that they saw behind efforts to block its further reform. In his polemic against the French merchants, Dubuc described the entire history of the trade restrictions as the product of a deliberate plot. When the policy of the *exclusif* was first implemented, he claimed, official knowledge of colonial affairs was "surrounded by a thick fog that particular interests had created, and which they took care to maintain". This explanation relied on a common theme of French conspiracy rhetoric, the idea of a well-intentioned monarchy led astray by the powerful influence of greedy conspirators. Dubuc claimed that whenever news of suffering in the colonies reached the French government, the merchants used their influence to deny the existence of food shortages, asserting that the colonists "had everything in the greatest abundance".[29]

The tendency to conspiracy rhetoric became even more pronounced during the Revolution. When a committee created by the National Assembly to examine the claims advanced by the planter representatives concluded that Saint-Domingue was not, in fact, experiencing a famine, the planter deputy Cocherel noted bitterly that four of the six deputies sitting on the committee were merchants.[30] According to proponents of the colonial famine plot, the Revolution had simply made it easier for the merchants of the port cities to exercise control over colonial policy.

27. "Très Humbles Représentations", ANOM, Series F–3, no. 126.
28. "Quelques observations de la Chambre d'Agriculture de la Guadeloupe", ANOM, Series F–3, no. 126.
29. [Dubuc and Dubuisson], *Lettres Critiques et Politiques*, pp. 101–108.
30. Nicholas-Robert de Cocherel, *Réflexions de M de Cocherel, député de Saint-Domingue, sur le Rapport du Comité des Six* (Paris, 1789), pp. 1–7.

In the minds of the planters, the motives behind the colonial famine plot were as devious as the means by which it was carried out. In their assessment, slave malnutrition was a winning proposition for the merchants because they benefited from both the high price of basic necessities and the increased indebtedness of planters whose work gangs had been wiped out. Even as the planters watched "their blacks succumb to misery and famine", Dubuc asserted, "the merchants never ceased to demand the repayment of their debts".³¹ As one Saint-Domingue planter wrote succinctly in 1785, the ultimate result of the *exclusif* was to "raise the price of provisions to enrich a few merchants", and he predicted that the end result would be to "kill our poor laborers and ruin their masters".³² The planters complained of their subjection to the trade restrictions in a language they knew all too well. In 1790, the absentee planter and deputy to the National Assembly Pierre de Thébaudières described trade restrictions as "the shackles that have long made the colonists moan", and asserted that the ultimate goal of the merchants was to "render us more enslaved than our Blacks".³³

Even as they refused to accept responsibility for starvation in the colonies, proponents of the colonial famine plot demonstrated that they understood the problems caused by their reliance on plantation slavery. In their campaign against the *exclusif*, planters frequently emphasized that the colonies were simply unable to supply their own needs. In 1761, the Port au Prince Chamber of Agriculture observed that "a country which absolutely lacks that which is necessary for the subsistence of its colonists [...] can only be thrown into violent crisis in seeing itself deprived of constant commerce that can supply all of its needs".³⁴

Several years later, the planters of Guadeloupe provided a more detailed discussion of this issue. The planters admitted that when the colony was first founded by a handful of adventurers in the seventeenth century, abundant natural resources had provided for "an easy subsistence". With the arrival of sugar and coffee cultivation at the end of the century, however, "the population began to accumulate rapidly, both from the number of Europeans who transplanted themselves to this country, and from the even greater number of blacks demanded by these new branches of agriculture". With this transformation, the planters noted, "hunting and fishing were exhausted, [and] dried cod became a necessary provision for the blacks and for many of the whites".³⁵

---

31. [Dubuc and Dubuisson], *Lettres Critiques et Politiques*, pp. 101–108.

32. "Observations d'un habitant de Saint-Domingue, sur le mémoire des négociants de Bordeaux", ANOM, Series F-3, no. 84.

33. Pierre-André-François de Thébaudières, *Vues générales sur les moyens de concilier l'intérêt du Commerce National avec la prospérité des Colonies* (Paris, 1790), pp. 6–8.

34. "Mémoire présenté", ANOM, Series F-3, no. 126.

35. "Quelques observations de la Chambre d'Agriculture de la Guadeloupe", ANOM, Series F-3, no. 126. On the turn-of-the-century environmental transformations described by the

In 1784, the Chamber of Agriculture in Cap Français described the nature of agriculture in the colonies, focusing specifically on the choice between the crops needed to feed the colonial population and those destined for export to Europe. "As for vegetables and other provisions", they asserted, "the colony can produce them only in detriment to colonial goods [i.e. sugar and coffee]". The Chamber recognized that the expansion of plantation agriculture threatened the ability of the colonies to supply their own needs. "To the extent that the [luxury] crops have been extended", the planters contended, "the mountains have been degraded, and the resources for provisioning have diminished". The ecological conditions in the colonies, the Chamber suggested, presented planters with a choice between growing enough foodstuffs to feed their enslaved laborers and extending the cultivation of colonial products. In order for the colonies to produce enough food to sustain their population, the planters asserted, "provisions must take the place of coffee, and this precious source of wealth will be lost to France". With these conditions in mind, the planters demanded, "Can you ask the colonist to plant provisions, which are necessarily sold at a low price, in place of the goods that can enrich him?"[36] This logic accounts for the unwillingness of the colonists to abandon either plantation agriculture or the slave trade, even as they decried the suffering caused by food shortages in the colonies.

On various occasions, the planters advanced exact figures to describe the loss of life that they attributed to the colonial famine plot. Dubuc claimed that the strict application of the *exclusif* since 1727 had "killed more than fifteen thousand human beings". The planters of Cap Français went much further, calculating that "the lack of rations has cost us a million blacks". Seeking to instill a sense of urgency in his colleagues in the National Assembly, in 1789 the planter deputy Jean-François Reynaud de Villeverde emphasized that, as a result of the trade restrictions, "10,000 to 12,000 die of hunger each year".[37]

While these statistics were used to discredit proponents of the *exclusif*, planters also consistently demanded permission to import even greater numbers of enslaved laborers. According to the Guadeloupe Chamber of Agriculture, French commerce "can supply us only with 3,000 blacks [per year], while replacing [the losses caused by] death and flight requires at least 5,000".[38]

---

planters, see Philip Boucher, *France and the American Tropics to 1700: Tropics of Discontent?* (Baltimore, MD, 2008), pp. 235–236.

36. *Mémoire sur le commerce étranger*, pp. 25–28.

37. [Dubuc and Dubuisson], *Lettres Critiques et Politiques*, pp. 89–92; *Mémoire sur le commerce étranger*, pp. 1–6; Jean-François Reynaud de Villeverde, *Motion de M. le comte de Reynaud, député de Saint-Domingue, a la séance du 31 Août* (Versailles, 1789), pp. 1–6.

38. "Quelques observations de la Chambre d'Agriculture de la Guadeloupe", ANOM, Series F–3, no. 126.

The Chamber of Agriculture in Cap Français noted pointedly that "the English [slave traders] furnish their blacks at half the price that French merchants demand from the colonists."[39] While admitting that the colonies were unable to produce sufficient provisions to prevent high rates of mortality, the planters firmly demanded the right to purchase even greater numbers of enslaved laborers.

In order to defend their demands for commercial reform, the planters asserted that opening the colonies to foreign merchants was the only means to ensure the continued expansion of the plantation system. In 1768 the planters of Cap Français lamented that the malnourishment of their labor force left them "very far from thinking of clearing new land or the perfection of agriculture".[40] Assessing the state of agriculture in the colony of Saint-Domingue twenty years later, Dubuc estimated that "its production can be augmented by more than a third, perhaps even by half" if the trade monopolies were done away with. Because the *exclusif* prevented planters from purchasing enough enslaved workers and sustaining those they could obtain, Dubuc argued, "a large portion of the land susceptible to exploitation still waits for cultivators". He also predicted that free trade would permit "more intense cultivation of the existing plantations, which requires improvements that the [current] lack of blacks renders impossible so long as more effective measures are not taken to support their nutrition and replenish the work gangs".[41] Even as proponents of the colonial famine plot persuasion admitted that plantation monoculture had made it impossible for the colonies to sustain themselves, they anticipated the further expansion of the plantation system promised by commercial reform.

French planters thus presented trade reform as the most effective means to ensure the prosperity of the colonies and the expansion of the French empire. The *exclusif*, the planters of Guadeloupe maintained, went against "the true interests of the state".[42] Their counterparts in Cap Français agreed, asserting that "unlimited freedom of foreign commerce is as useful to the aggrandizement of the Colonies as to the prosperity of national Commerce". The planters argued that the basis for establishing successful colonies "consists of the easing of the fate of the slaves", and while they were fully willing to claim credit for the supposedly humanitarian aspects of trade reform, the planters made it clear that their primary purpose in seeking a relaxation of the *exclusif* was to encourage the further development

---

39. *Mémoire sur le commerce étranger*, p. 22.
40. "Mémoire de la Chambre d'Agriculture du Cap" (2 December 1768), ANOM, Series F–3, no. 125.
41. [Dubuc and Dubuisson], *Lettres Critiques et Politiques*, p. 83.
42. "Quelques observations de la Chambre d'Agriculture de la Guadeloupe", ANOM, Series F–3, no. 126.

of the plantation system.[43] In this way, the colonial famine-plot persuasion constituted a response to the ecological catastrophes induced by European colonization of the Caribbean, but a response premised on the further expansion of the colonial system.

In advancing the cause of commercial reform, French planters suggested that the alternative was nothing less that the ruin of the colonies. As Dubuc explained, "every black with nothing to eat necessarily flees his master's plantation". Eventually, he predicted, "these unfortunates, who have been pushed by hunger and despair", would begin to organize brazen attacks against the plantations. In these circumstances, maintenance of the *exclusif* posed a grave danger to the security of France's colonies. If not checked, Dubuc claimed, the obstinacy of the merchants in clinging to their trade monopolies "will one day cause the throats of the masters to be slit by their own slaves, after having killed half of those through famine".[44] On the eve of the Haitian Revolution, the colonial representative Reynaud offered a similar warning to his colleagues in the National Assembly, asserting that "the lack of rations leads to thefts, quarrels, desertions, revolts, and even murders."[45]

This assessment reflected the general tendency of eighteenth-century Europeans to attribute slave resistance to outside influences, denying that the slaves on their own might be capable of defying the plantation system.[46] During the revolutionary crisis of the 1790s planters fixed the blame for slave resistance on abolitionist movements, but in the final decades of the *ancien régime* metropolitan merchants and the *exclusif* played a similar role for proponents of the colonial famine plot persuasion.

While the influence of the planter lobby in France suffered a sharp decline in the first half of the 1790s, by the end of the decade they had again succeeded in infiltrating the halls of power, guiding Napoleon's failed attempt to retake Saint-Domingue, as well as his successful efforts to restore slavery in France's other colonies.[47] From this perspective, the political activities of wealthy planters at the end of the *ancien régime* resemble less the death throes of a doomed aristocracy than a foreshadowing of later responses to the problems posed by colonial expansion. In particular, the adoption of famine-plot rhetoric to the campaign for commercial reform reflects a sophisticated, if ultimately self-serving,

---

43. *Mémoire sur le commerce étranger*, pp. 1–6.
44. [Dubuc and Dubuisson], *Lettres Critiques et Politiques*, p. 124.
45. Reynaud, *Motion de M. le comte de Reynaud*, pp. 1–6.
46. Michel-Rolph Trouillot, *Silencing the Past: Power and the Production of History* (Boston, MA, 1995), pp. 70–107.
47. On the resurgence of planter influence, see Laurent Dubois, *A Colony of Citizens: Revolution & Slave Emancipation in the French Caribbean, 1787–1804* (Chapel Hill, NC [etc.], 2004), pp. 277–307.

understanding of the ecological catastrophes that followed in the wake of European colonization and the growth of the plantation system in the Caribbean.

Rather than attempt to moderate the system of monoculture and environmental degradation that they had created, the planters called for free trade as a means of further sustaining the colonial enterprise. In this, their response anticipated that of later proponents of empire, who denied their own basic responsibilities for the devastating famines of the late nineteenth century even as they promoted the further integration of colonized regions into European-dominated global markets.

IRSH 55 (2010), Supplement, pp. 123–151 doi:10.1017/S0020859010000520
© 2010 Internationaal Instituut voor Sociale Geschiedenis

Environmental Changes, the Emergence of a Fuel Market, and the Working Conditions of Salt Makers in Bengal, c. 1780–1845*

S A Y A K O   K A N D A

Faculty of Economics, Keio University

E-mail: kanda@a7.keio.jp

SUMMARY: During the late eighteenth and early nineteenth centuries, the British East India Company monopolized salt production in Bengal, and the British sought a new market for English salt in India. As previous studies have emphasized, external political and economic forces devastated indigenous industry and its workers. However, working conditions were influenced more by the natural environments of the salt-producing localities, particularly the availability of fuel, which was indispensable to the process of manufacture. The industry had always benefitted from abundant grass and straw for use as fuel. However, as grasslands were lost due both to constant river encroachment and to land clearance for cultivation, straw prices increased with the emergence of a regional market for biomass fuels, so that increasing difficulties in procuring fuel gradually made the salt industry costly. That state of affairs was accelerated by the advance of economic activity in general and a shortage of coal in particular. The changes made workers much more dependent on the fuel market.

INDIGENOUS INDUSTRY IN THE AGE OF EXPANSION OF GLOBAL TRADE

In Indian history, the late eighteenth to the early nineteenth century was a period when the British East India Company [hereafter, the Company] gradually consolidated its rule over India by securing stable sources of revenue. Simultaneously, world trade expanded under the free trade system and the internal Indian market became increasingly connected to the world market.

* Research for this article was supported by the Japan Society for the Promotion of Science, Grant-in-Aid for Scientific Research (B), 18330074, 2006–2008. An earlier version of this article was read at the 15th World Economic History Congress, Utrecht, 6 August 2009. I would like to thank Professors Kaoru Sugihara, Kōhei Wakimura, Haruka Yanagisawa, Peter Robb, and Tirthankar Roy for their comments.

The growth of the export trade in opium and cotton for the Chinese market and the rapid expansion of the Company's territories involved an increase in production of cash crops as well as large-scale movements of troops, civil servants, commodities, and bullion. In eastern India the period saw the growth of internal trade as a result of a series of institutional reforms of the Company. The Company's directors tried to establish control over markets by making them "public property", what Sudipta Sen calls "a permanent settlement of marketplaces",[1] which deprived *zamindars* [landholders] and other landed and commercial interests of privileges and authority over them. The Company's interference in internal trade not only made it easier for it to obtain direct access to production sites, but also, as Rajat Datta argues, led to a proliferation of private marketplaces and enabled indigenous merchants "to expand their direct control over the internal market".[2]

The buoyancy of the economy created a new demand for safer, speedier, and larger means of transport, which led, for example, to Britain and north India's becoming connected by regular steamship routes via Calcutta in the 1830s. Furthermore, the introduction of steamships generated a demand for a new commodity – coal. The development of the coal industry was unable to keep up with the pace of demand, and the Company started looking eagerly for alternative fuels. The consequence was the emergence of a wider fuel market in Eastern India. Fuel-consuming indigenous industries were greatly affected by this new development in the early nineteenth century.

This essay explores the working conditions of salt makers, known as *malangis*,[3] in Bengal during the period of rapid economic and political change which occurred in the late eighteenth and early nineteenth centuries. The production of salt in Bengal and Bihar was monopolized by the Company in 1772, and, through a major institutional change in 1836, the monopoly lasted until 1863, when it was finally abolished. Then, Bengal salt was driven from the market and Cheshire salt imported from Liverpool became almost the sole variety of salt consumed in eastern India.

The dislocation of indigenous industries has been explained in the context of colonial rule and expanding global trade. It has been argued that the Company's monopoly, with its discriminatory practices, gradually devoured the established salt industry by depriving it of its competitiveness. Cheshire salt and Liverpool shipping interests applied political

---

1. Sudipta Sen, *Empire of Free Trade: The East India Company and the Making of the Colonial Marketplace* (Philadelphia, PA, 1998), chs 4–5.
2. Rajat Datta, *Society, Economy and the Market: Commercialization in Rural Bengal, c.1760–1800* (Delhi, 2000), pp. 200–206.
3. The salt manufacturers were commonly called *malangis*, but the term included several occupations without distinction, including boilers and coolies.

pressure which helped set the stage for the influx of Cheshire salt into eastern India.[4] Inherent in that and other established views is the assumption that the economic transition should be examined within the framework of dichotomies: free trade and monopoly; Britain and India; and Bengal salt and Cheshire salt. Such dichotomous approaches see the Company and British capital as the prime forces behind the globalization of trade and the transformation of the indigenous economy. In turn it is assumed that the indigenous society was a silent witness to the changes.

The working conditions of the *malangis* under the Company were also discussed in terms of such dichotomous approaches. The select committee appointed in 1836 to examine the salt monopoly in India was especially instructed to examine the working conditions of *malangis*. Those who opposed the monopoly, including British salt importers, insisted that the *malangis* were "the most wretched human beings" and their conditions were "in the state of slavery", because the Company relied upon a system of coerced labour.[5] The Company, which was in a position to preserve the monopoly, contradicted their claims, stressing that the *malangis* were better off than cultivators in the area, since salt production promised them an extra income in addition to what they cultivated on their own lands, and said that laws and regulations protected them from extortion.

Both views, however, failed to notice the changes in their conditions over the period under consideration. External political and economic forces were not the only influence on the fate of the salt industry and its workers. The present article attaches much importance to the environmental factors that influenced the performance of the industry and the conditions of its workers. The industry was located in the vast area along the Bay of Bengal, where raw materials, including seawater and fuel, were abundant. Thus, the industry was fortunate in having available such local environments, producing a large quantity of salt and profits both for the Company and the *malangis*. However, at the same time, the surroundings could make them very vulnerable. The salt industry and its workers were prone to tidal floods, cyclones, and tigers, to say nothing of constant changes in the river courses themselves. At least seven floods in the Ganges catchment and two in the Brahmaputra catchment areas were recorded during the period under consideration,[6] and salt production was hit severely by them, as was the case in 1787.

4. For instance, Indrajit Ray, "Imperial Policy and the Decline of the Bengal Salt Industry under Colonial Rule: An Episode in the 'De-Industrialisation' Process", *Indian Economic and Social History Review*, 38 (2001), pp. 181–205.
5. For these contradicting observations (between D.C. Aylwin, a member of Aylwin & Co., and F.J. Halliday, Secretary to the Government of India, Home Department), see Appendix F, no. 3, British Parliamentary Papers [hereafter, BPP], XXVI, 1856.
6. Thomas Hofer and Bruno Messerli, *Floods in Bangladesh: History, Dynamics and Rethinking the Role of the Himalayas* (Tokyo [etc.], 2006), pp. 63–69.

The availability of fuel was influenced by such environmental factors also, and began to be affected by the growth in economic activity during the same period. Since the supply of coal was insufficient to meet increasing demand, fuel consumers began to exploit local firewood as an alternative. The rise in general fuel prices had an adverse effect on the salt industry and began to reduce the profits of its workers. The Company's policy also had to deal with such changing local ecological and economic conditions in order to stabilize salt production. Thus, to assess the working conditions of the *malangis* and changes in them over the years, we need to examine those working conditions in relation to much wider ecological, economic, and social changes.

THE *MALANGIS* UNDER THE COMPANY'S SALT MONOPOLY

The Company's salt policies

Under increasing pressure to secure revenue to finance extensive military campaigns and to pay salaries for its servants, the Company began to take measures to maximize revenues from salt. By a series of reforms in production and marketing during the 1780s, the Company successfully established a stable system of monopoly, which was characterized by the high price of salt maintained by the Company's strict control of its supply. Salt then became the second largest revenue source for the Company, playing a crucial role in consolidating Company rule.

In 1780, the Company started to take direct control of production and prohibited the private production of salt and other saline substances such as byproducts of saltpetre manufacture and the ashes of certain plants.[7] The private importing of salt was banned too, both by land and sea, although it had been one of the most important sectors of Bengal's import trade. In the same year, the salt agency system was instituted under the Board of Revenue.[8] All the salt *aurangs* or manufacturing divisions along the Bay of Bengal were integrated into six agencies at Hijili, Tamluk, the Twenty-Four Parganas, Raymangal, Bhulua, and Chittagong.[9] Salt agents were appointed by the Board of Revenue to manage their respective agencies.

---

7. India Office Records, British Library [hereafter, IOR], Bengal Board of Revenue (Miscellaneous) Proceedings, Salt [hereafter, BRP–Salt], P/101/56, 13.10.1829, no. 1; West Bengal State Archives, Letter from the Superintendent of Western Salt Chokies, Proceedings of Bengal Board of Trade, Salt [hereafter, BT–Salt], CIII, 1.8.1815. The production of certain kinds of industrial salt unfit for human consumption in Bihar, known collectively as *khari nun*, was the only exception. BRP–Salt, P/101/56, 13.10.1829, no. 1; Letter from the Superintendent of Western Salt Chokies, BT–Salt, CIII, 1.8.1815.

8. The Board of Trade took over the salt business in 1793 until the establishment of the Board of Customs, Salt and Opium in 1819.

9. In the Sundarbans area, there were two major rearrangements of the agencies. In 1801, the Raymangal agency was abolished due to heavy costs. In 1819, the eastern half of the Twenty-Four

The agents would contract with the *malangis* and pay advances to them as well as supervise the entire process of salt production, the storage of salt in the Company's warehouses, and its delivery to merchants. Agents were also required to be on the lookout for illegal production and smuggling. A chain of native officers at different stages in the production process enabled a salt agent to manage the entire scope of commercial activities within his region. Under that system, the Company exercised direct control over production, abolishing customary intermediate interests between the Company and *malangis*, such as *zamindars*, European and native revenue farmers, and merchants.[10]

To centralize sale and distribution and allow it to raise prices further, in 1788 the Company introduced sales by public auction, abandoning the practice of making sales at a fixed price. Under the auction system, the annual quantity of salt supplied to the market was fixed at about 3,000,000 *maunds*,[11] and all salt, domestic and foreign, was sold in Calcutta at auctions held several times a year. The new sale system encouraged competition among salt purchasers.[12] In January, the annual quantity of supply and the production quota of each agency were determined on the basis of production estimates reported by the Company's agents, salt prices in Calcutta and major commercial centres, and the reserves of salt in the Company's warehouses. The reserves included foreign salt[13] and purchasers' salt that had not yet been shipped from the warehouses.

Bengal method of production and location of salt industry

In many parts of coastal India, where seawater was readily available, solar-evaporated salt was widely produced. In contrast, Bengal salt was a boiled variety, known as *panga*. The Bengal method followed a boiling process because Bengal's extreme humidity made it difficult to crystallize

Parganas agency was separated to form the independent Jessore agency. The Joynagar agency operated experimentally for two seasons in 1793–1794 and 1794–1795.

10. For details see Sayako Miki, "Merchants, Markets, and the Monopoly of the East India Company: The Salt Trade in Bengal under Colonial Control" (unpublished Ph.D. thesis, University of London, 2005), ch. 1.

11. One *maund* is the equivalent of about 37.3 kilograms.

12. Salt merchants also played a significant role in maintaining high salt prices, and consequently the monopoly system itself. They purchased salt at public sales and pushed up prices on the market. For details see Miki, "Merchants, Markets, and the Monopoly", chs 1, 3.

13. The import of salt was not included in the trade statistics, because salt was "a source of revenue, and not of commerce"; IOR, Report on the External and Internal Commerce of Bengal in the Year 1818–1819, Bengal Commercial Records, P/174/30, 1818–1819. However, foreign salt, particularly from Coromandel and Orissa, played a crucial role in tackling smuggling and illicit production in the monopoly system, accounting for roughly one-quarter share of the total supply of salt in Bengal and Bihar. For details see Miki, "Merchants, Markets, and the Monopoly", chs 1–2.

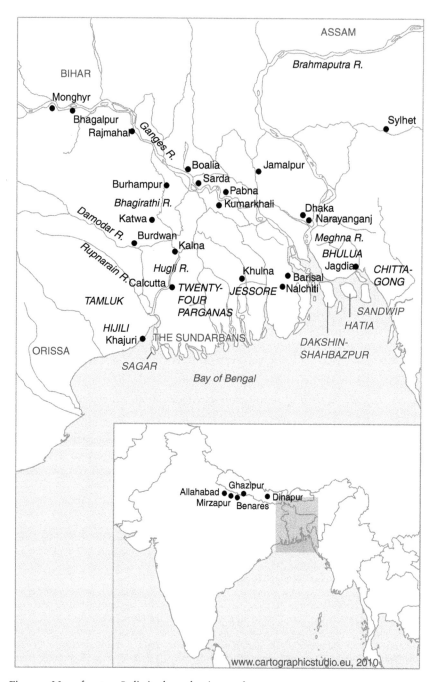

Figure 1. Map of eastern India in the early nineteenth century.

brine by solar power alone and the readily available fuel made *panga* production possible there. Fuel materials of low calorific value such as grass and paddy straw were generally used to boil brine, and even brushwood was occasionally used when no alternative was available. By boiling brine for long hours in small earthenware pots at low temperatures, finer and whiter salt was produced. Bengal salt was popular among consumers in Bengal, and thus fetched higher prices in the region's market.[14] Solar salt, which was imported mainly from the Coast of Coromandel, was unpopular because of its muddy appearance and inherent impurity. Such consumer preference had kept the price of solar salt low in most of Bengal, and it was supplied mostly to poorer and remote areas where Bengal salt was not generally available.[15]

The manufacturing season in Bengal began in October or November and ended in June or July before the seasonal rains began. Well before manufacturing began, *malangis* prepared by clearing salt grounds and making saltpans. From the saltpans that had been filled with salt water, they collected brine and then boiled it to make the salt. *Malangis* were responsible for producing a fixed amount of salt according to their respective *taidads* or contracted quantities and for delivering the product to the salt agent as it was produced. They settled their accounts with the agent at the end of the season. Since the advances given to *malangis* included all the costs incurred in the manufacturing process, it was their responsibility to procure sufficient fuel and pots for their season's work.

All the agencies followed similar production methods and time schedules, but geographical and environmental differences among them influenced their performance. The Hijili and Chittagong agencies, and to a lesser extent the Tamluk agency, had more suitable environments for salt production. Those agencies were able to produce salt of higher quality, because they were located far enough from the mouths of great rivers for the process of collecting brine to be less affected by fresh water or by natural changes in water flow, which caused soil erosion and devastated the land areas where fuel could be collected, and ruined the saltpans themselves.

Many production sites of the Twenty-Four Parganas, Raymangal, Joynagar, and Jessore agencies were situated within the Sundarbans jungle.

---

14. Until the mid-1820s the price of Bengal salt was generally about 100 rupees per 100 *maunds* higher than the average price of solar salt. For instance, the average price of Coromandel solar salt for 8 public sales from May to December 1825 was 317.08 rupees per 100 *maunds*, while that of Hijili salt was 419.5 rupees (calculated from *Calcutta Exchange Price Current*, 2, nos 332, 337, 341, 345, 350, 355, 359, and 363 (1825)).

15. For the difference in production method and taste, see Sayako Kanda, "Taste, Merchants and the Expansion of the Global Trade: Competition and Changes in the Salt Market in Eastern India, c.1820–1860", paper presented at Session H–5, 15th World Economic History Congress, Utrecht, 5 August 2009.

Figure 2. The interior of a boiling house in Tamluk, with two *malangis* boiling brine with grass or paddy straw.
Source: Notes on the Manufacture of Salt in the Tamluk Agency, *by H.C. Hamilton, Salt Agent, Dated September 23, 1852, Appendix B, BPP, vol. 26, 1856.*

Salt production for those agencies was environmentally challenging, since they had to overcome constant permeation of fresh water from the Ganges and its branches, as well as frequent tidal floods. Salt workers themselves also had to cope with diseases and wild animals. For instance, it was reported that the Raymangal agency lost 439 salt workers during the manufacturing season of 1788–1789 alone: 309 were killed by tigers, 3 killed by gavials – alligator-like creatures – 115 died of disease, 11 drowned, and 1 fell out of a tree.[16] The *malangis* of those agencies frequently

16. BRP–Salt, P/88/72, 12.11.1789. The reptiles that killed three people were called "alligators" in this report, but since the Ganges was not a natural habitat of the alligator, it is highly likely that they were in fact gavials.

petitioned the salt agents to take safety measures against tigers, and although attempts were made to set traps, and the huts were surrounded with fences of gram branches, and the men even used the noise of wooden sticks to keep the tigers away,[17] such measures proved ineffective.

Moreover, in contrast to the state of affairs in other agencies, the salt-pans were in the woods some way away from inhabited areas, so that the *malangis*, together with the coolies and woodcutters who cleared the woods for making the salt grounds, had to be sent to the manufacturing places along rivers which were difficult to navigate. In addition, supplies for these people and the boiling pots also had to be floated to the places of manufacture in a fleet of small boats of 1,500 to 2,000 *maunds*.[18]

The location of the Bhulua agency too was environmentally disadvantageous, since the production sites were scattered around the mouth of the mighty Meghna, as well as on several islands: Dakshin Shahbazpur, Sandwip, and Hatia. Salt production was often affected also by strong tides and the constant encroachment of rivers, which destroyed saltpans and grasslands.

The control of production and the welfare of the malangis

The total number of salt makers employed by the Company was estimated to be 60,000 between 1780 and 1836, assuming each *malangi* would produce 50 *maunds* of salt and that during that period the annual production level was set at 3,000,000 *maunds*.[19] According to a police estimate in 1823, the population of Bengal and Bihar was 35,593,307, of which 4,757,685 resided in the coastal districts of Midnapur, the Twenty-Four Parganas, Jessore, and Chittagong.[20] The *malangis* made up about 1.3 per cent of the total population of coastal districts. The population of the *malangis* in itself was not significant, but if we include their dependents and related workers such as coolies, woodcutters, potters, and boatmen, the number of people dependent on the salt industry was much greater.

The salt agents were responsible for producing the authorized annual quota, an important task because success or failure in production would determine the Company's salt revenues. Weather conditions, such as excessive rainfall, storms, and unusually high tides during the preparing and manufacturing seasons, often caused production failures. For example, the failure in 1794–1795 in Tamluk was caused by excessive rain and uncommonly high spring tides in late October that overflowed the

---

17. *Ibid.*
18. BRP–Salt, P/88/74, 17.11.1790.
19. BRP–Salt, P/101/11, 13.1.1826, no. 12.
20. This estimate included Bengal, Bihar, and foreign settlements (BRP–Salt, P/101/44, 11.11.1828, no. 1).

salt grounds.[21] The severe storm that hit Tamluk in May 1833 not only destroyed salt but also made food collection difficult for the next season.[22] Constructed at the discretion of the agents, secure embankments around saltpans and warehouses were built to prevent damage from floods and high tides – although not always successfully so, in spite of the agents and their assistants making regular trips to inspect such embankments.[23]

The salt agents were also expected to take immediate relief action whenever the *malangis* themselves suffered from natural disasters, which of course hampered the level of production. For instance, when floods damaged a vast area of the Hijili Agency in July 1824, the salt agent immediately supplied the *malangis* with rice, beans, and chilli peppers to help the people recover and get back to work.[24] On another occasion, to mitigate the difficulties of the *malangis*, the salt agent of Hijili asked the Company for permission to produce 100,000 *maunds* of salt in addition to the authorized quantity of 800,000 *maunds*.[25]

Workers were also exposed to various diseases. The failure in 1798–1799 in Bhulua was due to unseasonable rain from January to May that helped spread contagious diseases among the *malangis*.[26] According to C. Herd, who toured the Tamluk agency after the severe storm in May 1833, many of the *malangis* had fallen victim to *cholera morbus* and an unspecified fever.[27] Although no malaria was reported from the salt districts during that period,[28] people were prone to "apoplexy, paralysis, inflammatory fever, and sudden attacks of cholera", due to the unhealthy circumstances of a tropical climate.[29] The first priority of the salt agents was to make sure that victims of such natural calamities recovered as soon as possible so that they could continue to work through the rest of the current and following seasons.

The timing of advance payments to the *malangis* also played a crucial role in the success or failure of production. According to Richard Goodlad, the salt agent at the Twenty-Four Parganas, "the success of the salt manufacture depends in a great measure on the funds which are

21. IOR, Bengal Revenue Consultations (Salt, Opium and c.) [hereafter, BRC–Salt], P/98/32, 18.7.1796, no. 1.
22. BRP–Salt, P/104/84, 7.1.1834, no. 1.
23. BRP–Salt, P/101/56, 6.11.1829, no. 8.
24. BRP–Salt, P/100/70, 17.8.1824, nos 11–12.
25. BRC–Salt, P/100/3, 26.4.1816, nos 6–8.
26. BRC–Salt, P/98/38, 21.8.1800, no. 1.
27. BRP–Salt, P/104/84, 7.1.1834, no. 1. According to his estimates, about one-third to one-half of the coolies had died or left the area.
28. According to Ira Klein, "the deadly form of malaria which became known ultimately as Burdwan fever [...] originated in Jessore, in the late 1830s"; Ira Klein, "Malaria and Mortality in Bengal, 1840–1921", *Indian Economic and Social History Review*, 9 (1972), pp. 132–160, 138.
29. Khondker Ifthkhar Iqbal, "Ecology, Economy and Society in the Eastern Bengal Delta, c.1840–1943" (unpublished Ph.D. thesis, University of Cambridge, 2005), p. 68.

necessary for carrying it on, being forthcoming at the exact periods at which they are wanted".[30] In 1793, when the remittance of the advance money was delayed from the Company's treasury because of a general shortage of silver rupees, he used his private account to borrow money from Gopal Das Hari Kissen Das, a large Benares banking concern, and distributed those funds to the *malangis* without delay.[31]

In the Hijili agency, the first advance was made in the middle of November at the office of each manufacturing division to enable the *malangis* to prepare their lands for manufacture and to give necessary advances to their coolies and potters.[32] The agent and his assistants visited all the manufacturing divisions to make the second advance in February. The third advance was made in April. After concluding the season in early June, the *malangis* came to the division office to settle their accounts. There were also intermediate advances, known as *howlath*, to meet the occasional exigencies of the *malangis* for the supply of fuel. Such intermediate advances enabled the *malangis* to buy straw for fuel when it was plentiful and cheap. In Tamluk, the *malangis* were in the habit of using such intermediate advances to go to the banks and sandbanks of the Rupnarayan to obtain various types of reed during the cold season when rivers were easily navigable.[33]

In the Twenty-Four Parganas, where salt was manufactured in the jungle, an extra concession for *malangis* seems to have been necessary. At the end of July, the early advance was made soon after the *malangis* returned from the woods, when "they are greatly distressed, the manufacture of salt is at an end and their lands at that season are entirely unproductive".[34] In early October, the second advance was given to the *malangis* when they were dispatched to the woods to prepare salt grounds and cut sufficient fuel for the entire boiling season. When they returned from the woods after about forty days to look after their cultivated lands, the December advance was made to enable them to "settle their revenue accounts and quit the cultivated country" by early January to manufacture salt. Besides, whenever necessary, the agents helped poorer *malangis* with small, extra advances. The time schedule of payment was determined at the discretion of the salt agents. The diversity of manufacturing locations, the availability of fuel and coolies, and the relationships between *malangis* and landholders helped to determine the timing of payment.[35]

The salt agents also had to make sure that *malangis* spent the advances exclusively on the manufacture of salt and that none of them pocketed a portion of it. It was a well-known saying that the salt agencies were "a

30. BRC–Salt, P/98/25, 26.7.1793, no. 2.
31. BRC–Salt, P/98/25, 11.11.1793, no. 4.
32. BRP-Salt, P/101/56, 6.11.1829, nos 7–8.
33. BRP-Salt, P/104/84, 7.1.1834, no. 17.
34. BRC–Salt, P/98/25, 26.7.1793, no. 2.
35. BRP–Salt, P/101/56, 6.11.1829, nos 9–12.

pagoda tree". The officers of the salt agencies were not only relatively well paid but also well placed to take bribes from *malangis*.[36] To avoid any sense of impropriety, some *malangis* even asked for paddy straw, baskets, and earthenware pots instead of cash.[37] While the Company protected them from extortion by regulation (Clause 2, Section II, Regulation X of 1819), the salt agents tried to hand small sums at a time to the *malangis* in person without depending on agency officers. Since the amount of the first advance was larger than other instalments, they took particular care in the handling of that payment.

The availability of fuel influenced the performance of the salt agencies. It was necessary for the *malangis* to collect enough fuel for the boiling season, using the advance money paid by the Company. In and around the salt producing districts, "the lands bearing fuel the produce of which has from time immemorial been appropriated to the boiling of salt, have ever been considered as reserved to the use of the manufacture", and the *malangis* were allowed to use the grass without paying for it.[38] In some areas, "the ryots [*raiyats*] when they reap the harvest, just cut off the ears and leave the straw which the molunghees [*malangis*] collect for fuel, and the ryots [*raiyats*] are paid at the rate of 4 annas per begah [*bighas*] though the straw is worth much more".[39] When the *malangis* failed to gather enough fuel through such customary means, they had to purchase straw in the market or obtain other kinds of grass from distant places at their own cost.

The salt agents occasionally helped the *malangis* procure fuels in order to prevent delay to production. For example, when the grasslands in Hijili were flooded because of the collapse of dykes in 1788, the salt agent asked permission to cut brushwood in the neighbouring Tamluk jungle to make up the deficiency.[40] In Twenty-Four Parganas the proprietors of grasslands began to claim their right to receive annual rent from the salt agent, a practice that interfered with the customary right of the *malangis* to obtain grass there. In such cases, the agent was forced to pay the rent to facilitate the smooth running of the *malangis*' business.[41]

---

36. Girishchandra Bose, *Sekaler Darogar Kahini* [The Memoirs of a Chief Constable] (Calcutta, 1888, reprinted 1983), pp. 165–166. Bose was the *kerani* [head writer] of the Tamluk agency before he became the police *daroga* [superintendent] in 1853. He recollected the earlier prosperous days of the salt agencies, when every servant had some share, and when *malangis* gathered at the agency headquarters to receive the season's advances. He also pointed out that the salt agent usually connived at this abuse.
37. BRP–Salt, P/101/56, 6.11.1829, no. 8.
38. BRC–Salt, P/98/25, 9.12.1793, no. 1.
39. *Ibid.* A *raiyat* is generally translated as a peasant. One rupee equals sixteen annas, and one *bigha* is about one-third of an acre.
40. BRP–Salt, P/88/72, 3.2.1789; 25.2.1789; 10.3.1789.
41. BRC–Salt, P/98/25, 9.12.1793, nos 1–2. The lease of 4,000 *bighas* of grasslands in Calcutta Pargana alone cost the agency about 2,600 rupees annually.

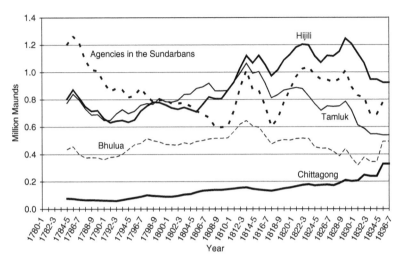

Figure 3. Salt production of Bengal agencies, 1780–1837 (4-year moving average).
Note: Production for the years 1830–1831 and 1832–1833 has been estimated. Agencies in the Sundarbans include the Twenty-Four Parganas, Raymangal, Joynagar, and Jessore.[43]

Production and cost

The Company set a production ceiling of 3,000,000 *maunds* and increased it to 4,000,000 *maunds* in the early 1820s. Production decreased from the late 1820s, mainly due to unfavourable weather conditions. The 1824, 1827, and 1831 seasons were especially bad in Bengal, and annual production then dropped to 2,500,000 *maunds*. The total annual supply of salt including foreign salt was about 3,500,000 *maunds* in the 1780s and 1790s, 4,500,000 *maunds* in the latter part of the first decade of the nineteenth century, and reached a level as high as 5,000,000 *maunds* in the mid-1820s. However, consistent with the decline in salt production in Bengal, that figure began to decrease in the late 1820s and fell to 3,800,000 *maunds* in 1835.[42] The deficiency in Bengal salt was made good by Coromandel and Orissa salt.

As Figure 3 shows, environmental differences were reflected in the levels of production and productivity of the salt agencies. Hijili was the

42. BRP–Salt, P/101/52, 10.7.1829, no. 16; P/102/9, 27.1.1832, no. 20; P/105/35, 28.2.1837, no. 12.
43. BRP–Salt, P/89/2, 5.12.1792; P/100/13, 26.12.1817, no. 4; P/100/23,16.12.1818, no. 1; P/100/28, 24.9.1819, no. 2; P/100/36, 20.10.1820, no. 4; P/100/43, 14.9.1821, no. 3A; P/100/52, 24.9.1822, no. 8A; P/100/61, 30.9.1823, no. 11; P/100/72, 19.11.1824, no. 29; P/101/12, 28.2.1826, no. 5; P/101/31, 4.12.1827, no. 7; P/101/42, 16.9.1828; no. 68; P/102/7, 23.12.1831, no. 3; P/102/28, 27.12.1832, no. 27; BRC–Salt, P/98/26, 28.7.1794, no. 5; P/98/27, 8.5.1795, no. 4; P/98/27, 20.7.1795, no. 2; P/98/32, 18.7.1796, app. no. 1; P/98/35, 25.7.1799, no. 8; P/98/43, 5.8.1802, no. 3; P/99/16, 30.1.1806, no. 2; P/99/26, 11.9.1807, no. 2; P/99/30, 12.8.1808, no. 3; P/99/34, 25.8.1809, no. 2; P/99/39, 29.10.1810, no. 3; BT–Salt, General Statement of the Produce etc., vol. 75, 4.8.1812; vol. 85-2, 17.8.1813; vol. 95, 23.8.1814; vol. 113, 16.8.1816.

Table 1. *Average sale prices at public auction, 1823–1824 to 1832–1833.*

Agency	Price (per 100 *maunds*)	Agency	Price (per 100 *maunds*)
Hijili	387.9	Jessore	408.46
Tamluk	406.64	Bhulua	376.17
Twenty-Four Parganas	419.15	Chittagong	388.94

Source: BRP–Salt, P/105/21, 2.2.1836, no. 11H.

largest producer and its production level increased more quickly than that of other agencies, particularly in the 1820s. Hijili's production quota was set at 800,000 *maunds* initially but was later increased to 1,100,000 *maunds*. Chittagong too showed a steady increase in the same period. The Twenty-Four Parganas agency produced as much salt as Hijili and Tamluk in the early years, but its production fluctuated dramatically because of the manufacturing challenges in the Sundarbans. The Raymangal and Joynagar agencies were closed due to heavy expenses. Even so, the Company expanded salt production in the Sundarbans. In 1819, the eastern half of the Twenty-Four Parganas agency was separated, creating the Jessore agency; this measure was taken because the salt produced in those agencies fetched much higher prices on the market in spite of its inferior quality.

As Table 1 demonstrates, Twenty-Four Parganas and Jessore salt was sold at a higher rate than superior Hijili and Chittagong salt. Consumers appreciated the salt made from the sacred Ganges water, which raised the ritual value of these varieties of salt.[44] A general decline in the salt production from Tamluk and Bhulua, shown in Figure 3, was largely due to fuel problems.

As Figure 4 shows, the cost of production in the agencies situated in the Ganges Delta was high from the beginning, and increased further in the 1820s, while the cost of Hijili and Chittagong was relatively stable throughout the period. Production costs in Tamluk remained as low as in Hijili, but began to increase from the mid-1810s to almost the same level as that of other costly agencies.

The costs incurred in the production of Bengal salt can be classified into two groups: production costs and administrative costs, which were related chiefly to management. The administrative costs included commission paid to the superintendents of the salt *chokis* or toll stations, commission paid to agents and their assistants, and the proportions taken by the salt office and *choki* establishment. Figure 5 compares the average costs of production for 1815–1816 and 1816–1817 with that for 1825–1826 and 1826–1827. The administrative costs were relatively unchanged between

44. Appendix F, no. 2, BPP, vol. 26, 1856.

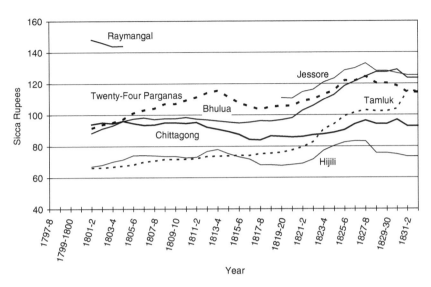

Figure 4. Costs and charges for producing 100 *maunds* of salt (5-year moving average).[45]

the two periods.[46] In the Twenty-Four Parganas and Tamluk, the increase in administrative costs was due to cash rewards granted to the merchants, an idea introduced in 1824 to encourage them to deliver their salt to market.[47]

Because administrative costs remained stable, it is likely that the cause of increasing costs lay in production. The main categories of production

45. BRP–Salt, P/100/13, 26.12.1817, no. 4; P/100/23, 16.12.1818, no. 1; P/100/28, 24.9.1819, no. 2; P/100/36, 20.10.1820, no. 4; P/100/43, 14.9.1821, no. 3A; P/100/52, 24.9.1822, no. 8A; P/100/61, 30.9.1823, no. 11; P/100/72, 19.11.1824, no. 29; P/101/12, 28.2.1826, no. 5; P/101/31, 4.12.1827, no. 7; P/101/42, 16.9.1828, no. 68; P/101/70, 21.1.1831, no. 81; BRC–Salt, P/98/35, 25.7.1799, no. 3; P/98/43, 5.8.1802, no. 3; P/99/16, 30.1.1806, no. 2; P/99/26, 11.9.1807, no. 2; P/99/30, 12.8.1808, no. 3; P/99/34, 25.8.1809, no. 2; P/99/39, 29.10.1810, no .3; BT–Salt, General Statement of the Produce, etc., vol. 75, 4.8.1812; vol. 85-2, 17.8.1813; vol. 95, 23.8.1814; vol. 113, 16.8.1816.

46. The proportions taken by the salt office and *choki* establishment remained almost unchanged at 5.19 rupees per 100 *maunds* of salt between 1801–1802 and 1828–1829. The rate of commission to the salt agents fluctuated until the mid-1810s, because of the reward system, by which agency officers were entitled to receive rewards when they apprehended smugglers. It later decreased and eventually stabilized to an average of 7.63 rupees between 1814–1815 and 1828–1829. The rate of commission paid to the superintendents of the salt *chokis* was only 2.69 rupees throughout. Calculated from the sources for Figure 5.

47. Due to their financial difficulties, the stock of merchants' salt in the Company's warehouses increased in the 1820s. To solve this problem, which caused a shortage of salt in the remote markets, this new system was introduced. Although at first deemed a temporary solution, it was reintroduced in 1827 and 1830. Thereafter the cost became the second largest item for agencies after the prime cost. For details see Miki, "Merchants, Markets, and the Monopoly", ch. 3.

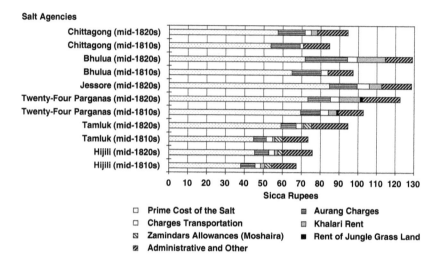

Salt Agencies

Figure 5. Average costs of production per 100 *maunds* of salt.
Note: The figures for the mid-1810s and the mid-1820s refer to the average costs for 1815–1816 and 1816–1817, and those for 1825–1826 and 1826–1827 respectively.[48]

costs were the "prime cost" of the salt, the charges of the *aurang* or manufacturing divisions, transport charges, the *khalari* rent, *zamindars'* allowances in Hijili and Tamluk, known as *moshaira*; and the rent of jungle grasslands in the Twenty-Four Parganas. The prime cost of the salt, amounting to 60 per cent of all production costs, included the total amount advanced to the *malangis* during a season. *Aurang* charges included all costs and charges related to managing production sites, such as the salaries of native officers in manufacturing and weighing establishments, expenses for building and repairing offices and warehouses, the purchase of fuel by the salt agent, gifts to industrious *malangis*, and any other small disbursements relating to the manufacturing divisions.[49] Transport costs were related primarily to the shipment of salt from production sites to the salt wharves, where it was stored for later shipment. The *khalari* was the rent paid to the landowners of the saltpans.

Production costs increased for reasons which varied among agencies, except for a general increase in the prime cost. Figure 5 shows that the prime cost of the Twenty-Four Parganas, Raymangal, and Jessore agencies was higher because, as we saw earlier, those located in geographically

48. BRC–Salt, IOR P/100/13, 19.12.1817, no. 1; P/100/23, 16.12.1818, no. 1; P/101/31, 4.12.1827, no. 7; P/101/42, 16.9.1828, no. 68.
49. Letter from the Agent at Hijili, BT–Salt, vol. 77-1, 14.10.1812.

challenging areas generated additional expenses. Another problem in those agencies was that some *malangis* absconded with their advance money.[50] The locations of manufacturing sites in the woods made it difficult for the salt agents to search them. In the case of the Twenty-Four Parganas, there was a wide gap in the rate of the advance money to the *malangis* between the distant divisions in wooded areas and those near Calcutta. The difference was so large that *malangis* around Calcutta deserted to wooded areas to obtain higher rates. Some of them even registered under fictitious names in distant divisions.[51] The salt agent tried to solve the problem by increasing the rate in the divisions near Calcutta to reduce the gap. The highest rate given to the *malangis* of the Twenty-Four Parganas was fixed at 87.5 rupees per 100 *maunds*, but the lowest rate, which was 56.25 rupees in the 1810s, increased to 75 rupees in the 1820s.[52] Those measures, however, led to a general increase in costs for these agencies.

Difficulties in procuring fuel and a rise in its price began to affect distributions of advance money. The problem was most strongly felt in Bhulua due to its geographical location. According to J. Irwin, the salt agent of Bhulua and Chittagong, because one production area, Sandwip Island, produced no fuel it had to be supplied from the vast alluvia of its southern and eastern shore.[53] The numerous shoals in the sea that became dry at low tide made it laborious and sometimes dangerous for the boats, laden with fuel, to reach the shore. In the season of 1810–1811 alone, at least seventeen fuel boats were lost in the surf.

The *malangis* on Hatia Island had formerly procured sufficient fuels from the "Neeluky Jungle" on the island, but the island's large tracts of fuel land were devastated by the encroachment of the Meghna, by constant soil erosion, and by the expansion in cultivation of other crops. The *malangis* on the island therefore had to depend on the southern extremity of Dakshin Shahbazpur Island for fuel, and the labour and transport costs of doing so weighed heavily on them. The Jagdia division too at the mouth of the Little Feni faced difficulties in the conveyance of fuel by boat because of the alluvial choking of the river. The agent's need to supply additional fuel explains the high rate of *aurang* charges of that agency.

Tamluk too faced difficulties in collecting fuel. Straw was sold at between 0.57 and 0.67 rupees per *kahan* during the period 1800 to 1807, but the rate rose to as high as 2 rupees per *kahan* in 1818.[54] The agent saw the increase in straw price as incidental, but the growth of the straw

50. BRP–Salt, P/98/28, 21.8.1800, no. 1; /P/100/47, 25.3.1822, no. 7.
51. BRP–Salt, P/100/47, 25.3.1822, no. 7.
52. Letters from the Several Agents, BT–Salt, vol. 86, 21.9.1813; BRP–Salt, P/101/22, 26.1.1827, nos 9–21; P/101/49, 14.4.1829, nos 11–24.
53. Extract from the Agent's letter dated 18 August 1812, BT–Salt, vol. 86, 21.9.1813.
54. BRC–Salt, P/100/22, 2.10.1818, no. 6. The *kahan* was a measure of grain or straw.

market in Calcutta gradually affected the price of it in surrounding areas.[55] Straw was used to thatch houses and as a domestic fuel by mixing it with cow dung. The fact that the smoke generated by the burning of dung cakes was one of the major causes of air pollution in early nineteenth-century Calcutta suggests a growth in straw consumption there.[56] It is highly likely that the growth of the market gave landowners, merchants, and peasants a strong incentive to sell the commodity on the open market. Under such circumstances, the *malangis* lost their customary right to collect paddy straw and had to buy more straw when they had no alternative. Moreover, it can be suggested that the growth of the silk industry, another major fuel-consuming industry in Bengal in the neighbourhood of the salt agency, increased competition for fuel.

The Twenty-Four Parganas, Jessore, and Bhulua agencies, which had comparable prime costs, bore higher costs in their salt production. When comparing the two periods in Figure 5, we can observe a significant increase in the *khalari* rent. Because of the particular geography of agencies in the Sundarbans area, saltpan sites there were vulnerable and it became necessary to lease ground for saltpans from landowners to maintain production levels.

Employment opportunities and bargaining power of the malangis

The Company tried to prevent not only production failures but also overproduction, as a large part of any surplus salt would enter the market illegally and reduce the price of legitimate supply. To control the total supply of salt, the Company kept the amount of Bengal salt below a certain level by reducing its production. Accordingly, each salt agent was responsible for keeping his agency's production level well below its actual capacity.

Constant cutbacks in production therefore reduced the income of *malangis* and undermined their trust in working under the Company monopoly. That provided a strong impetus to make extra salt illegally, by which salt makers could recoup losses caused by production cutbacks. Such illicit salt production was attractive, since the rate offered by smugglers was much higher than the rate of advances made by the Company, which was between 0.5 and 0.875 rupees per *maund*. For instance, the *zamindars* in Hijili, who smuggled to the interior, purchased salt from the *malangis* at a per *maund* rate of between 1.41 and 2.56 rupees.[57]

---

55. BRP–Salt, P/101/24, 3.4.1827, no. 24.
56. M.R. Anderson, "The Conquest of Smoke: Legislation and Pollution in Colonial Calcutta", in David Arnold and Ramachandra Guha (eds), *Nature, Culture, Imperialism: Essays on the Environmental History of South Asia* (New Delhi [etc.], 1995), pp. 293–355, 297–298.
57. BRC–Salt, P/100/32, 21.4.1820, no. 3. The *zamindars* employed peasants to purchase salt from the *malangis* and received it as their rents.

To tackle the problem of illicit production, salt agents tried to use a sur-
veillance system, composed of networks of native officers and informers
known as *goindas*, to limit illegal activities by the *malangis*. More importantly, they had to look after the welfare of the *malangis* to prevent them
from seeking other employment with better wages. In the 1811–1812 season,
the Company decided to buy up surplus quantities of salt from the *malangis*
to prevent it from flowing into the market illicitly, and the leap in production
shown in Figure 3 was the direct consequence of that plan. The Company
was satisfied with the result of its measure, stating that

> [...] a large increase in [the] quantity of salt delivered by the manufacturers at the
> Company's Golahs [warehouses] and a consequent diminution in the quantity
> formerly smuggled by them from the *aurangs* [manufacturing divisions], it also had
> the effect of affording general satisfaction to the Molunghees [*malangis*] and
> operated as a check to smuggling in general throughout the country.[58]

In the season of 1812–1813 too, the Company purchased surplus salt in
expectation of an abundant production season. After that point, many
agencies employed such purchase strategies. As the Board of Customs,
Salt and Opium stated in 1822, the prevention of illicit traffic in the salt
districts "can only be accomplished by granting to the Molunghees
[*malangis*] an enhanced price for the salt which they may deliver in excess
of their respective taidads [contracted quantities]".[59]

However, the purchase of surplus salt was costly. Such purchases were
intended to be only temporary, stopgap measures, but, as Figures 4 and 5
suggest, the practice became extremely difficult for the Company to eliminate once the *malangis* became used to higher prices. Unlike other agents,
the salt agent of Hijili was unwilling to take the measure, judging it too
expensive because Hijili could probably manufacture twice as much as the
annual quota of production.[60] Instead, the level of production was raised
from 800,000 *maunds* to about 1,100,000 *maunds* in the late 1810s to increase
the regular income of the *malangis* and prevent them from producing salt
illegally. In addition, the successive agents of Hijili distributed rewards in
kind to the most deserving and industrious *malangis* who reached a certain
level of deliveries. Rewards consisted of pieces of broadcloth, various other
types of cloth, red woollen lascars' caps, and small looking glasses. That
unique reward system can be explained by the fact that employment
opportunities for people in the district were limited to agriculture, and salt
manufacture at John Palmer's estate on Sagar Island.[61]

---

58. Letter to the Governor General in Council, BT–Salt, vol. 86, 21.9.1813.
59. BRP–Salt, P/100/47, 19.3.1822, no. 16.
60. BRP–Salt, P/101/56, 6.11.1829, no. 7.
61. Bodleian Library, Palmer Papers (MS English Letters, c.105), Letter from John Palmer to J.
Reed (29.12.1826), pp. 17–18; Letter from John Palmer to J. Reed (26.1.1826), pp. 104–106;

In contrast to circumstances at Hijili, there was growing competition among different industries for the workforce in and around the salt agencies of Tamluk particularly, and in the Twenty-Four Parganas and Jessore. In Tamluk, the number of silk factories increased from 3 in 1803 to 37 in 1818,[62] as wages for silk factory labourers rose from 2.69 rupees per month in 1803 to 3.19 rupees in 1818. That was a much higher wage than that of normal labourers, which ranged from 1.75 to 2.125 rupees in 1818, and more locals seem to have been attracted to silk factories by it; the number of locals employed increased from 825 out of 1,781 in 1803 to 2,979 out of 3,104 in 1818. In the Twenty-Four Parganas and Jessore agencies, the *malangis* sought employment in the indigo and sugar cane cultivation sectors.[63] The above observations suggest that the *malangis* were in a strong bargaining position vis-à-vis the Company, largely owing to the existence of smuggling fostered by the Company's high price strategy and because of labour scarcity in and around the salt agencies.

In other industries too, workers seemed to have enjoyed strong bargaining power with the Company. The opium industry in Bihar, which was also under Company monopoly, faced competition from the cultivation of other crops such as potatoes, and the illicit siphoning off of the workforce into other commercial pursuits.[64] Similarly to what was done in the salt monopoly, the rate of advances to opium growers was, therefore, increased in 1823. Even though they too received advances, the weavers employed by the Company were able also to sell their products clandestinely to other buyers, such as private traders of various nationalities. As Shubhra Chakrabarti puts it, "the English Company never could establish a total monopoly in the buyers' market".[65] Producers of cash crops, excluding those of indigo and opium, sold their produce in open markets.[66] Even indigo cultivators "looked better clothed and better conditioned than their neighbours" in the late 1820s, as Rammohan Roy observed.[67]

Letter from Ragoo Ram to J. Reed (7.3.1827), pp. 208–210. The *malangis* were usually brought from Hijili to John Palmer's estate through a *sardar* [recruiter] from Khajuri.

62. BRC–Salt, P/100/22, 2.10.1818, no. 6.

63. Narendra Krishna Sinha, "Introduction", in *idem* (ed.), *Midnapore Salt Papers: Hijili and Tamluk, 1781–1807* (Calcutta, 1954), pp. 1–24, 9.

64. Benoy Chowdhury, *Growth of Commercial Agriculture in Bengal, 1757–1900* (Calcutta, 1964), I, pp. 27–36.

65. Shubhra Chakrabarti, "Collaboration and Resistance: Bengal Merchants and the English East India Company, 1757–1833", *Studies in History*, 10 (1994), pp. 105–129, 117–124.

66. S. Bhattacharya and B. Chaudhuri, "Regional Economy: Eastern India", in Dharma Kumar (ed.), *The Cambridge Economic History of India*, 2 vols (Cambridge, 1982–1983), II, pp. 270–332, 324–329.

67. Sugata Bose, *Peasant Labour and Colonial Capital: Rural Bengal since 1770* (Cambridge, 1993), pp. 47–48.

These observations do not necessarily mean that the workers of various industries and those cultivating cash crops were well off. It is more likely that high revenue demand during the period meant that workers had to have multiple income sources to increase their earnings. As Sugata Bose points out, the production of cash crops such as indigo "not only promised a larger income but came with cash advances which could be used to pay the rent".[68] And an individual's relationship with other members of the community, such as landowners, moneylenders, and peasants, certainly influenced how much he or she earned. In the 1830s, however, the conditions of indigo cultivators and weavers deteriorated.[69] So, consequently, did those of the *malangis*, as the next section shows.

THE EMERGENCE OF THE FUEL MARKET AND ITS IMPACT ON THE SALT INDUSTRY

Growing demand for coal

The ever growing demand for safer, cheaper, and faster water transport for conveying goods, passengers, troops, and treasure between Calcutta and the upper provinces hastened the Company in establishing a stable river navigation. Lower Bengal had been well connected by water to north India and Assam, but although sophisticated the indigenous water communications were no longer sufficient for the growing demand in terms of volume as well as speed. According to J.H. Johnston, Controller of Government Steam Vessels, "the demand for water carriage frequently exceeds the available tonnage – it is always difficult to obtain boats for the service of the Government, and in cases of emergency they can only be procured by compulsion".[70] In 1830, Johnston estimated that about 60,000 boats with a total capacity of 320,000 tons were employed in Bengal, among which more than 25,000 tons had been annually engaged for the service of government. However, "the quantity of goods actually embarked had not perhaps exceeded in each year seven or eight thousand".[71] This was because the conveyance of goods needed to be accompanied by a fleet of boats with armed guards.

According to Cyril S. Fox, who served as the superintendent of the geological survey of India, evidence of burnt debris and outcrop fires in the Damodar Valley coalfields in Western Bengal suggests that "coal had been known in India from time immemorial, [...] yet when we turn to the

68. *Ibid.*, p. 47.
69. *Ibid.*, pp. 47–48; B.R. Tomlinson, "Bengal Textiles, British Industrialisation, and the Company *Raj*: Muslins, Mules and Remittances, 1770–1820", *Bulletin of Asia-Pacific Studies*, 10 (2000), pp. 197–214, 209.
70. J.H. Johnston, *Précis of Reports, Opinions, and Observations on the Navigation of the Rivers of India, by Steam Vessels* (London, 1831), p. 29.
71. *Ibid.*

literature and language of the country we find no mention of coal – there is no folk-lore, no legend, no story of any kind relating to these mysterious fires".[72] He further concluded that "it appears certain at all events that coal was not mined nor traded in by the people until John Sumner and Suetonius Grant Heatly discovered it in Bengal in 1774 and applied to Warren Hastings for permission to work coal mines".[73] Commercial coal mining started in 1815 when the first shaft mine was open at Raniganj in the Burdwan Coalfield.[74] After the successful experimental voyage of the *Hugli* steamer on the Ganges in 1828, the demand for coal rapidly increased and the Company emerged as the largest consumer of coal. The demand for bunker coal therefore created a market for coal in India for the first time in history.

After the *Hugli*, the Company launched 4 more river steamboats by 1840,[75] and the number had increased to 10 by 1849. In addition, it owned 19 seagoing steamships, and private companies had 15. Other consumers of coal were flour mills, foundries, and other powered factories in the Haora area near Calcutta.[76] The demand for coal stimulated the development of the coal-mining industry in eastern India where the largest coalfield was situated in Burdwan. The annual production of Burdwan coal was 1,000,000 *maunds* in the late 1830s, a figure which had increased to 2,500,000 *maunds* by 1846.[77] New coalfields in Palamau, Sylhet, Assam, Cuttack (Orissa), and other places on the fringes of eastern India were investigated and developed at the same time.[78]

To achieve stable and regular steam navigation, it was inevitable that the Company would need to secure a consistent source of coal for its steamboats. The Company therefore introduced a contract system, in which contractors were expected to procure coal and convey it to the Company's coal depots along the main river routes between Calcutta and Allahabad, as well as between Calcutta and Assam (see Figure 1). The Company's contract system, however, did not work well and many cases were reported of broken contracts. Particularly at the north Indian depots of Allahabad, Mirzapur, and Benares, firewood was frequently supplied instead of coal. The long

72. Cyril S. Fox, *Coal in India: I (The Natural History of Indian Coal), Memoirs of the Geological Survey of India*, LVII (Calcutta, 1931), p. 2.
73. *Ibid.*
74. About the earlier development of the Burdwan Coalfield, see Blair B. Kling, *Partner in Empire: Dwarkanath Tagore and the Age of Enterprise in Eastern India* (Calcutta, 1981), pp. 94–121.
75. *Ibid.*, p. 99. For the details of steamboats, see Henry T. Bernstein, *Steamboats on the Ganges: An Exploration in the History of India's Modernization through Science and Technology* (Hyderabad, 1960).
76. Kling, *Partner in Empire*, p. 98.
77. *Ibid.*, p. 105.
78. IOR, Marine Department, Reports of Committee for Investigating the Coal Resources of India for 1841 & 1842, L/MAR/C/604.

Table 2A. *The price of firewood at various places in eastern India,*
1836–1840.

Places	(Company's rupees per 300 *maunds*)*		
	Month and Year	Prices	Remarks
Mirzapur Allahabad	Late 1836–early 1837	156.0	
Allahabad	August 1839	110.7	
City of Benares	February 1839	76.5	
City of Benares	May 1839	77.4	
City of Benares	July 1839	76.5	
Ghazipur	May 1839	65.4	
Dinapur	August 1838	80.1	Contract
Monghyr	August 1838	80.1	Contract
Khulna	August 1838	80.1	Contract
Boalia	October 1840	30–33	
Boalia	November 1840	54.3	
Kumarkhali	November 1840	60.0	

distance from Calcutta to those depots made it difficult to transport coal in
abundance and on time. In September and October 1836, the master of the
Lord William Bentinck was forced to purchase coal at Monghyr and Dinapur
because there was no coal owing to the failure to deliver by the contractor.[79]
In such places, firewood seems to have been readily available from local
suppliers,[80] although the price was extremely high. Tables 2A and 2B,
compare firewood and coal prices in the late 1830s. Clearly, the price of
firewood was much higher than that of coal, even though the price of
Burdwan coal was as high as that of imported English coal.[81] The distance
from Calcutta determined the price of coal at each depot. In the case
of firewood, local availability seems to have influenced prices. Higher prices
in Allahabad and other cities in north India no doubt resulted from the fact
that the area along the Ganges had already suffered from very extensive
deforestation, so that wood had to be brought from distant places.[82]
In Lower Bengal by contrast, the trade in wood for fuel was extremely
limited and the Company's records of the procurement of firewood for

79. Bengal Steam Proceedings [hereafter, BSP], P/173/16, 10.10.1836, nos 5, 8.
80. For instance, in order to make good a deficiency in coal at the Dinapur Depot, Jaggarnath
Doss, a coal contractor, purchased 1,135 *maunds* of firewood from Byjun Bhuggut, a local
merchant, through the agency of Toraub Khan, the Company's coal agent on the spot (BSP, P/
173/18, 28.9.1837, no. 14).
81. The main reason for the high price of Burdwan coal was the cost of transport via the
Damodar to Calcutta and the difficulty in chartering sufficient numbers of boats and boatmen.
The dominance of Carr, Tagore and Co. in the coal trade in Calcutta was also a factor. See
Kling, *Partner in Empire*, p. 98.
82. Bernstein, *Steamboats*, p. 111.

Table 2B. *The price of Burdwan coal at various coal depots in eastern India, 1836–1842.*

Coal depots	(Company's rupees per 100 *maunds*)		
	Month and Year	Prices	Remarks
Allahabad	October 1836–February 1837	109.8	Contract
Mirzapur	October 1836–February 1837	86.7	Contract
Ghazipur	October 1836–February 1837	80	Contract
Dinapur	March–July 1838	80	Contract
Monghyr	March–July 1838	74	Contract
Colgong	March–July 1838	70	Contract
Sarda	March–July 1838	70	Contract
Rajmahal	March–July 1838	67	Contract
Kumarkhali	March–July 1838	64	Contract
Burhampur	March–July 1838	56	Contract
Katwa	March–July 1838	55.5	Contract
Kalna	March–July 1838	54	Contract
Khulna	March–July 1838	54	Contract
Calcutta	June 1839	45	Contract
Calcutta	Early 1842	50	
Calcutta	March–April 1842	75–81	

steamers provide a picture of the state of the firewood market there. When coal contractors failed to supply depots with coal or alternatively wood, the Controller of Government Steam Vessels had to act to obtain firewood for steamers from district collectors and magistrates. In June 1839, W. Swarman of the Dhaka Commissariat Office managed to obtain firewood for the Jamalpur coal depot from merchants who had stored it for the consumption of the troops. He stressed, however, that for future orders he would need advance notice because firewood was brought from "the place of growth".[83] That meant there was no ready market for firewood in the vicinity of Jamalpur. Similarly, W.J. Allen, Joint Magistrate of Pabna District Criminal Court, claimed that it was impossible to procure the wood required for steamers, and in Pabna District firewood was consumed only in the Company's Kumarkhali silk filatures, it being obtained from the Sundarbans.[84] In November 1840, W.M. Dirom, the Collector of the same Pabna District, did manage to find wood suppliers to feed the coal depots at Boalia, Kumarkhali, and Khulna, although since the price was much higher than the highest price of coal the Controller had to decline the offer.[85]

83. BSP, P/173/25, 10.6.1839, no. 6.
84. BSP, P/173/31, 16.11.1840, no. 11.
85. BSP, P/173/31, 9.11.1840, no. 26.

The relative cheapness of firewood in Boalia and Kumarkhali (see Table 2A) can be explained by their easier access to the Sundarbans, where the Company procured wood for its filatures. In the Sundarbans area, there was a brisk trade in wood as building material. In particular, Nalchiti was the major wood market in eastern Bengal, dealing in wood from the Sundarbans and supplying chiefly to Narayanganj and Calcutta.[86] It can be said that the existence of a buoyant timber trade began to facilitate the Company's procurement of wood as fuel.

Fuel crisis and the decline of the salt industry

There were several kinds of fuel-consuming industry in eastern India. Although a large amount of fuel was consumed, indigenous fuel markets developed on only a limited scale. Fuels were obtained locally through both non-market and market transactions, as in the case of the salt industry, which depended largely on straw and grass. In the indigenous silk industry in Birbhum District, cow dung was used for cocoon boiling in earthenware pans.[87] In the vicinity of Dhaka, people depended on brushwood, reeds, and other plant stalks for fuel.[88] A French army officer witnessed on the shore near Khajuri at the mouth of the Hugli "dry wood, consisting of branches of dead trees", which was to be sold in Calcutta.[89] That officer's observations suggest that commercial logging to make firewood had been limited, largely because other biomass fuels were easily available. Thus, local vegetation influenced the choice of fuel, and industries seem to have adapted themselves to the use of local fuels.

As the previous section shows, the production of Bengal salt became costly in the 1820s, and accordingly salt revenues began to decline in the late 1820s and early 1830s.[90] To save the monopoly as one of the most important sources of revenue in the face of the pressure to open the market to British industrial capital, the Company tried to reduce the cost

86. Bangladesh National Archives, Letter from R. Hunter, the Collector of Zillah Backergunge, on 27 June 1818, Barisal Records, letters issued, vol. 226.
87. Ranjan Kumar Gupta, "Birbhum Silk Industry: A Study of its Growth to Decline", *The Indian Economic and Social History Review*, 17 (1980), pp. 211–226, 213. In the sugar industry in Gorakhpur in North India, various kinds of fuel materials were used: firewood imported from Nepal, bagasse, dried plant stalks, and shrub wood. See Shahid Amin, *Sugarcane and Sugar in Gorakhpur: An Enquiry into Peasant Production for Capitalist Enterprise in Colonial India* (Delhi, 1984), p. 82.
88. BSP, P/173/25, 10.6.1839, no. 6.
89. P. Thankappan Nair, *Calcutta in the 18th Century: Impressions of Travellers* (Calcutta, 1984), p. 217.
90. The average net revenue between the years 1822–1823 and 1827–1828 was £1,342,210 sterling, but between the years 1828–1829 and 1833–1834 it was £1,251,951 sterling (calculated from Appendix no. 77 to the Report from the Select Committee on Salt, British India, BPP, vol. 17, 1836).

of production, and the reward system of Hijili was one of the targets for abolition. Although J. Donnithorn, the salt agent of Hijili, expressed anxiety that its abolition "will cause a vast number of them [*malangis*] to abandon altogether the occupation",[91] it was indeed abolished in 1829. From the late 1820s, the abolition of the costly agencies themselves began to be discussed. However, since the Company depended heavily for large revenues on the high price of Bengal boiled salt, which was preferred by consumers, there was little incentive to abandon the Bengal method of production altogether or to search for alternative fuels. The boiling of brine using high-calorie fuels would have changed the quality of salt, and that would have met with strong opposition in the market.

When the abolition of the Bhulua agency was discussed in 1830, the Company insisted that the deficiency had to be made up for by Hijili, Tamluk, or Cuttack (Orissa) boiled salt, not by solar salt imported from south India.[92] Moreover, energy conversion to higher calorific materials such as wood and coal was financially unrealistic for the Company when salt revenues had been on the decline. The fuel market had already been tight, and a switch of fuels would require large investment in new skills, and equipment such as tougher boiling pans to withstand higher temperatures.

In 1836 the Company abandoned its high-price policy and introduced several measures to reduce the price of salt, since the widespread existence of problems caused by illicit production was one of the major reasons for rising costs. Salt began to be sold at a fixed price and the market was opened to private imports on which excise duties could be levied. The Company was able to break through its difficult situation and so saved its monopoly.

All the same, the new system did not solve the fuel problem. In Tamluk, in the 1830s, the industry seems to have depended ever more on wood whenever it failed to procure sufficient grass and straw. According to the salt agent's report in 1834, utilizing branches of trees in the small jungles on the Company's embankments and procuring firewood from Sagar Island could solve the deficiency in fuel.[93] Firewood, which was probably brushwood or small branches of trees, was also brought to Tamluk from the jungle in the interior.[94] The increasing difficulties in procuring fuel made the Tamluk agency look for alternatives. In the meantime, land cultivation and reclamation of the Sundarbans began on a large scale, and a large tract of wasteland was brought under cultivation.[95]

---

91. BRP–Salt, P/101/56, 6.11.1829, no. 7. He estimated that about one-quarter of the workers would seek employment in other districts and economic sectors.
92. BRP–Salt, P/101/54, 18.8.1829, no. 63.
93. BRP–Salt, P/104/84, 7.1.1834, no. 17.
94. *Ibid.*
95. Iqbal, "Ecology, Economy and Society", pp. 6, 16, 35–44.

The fuel problem became more serious in the early 1840s. The tight supply and demand situation for coal became tighter still because of the outbreak of the Opium War in late 1839 and due to severe floods in Burdwan in 1840. The price of the best Burdwan coal in Calcutta before the war was 0.45 rupees per *maund*, but this surged to 0.81 rupees in 1842 (see Table 2B). The rise in coal prices in the early 1840s seems to have affected the price of firewood, because the shortage of coal, due to a great rise in demand from river steamers, increased demand for wood as an alternative fuel, helping to make it a commodity. For instance, the price of firewood at Boalia increased 70 per cent in just a month in the late 1840s (see Table 2A). The straw price too rose rapidly in Tamluk, from 1.25 rupees per *kahan* in December 1839 to 2 rupees in 1842.[96] As the price of coal returned to normal, the price of straw went down also to 1.5 rupees per *kahan* in December 1845 and 1847.[97] Such price information is limited, but similar fluctuations in various fuel prices suggest the emergence of an integrated fuel market.

Although recovery from it in the early 1840s was quick, the fuel crisis had an enormous impact on the salt industry. The Bhulua agency was abolished in 1840, and the costly separate operations in the Twenty-Four Parganas and Jessore agencies were also closed down, resulting in the integration of the management of the two agencies. In the remaining salt agencies of Hijili, Tamluk, and Chittagong, the Company secured fuels and at the same time saved expense by giving up distant grasslands and concentrating them close to the manufacturing sites. In so doing, the Company not only facilitated the *malangis'* fuel gathering but also converted distant grasslands into agricultural cultivation, thereby creating a new revenue stream from leases on those lands.[98] In consequence, wood began to be more extensively used in salt manufacture. Even so, lack of fuel frequently halted production.[99] The northern divisions in the Chittagong agency occasionally faced high prices or a severe scarcity of firewood,[100] and of course when firewood prices were high the *malangis* suffered a great loss because the cost of fuel made up about 40 per cent of their total expenses.[101]

In the 1840s production of Bengal salt decreased by half, because of the closure of Bhulua, Jessore, and eventually the Twenty-Four Parganas, but

96. BRP–Salt, P/106/9, 11.2.1840, no. 10; P/106/38, 9.1.1843, no. 17.

97. BRP–Salt, P/106/65, 2.1.1846, no. 59; P/109/28, 6.1.1848, no. 14.

98. Note on the Manufacture of Salt in the Tamluk Agency, Appendix B, BPP, vol. 26, 1856, pp. 443–444.

99. BRP–Salt, P/106/65, 2.2.1846, no. 36.

100. BRP–Salt, P/111/24, 25.2.1857, nos 6-7.

101. Note on Manufacture, Storage, Sale and Delivery of Salt in the Chittagong Agency, Appendix C, no. 2, BPP, vol. 26, 1856, p. 478.

the production of Bengal salt had already been in decline before the arrival of large quantities of Cheshire salt in the 1850s. Further research is needed on the fate of former *malangis* in the 1840s, but it is likely that the growing demand for labour in land reclamation in the Sundarbans absorbed them. However, by the mid-1830s western and central Bengal had become heavily populated, reaching densities of more than 700 per square mile, and as it did so the area gradually became malarial in the 1840s.[102] Such increasing demographic pressure and unhealthy environments would have aggravated the working conditions of former *malangis* as well as of agricultural and industrial workers in general.

CONCLUSION

The salt industry in Bengal was able to produce a large amount of superior salt as well as considerable profits for the Company, thanks to the abundance of seawater and fuel. At the same time, the industry and its workers had to cope with the environmental difficulties surrounding them. They faced the constant danger of natural calamity, wild animals, and diseases. Occasional tidal floods, storms, and constant river encroachment were major causes of devastated saltpans and grasslands, which caused failures of production. The Company was responsible for giving the necessary assistance to the *malangis* whenever they faced difficulties in producing salt, since their level of productivity would affect salt revenues.

That did not ensure the well-being of the *malangis*, but at least circumstances were favourable for them. Severe competition from other employment opportunities also increased the *malangis'* income and bargaining power with the Company. As the Company at least liked to claim, the working conditions of the *malangis* were comparatively favourable, at least until the late 1820s.

However, working conditions began to deteriorate. Rising fuel costs contributed much to the weaker position of the *malangis*. In addition to the loss of grassland to environmental changes, reclamation of grassland for cultivation, which advanced particularly in the 1830s, also reduced the availability of fuel for industrial activity. Expanding economic activities led to increased straw prices, as straw was used as a building material as well as fuel for domestic and industrial purposes. Further, the shortage of coal in the 1830s encouraged commodification of other fuels, particularly wood. Straw prices also began to fluctuate in accordance with coal prices. Such new developments deprived the *malangis* of the customary right to procure straw and grass, and forced them to depend more on the market for fuel.

In the early nineteenth century, along with environmental changes, industrial and agricultural development as part of the globalization process

---

102. Klein, "Malaria and Mortality", p. 156; Bose, *Peasant Labour*, pp. 22–24.

led various industries to compete for energy resources. Because of the rise in production-related costs, the salt industry lost its competitiveness, long before the influx of Cheshire salt into its market. The fuel crisis in the early 1840s, caused largely by the Opium War, came as a devastating blow to the salt industry and led to rapid shrinkage of the Company's monopoly. As Tomlinson points out, "once their exports became uncompetitive [...], the Company [...] moved on to other commodities and other producers, turning colonial Bengal into an exporter of primary products rather than manufactured goods".[103] A large number of the salt workers lost one of their major sources of income, and it can be speculated that they were absorbed into agriculture and manual labour.

---

103. Tomlinson, "Bengal Textiles, British Industrialisation, and the Company *Raj*", p. 209.

IRSH 55 (2010), Supplement, pp. 153–174 doi:10.1017/S0020859010000532
© 2010 Internationaal Instituut voor Sociale Geschiedenis

Industrial Life in a Limiting Landscape: An Environmental Interpretation of Stalinist Social Conditions in the Far North*

ANDY BRUNO

History Department, University of Illinois at Urbana-Champaign

E-mail: andy.bruno@gmail.com

SUMMARY: This paper offers an environmental history of a group of forced migrants who were sent to work on a Soviet industrial project in the far north during the 1930s. As part of the drive to industrialize the country rapidly, the Soviet state deported thousands of peasants who had been declared class enemies to the previously desolate Khibiny Mountains in order to serve as the labor force for a new socialist mining town. These forced migrants became known as "special settlers". I argue that the integration of the environment as a dynamic force in the social history of Stalinism enriches current explanations for why the Soviet state was often unable to carry out its intentions during industrialization. I also maintain that through the pursuit of the global process of industrialization, the Soviet government contributed to making the special settlers in the Khibiny Mountains vulnerable to natural hazards.

After what she recalled was a happy childhood in a village in the Krasnodar region, L.E. Gudovskaia's life changed abruptly on a February night in 1930. Police came and arrested her father, E.A. Zinchenko, as a *kulak* – a comparatively well-off peasant deemed a class enemy by the Soviet state. Stripped of their property, the entire family was sent to the Urals region and forced to collect wood from the surrounding forests. At the end of the summer the government again relocated the family. Contrary to seventeen-year-old Gudovskaia's hope of returning home, they landed in

* I would like to express my appreciation to the many individuals who have read and commented on this manuscript at varying stages, including Alan Barenberg, Peter Boomgaard, Donald Filtzer, Sarah Frohardt-Lane, Zsuzsa Gille, Marjolein 't Hart, Diane Koenker, John Randolph, Jesse Ribot, Mark Steinberg, and Maria Todorova. The research for this essay was supported by an International Dissertation Research Fellowship from the Social Science Research Council with funds from the Andrew W. Mellon Foundation and with a fellowship from the US Student Fulbright Program.

a new settlement in the Khibiny Mountains in the far north-west corner of the country. In the 1990s she described their arrival to local members of the Memorial society:

> The settlement at thirteenth kilometer, where we were unloaded, consisted of *shalmany* and tents. After sanitation processing and baths our families moved into a *shalman*. The *shalman* was built from boards and on the outside it was covered with roofing felt. On the sides there were plank beds. De-kulakized families already resided in this *shalman*. On the edges of the *shalman* stood two iron stoves. Lanterns lit the *shalman*. Our family took eight meters of space on the plank beds. We slept, ate, and sat on these boards. Sometimes, waking up on cold days, your hair would be frozen to the wall.[1]

The family lived in this residence for two years while the father worked in a mine, extracting the phosphorous mineral apatite for fertilizer production, and Gudovskaia took various jobs. They survived on meager food rations and the mushrooms and berries they collected. Upon moving to an apartment, Gudovskaia summarized life during those first years:

> [...] we, the *kulaks*, lived as morally dead, dejected people. Thousands of people went hungry and grieved in the tents and *shalmany* over the whistling of the raging northern wind, over the wailing blizzards, and, yes, over the cries of our own young children trembling from the cold in tarpaulin tents and in crowded, hard to heat, *shalmany*.[2]

EXPLAINING STALINIST SOCIAL CONDITIONS

Historians of the Soviet Union have interpreted the common stories of personal suffering in the 1930s like Gudovskaia's in several ways. In works produced in the Soviet Union under the auspices of regime censorship, such accounts were often incorporated into heroic narratives of citizens struggling in adverse conditions to build socialism without any reference to the coerced character of their labor.[3] For an array of other observers and scholars such indignities reflected the callousness of Joseph Stalin and other Soviet leaders and the inhuman character of the communist system.[4] Hunger, the cold, and material deprivations were intentional elements of a campaign to punish the peasantry.

1. L.E. Gudovskaia, "Chto sokhranila pamiat", in *Spetspereselentsy v Khibinakh: Spetspereselentsy i zakliuchennye v istorii osvoeniia Khibin (Kinga vospominanii)* (Apatity, 1997), pp. 34–41, 36.
2. *Ibid.*, p. 37.
3. An example of this literature that discusses the industrialization of the Khibiny region is the first edition of A.V. Barabanov, A.A. Kiselev, and A.I. Krasnobaev, *Gigant v Khibinakh: Istoriia ordena Lenina i ordena Oktiabr'skoi revoliutsii proizvodstvennoi ob"edineniia "Apatit" im. S.M. Kirova (1929–1979)* (Murmansk, 1981).
4. Alexander Solzhenitsyn, *The Gulag Archipelago*, Thomas P. Whitney and Harry Willetts (trans.), 3 vols (New York, 1973); Robert Conquest, *The Great Terror: Stalin's Purges of the*

Figure 1. Many "special settlers" in the Khibiny Mountains lived in ad hoc structures like this one made of boards and roofing. In Russian it was known as a *shalman*.
Source: Sergei Tararaksin, Sudeb sgorevshikh ochertan'e [Outlines of Burnt Fates] *(Murmansk, 2006), p. 26.*

Another line of scholarship takes intentional oppression as a given, but stresses the extent to which such brutality aligned with Soviet ideology. Stalinist industrialization relied on using rehabilitative labor to attempt to turn peasant class enemies into modern socialist citizens.[5] The hubris that accompanied this desire to transform society rapidly and totally helped blind ideologues to the easily anticipated deprivations that would result from their schemes.

Historian Lynne Viola concurs with the assessments that emphasize the deliberately punitive elements of Soviet agrarian politics in the early 1930s, labeling this era a "war on the peasantry".[6] She, nevertheless,

Thirties (New York, 1968); *idem, The Harvest of Sorrow: Soviet Collectivization and the Terror-Famine* (Oxford, 1987); Oleg V. Khlevniuk, *The History of the Gulag: From Collectivization to the Great Terror* (New Haven, CT, 2004); *idem, The Master of the House: Stalin and His Inner Circle,* Nora Seligman Favorov (trans.) (New Haven, CT, 2008). On the brutal social conditions of the 1930s and their connection to communist economic organization, see Elena Osokina, *Our Daily Bread: Socialist Distribution and the Art of Survival in Stalin's Russia, 1927–1941* (Armonk, NY, 2001).

5. Stephen Kotkin, *Magnetic Mountain: Stalinism as a Civilization* (Berkeley, CA, 1995); David Hoffmann, *Stalinist Values: The Cultural Norms of Soviet Modernity, 1917–1941* (Ithaca, NY, 2003); Jochen Hellbeck, *Revolution on My Mind: Writing a Diary Under Stalin* (Cambridge, MA, 2006).

6. This phrase appears primarily in Viola's earlier works: Lynne Viola, *Peasant Rebels Under Stalin: Collectivization and the Culture of Peasant Resistance* (New York, 1996); *idem et al.*

explains the hardships of former *kulaks* somewhat differently. In the first major English-language study of the fate of "special settlers" like Gudovskaia's family, Viola highlights the unintended consequences of policy decisions and the inability of the state to enact its will fully.[7] This chaos undermined the imperatives of economic development. She also sees the role of re-education efforts as primarily rhetorical and therefore less constitutive of special settler experience than other scholars. Summarizing her position, Viola writes that the "combination of an infrastructurally weak state, an interventionist state bent on a totalizing vision of societal transformation (all too often in the abstract), and an ideological Weltanschauung of prejudice, fear, and limitless hatreds were at the roots of Stalinist repression".[8] The interaction of these three factors explains the overall brutal experience of forced peasant migrants, including weather-related afflictions like the frozen trembling of Gudovskaia's younger brothers and sisters.

What is missing from these overall illuminating attempts to account for the miserable conditions faced by forced peasant migrants is an adequate assessment of the role of the natural environment in causing these hardships. The environment is more than a set of stable natural features of a place that obviously influence human populations. Instead, humans interact with the environment through a negotiated process. The responses of nature and social actors to changing circumstances frequently alter the situation further.[9]

The purpose of embracing this methodological perspective is twofold. First, it helps highlight the ubiquity and multifaceted significance of the environment in social history more thoroughly. The raging winds, wailing blizzards, and frozen hair of Gudovskaia's reflections become not only examples of human suffering, but key components of the world created by Stalinist modernization. Secondly, a focus on the responsiveness of the

(eds), *The War Against the Peasantry, 1927–1930: The Tragedy of the Soviet Countryside* (New Haven, CT, 2005).

7. Idem, *The Unknown Gulag: The Lost World of Stalin's Special Settlements* (Oxford, 2007). This interpretation aligns with much of the historiography on the social history of Stalinist industrialization. See, for example, Kendall Bailes, *Technology and Society under Lenin and Stalin: Origins of the Soviet Technical Intelligentsia, 1917–1941* (Princeton, NJ, 1978); Donald Filtzer, *Soviet Workers and Stalinist Industrialization: The Formation of Modern Soviet Production Relations, 1928–1941* (London, 1986); Hiroaki Kuromiya, *Stalin's Industrial Revolution: Politics and Workers, 1928–1932* (Cambridge, 1988); David Shearer, *Industry, State, and Society in Stalin's Russia, 1926–1934* (Ithaca, NY, 1996); Sheila Fitzpatrick, *Everyday Stalinism: Ordinary Life in Extraordinary Times: Soviet Russia in the 1930s* (Oxford, 1999).

8. Viola, *The Unknown Gulag*, p. 190.

9. On how humans interact with nature through a negotiated process, see Timothy Mitchell, *Rule of Experts: Egypt, Techno-Politics, Modernity* (Berkeley, CA, 2002); Bruno Latour, *Reassembling the Social: An Introduction to Actor-Network-Theory* (Oxford, 2005); Zsuzsa Gille, *From the Cult of Waste to the Trash Heap of History: The Politics of Waste in Socialist and Postsocialist Hungary* (Bloomington, IN, 2007).

environment enriches our perspective on the interplay of intentions and inadvertent results in this industrial project. The failure of initial government efforts to implement the intended punishment of former *kulaks*, which would have used them as productive workers, was due not only to the Soviet state's limited abilities and the naive hubris of central planners. The environment also undermined Soviet intentions; natural responses to industrial interference reduced the state's control over the situation further.

The present essay also connects the experience of former *kulaks* to industrialization: a global phenomenon that helped cause their vulnerability to natural hazards. The Stalinist state took rapid industrialization as a non-negotiable imperative. Many scholars have commented on the obsession of Soviet policymakers with catching up the West. They root it variably in the practices of modern statecraft, legitimate economic needs, communist ideology, and a national pathos of Russia.[10] It is also important to see Stalinist industrialization as a specific permutation of one of the most important global processes of the past two centuries.

In many places industrialization produced an increased vulnerability of social groups to natural hazards. Theoretical literature on vulnerability has emphasized that the outcomes of presumed natural calamities – such as famines, droughts, earthquakes, and climate change – are always embedded in social circumstances and existing political economy.[11] Examinations of the social production of vulnerability often concentrate on a single disaster, but can extend to a more elusive array of risks. Piers Blaikie, Terry Cannon, Ian Davis, and Ben Wisner, for instance, elaborate several vulnerability-creating processes for biological hazards: conditions of the micro-environment such as diet, shelter, sanitation, and the water supply; migration and especially forced displacements; and the degradation and limited capacities of a physical environment.[12] All of these processes were at work in shaping the experience of the forced migrants in the Khibiny Mountains.

10. For example, see Hoffmann, *Stalinist Values*; Kotkin, *Magnetic Mountain*; Moshe Lewin, *The Making of the Soviet System: Essays in the Social History of Interwar Russia* (London, 1985); Alexander Gerschenkron, *Economic Backwardness in Historical Perspective* (Cambridge, MA, 1962); Andrzej Walicki, *Marxism and the Leap to the Kingdom of Freedom: The Rise and Fall of the Communist Utopia* (Stanford, CA, 1995); Martin Malia, *Russia under Western Eyes: From the Bronze Horseman to the Lenin Mausoleum* (Cambridge, MA, 1999); idem, *The Soviet Tragedy: A History of Socialism in Russia, 1917–1991* (New York, 1994).

11. Michael J. Watts and Hans G. Bohle, "The Space of Vulnerability: The Causal Structure of Hunger and Famine", *Progress in Human Geography*, 17 (1993), pp. 43–67; Piers Blaikie *et al.*, *At Risk: Natural Hazards, People's Vulnerability, and Disasters* (London, 1994); Jesse C. Ribot, "The Causal Structure of Vulnerability: Its Application to Climate Impact Analysis", *Geo-Journal*, 35 (1995), pp. 119–122; Greg Bankoff, Georg Frerks, and Dorothea Hilhorst (eds), *Mapping Vulnerability: Disasters, Development, and People* (London, 2004).

12. Blaikie, *At Risk*, pp. 106–108.

THE KHIBINY MOUNTAINS AS A SITE OF GLOBAL
INDUSTRIALIZATION

The Soviet project in the Khibiny Mountains was part of a campaign to make the country an international power. It had its roots in the global ideologies of the time. The venture aimed at setting up apatite mines and processing plants on the Kola Peninsula (the Murmansk region) and constructing a socialist city from scratch north of the polar circle during the hectic first Five-Year Plan (1928–1932). Its history, therefore, fits just as much within the story of Stalinist industrialization in similar well-researched cities like Magnitogorsk as within accounts of forced labor in the Soviet Union and the development of the Gulag.[13]

Soviet leaders considered industrialization necessary to render the country's economy more powerful, increase its defensive capacity, and bring it closer to modernity and communism. The conviction that modernization and socialist construction required industrial economic forms resonated with the teleological thought of the era. Contemporary versions of both Marxism and liberal economics took the industrialized countries of western Europe and North America as "advanced" in comparison to "backward" places like Russia and most of the rest of the world. In both of these modernist frameworks the natural environment was understood as an object of conquest and mastery that would be subdued by human ingenuity and rationality in the name of progress. The Bolsheviks embraced an innovation in Marxist theory that claimed that an avant-garde communist party could steer their country rapidly through historical stages. Russia would be able to acquire the material base of such advanced countries while avoiding the social structure and cultural superstructure of capitalism.[14] Instead the Soviet Union would build "socialism in one country", in Stalin's memorable phrase, through rapid industrialization as a method of skipping stages of development.

Beyond the ideologies of the time that made industrial economies seem paramount, industrialization has also been one of the most transformative aspects of global environmental history. Understanding its Soviet variant can reveal much about how a large part of the world under a distinct political regime changed physically and socially. Stalinist industrialization involved the exclusive impetus of the state, the creation of a command

---

13. Kotkin, *Magnetic Mountain*. Recent works that treat regional industrialization and forced labor are Nick Baron, *Soviet Karelia: Politics, Planning and Terror in Stalin's Russia, 1920–1939* (London, 2007); James R. Harris, *The Great Urals: Regionalism and the Evolution of the Soviet System* (Ithaca, NY, 1999); Alan Barenberg, "From Prison Camp to Mining Town: The Gulag and its Legacy in Vorkuta, 1938–1965" (unpublished Ph.D. dissertation, University of Chicago, 2007); Paul R. Gregory and Valery V. Lazarev (eds), *The Economics of Forced Labor: The Soviet Gulag* (Stanford, CA, 2003).
14. Robert C. Tucker (ed.), *The Lenin Anthology* (New York, 1975).

economy with centralized planning, and a revolutionary enthusiasm that positioned gritty development projects as springboards to communism. These features would later be transferred globally to other communist countries after World War II.

The Soviet Union in the 1930s also endeavored to create new industrial towns with forced labor. This program was meant to colonize extremely peripheral and sparsely populated territories and extract their natural resources. The scale of the endeavor, the pomp and circumstance that justified it, and the excess of the contradiction between the utopian visions and brutal reality distinguish it among industrial development schemes. Nevertheless, the situation at sites such as the one in the Khibiny Mountains reflects a global pattern; industrializing states often treated the natural environment primarily as an exploitable resource and produced heightened vulnerability among laboring populations.

Industrial interest in the Khibiny Mountains emerged in the 1920s when the first systematic assessment of the geological content of the range revealed large veins of mixed apatite-nepheline ore in a massive igneous intrusion of nepheline rock.[15] Apatite ($Ca_5(PO_4)_3(F,Cl,OH)$) is a form of calcium phosphate with an extra ion of fluorine, chlorine, or hydroxyl. It can be used to manufacture phosphate fertilizer. Soviet economic planners sought to turn this rock into chemical fertilizer in order to help reduce imports and create a new export commodity. They viewed adjustment to the trade balance as a necessary step to help capitalize other industrial projects.[16] The expanded use of phosphate fertilizers could also increase agricultural productivity and help resolve the grain shortfalls that struck the country in 1927–1928.[17]

The Khibiny Mountains were an extremely remote location at the time; the site of the apatite deposits was virtually uninhabited except for a few Sami reindeer herders who would come to the area to release their animals in the highlands for summer grazing.[18] The lack of an available labor force in the region left open a variety of possibilities for how to exploit this resource. Initial ideas involved hiring temporary miners to extract the ore and then ship it to Leningrad on the nearby Murmansk railroad for processing.[19] During the planning stage in 1929, the Unified State Political

15. Victor Yakovenchuk *et al.*, *Khibiny* (Apatity, 2005), pp. 1–31.

16. G.N. Solov'ianov, *Kol'skii promyshlennyi uzel* (Moscow, 1932).

17. Viola, *The Unknown Gulag*, p. 14.

18. V.V. Charnoluskii, *Materialy po bytu Loparei: opyt opredeleniia kochevogo sostoianiia Loparei vostochnoi chasti Kol'skogo poluostrova* (Leningrad, 1930); A.E. Fersman, *Nash Apatit* (Moscow, 1968), p. 24.

19. Rossiiskii gosudarstvennyi arkhiv ekonomiki [hereafter, RGAE], f. 3106 [Glavnoe upravlenie khimicheskoi promyshlennosti (Glavkhimprom) VSNKh SSSR], op. 1/2, d. 367, ll. 62–79; A.V. Barabanov *et al.*, *Gigant v Khibinakh: Istoriia otkrytogo aktsionernogo obshchestva "Apatit" (1929–1999)* (Moscow, 1999), p. 16.

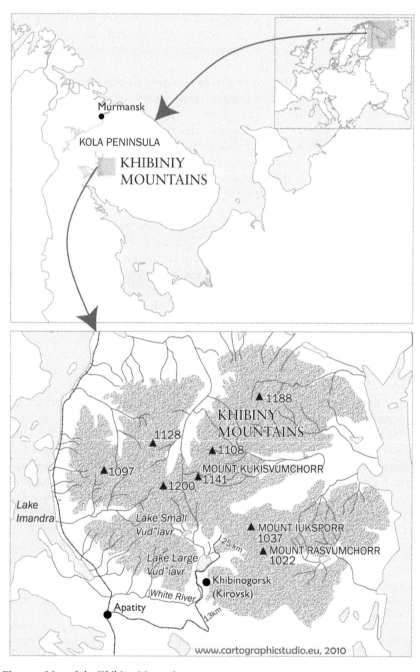

Figure 2. Map of the Khibiny Mountains.

Administration (OGPU) made a bid to use prisoner labor to construct and operate the apatite works in the Khibiny Mountains.[20] Government agencies ultimately rejected this proposal. Instead, revolutionary enthusiasm for the Stalinist Great Break inspired grandiose plans of building an entirely new socialist city in the region: one that would process the mined ore on site and strive to create an ideal communist environment, including harmony between proletarians and a subdued natural world.[21] Ideas about how to supply adequate labor for the project remained vague at this point; the recruitment of voluntary workers and the selected use of contracted prisoners would supposedly meet the needs of the enterprise, the *Apatit* trust.[22]

Around the same time, the government commenced a campaign to reform rural Russia. The twin policies of collectivization and de-*kulaki*-zation aimed at giving the state control of agricultural output, which had been market-based in the 1920s. As part of a mass collectivization campaign during the winter of 1929–1930, millions of comparatively well-off peasants became targeted as class enemies, *kulaks*. They were stripped of their property and excluded from membership in the new collective farms. The government slated a huge portion of these households for exile. Deportations began in the winter of 1930 at a time when there was no clear plan for resettlement, but only a general idea of using these de-*kulak*ized peasants to exploit natural resources in distant peripheries. Families arrived in new inhospitable and unfamiliar environments with minimal accommodations arranged.[23]

In April 1930, OGPU head Genrikh Iagoda outlined the idea of turning these camps into more or less permanent self-sustaining "colonization settlements". Former *kulak* families would work in timber, agriculture, and mining, and help "colonize the north in the shortest possible time".[24] This agency also specifically believed it was "impossible" to meet the needs of the *Apatit* trust by "hiring a free labor supply" because of the "remoteness and natural wildness of the Khibiny".[25] Former *kulak* migrants, who became defined in state parlance as "special settlers" (*spetspereselentsy*), occupied an intermediate status between citizens and

20. "Chast' ofitsial'naia", in A.E. Fersman (ed.), *Khibinskie Apatity: Spornik*, I (Leningrad, 1930), pp. 281–296, 284–286.

21. Gosudarstvennyi arkhiv Murmanskoi oblasti [hereafter, GAMO], f. 773 [Lichnyi fond V.I. Kondrikova (1929–1936 gg.)], op. 1, d. 1, ll. 18, 107–108; M.D. Petrova, S.M. Salimova, and T.I. Podgorbunskaia (eds), *Kirovsk v dokumentakh i faktakh, 1920–1945 gg. Khrestomatiia* (Kirovsk, 2006), pp. 33–34.

22. GAMO, f. 773, op. 1, d. 1, ll. 22, 100–106.

23. Viola, *The Unknown Gulag*, pp. 14–88.

24. Khlevniuk, *The History of the Gulag*, pp. 23–24.

25. Rossiiskii gosudarstvennyi arkhiv sotsial'no-politicheskoi istorii [hereafter, RGASPI], f. 17 [Tsentral'nyi komitet KPSS], op. 120, d. 26, l. 151.

labor-camp prisoners, being deprived of mobility and civil rights but contractually entitled to wages and (frequently unfulfilled) amenities.[26]

The special settlers became the main source of labor at this industrial site in the Khibiny Mountains. During the first few years of the 1930s, more than 45,000 special settlers came to the Kola Peninsula, which had a total population of only 27,000 in 1927. All but a few thousand of them directly served the apatite works.[27] In comparison to the majority of special settlers who worked in small isolated settlements for the forest industry, the labor needs of this project required greater integration of these forced migrants with the new socialist city of Khibinogorsk (Kirovsk after December 1934). In addition to the 6 special settlements outside the city and the ones serving the construction of the Niva Hydroelectric Station, close to 20,000 former *kulaks* in the Khibiny region lived in Khibinogorsk by 1933.[28] The special settlers came from numerous places in the country, but the largest percentage of them was relocated from parts of the Leningrad region. Excluding the construction site of the Niva Hydroelectric Station, special settlers made up 69 per cent of the total population (25,485) of the Khibiny region in October 1931. At this point the gender ratio was near equal and 32 per cent were under 16 years old.[29]

AN ENVIRONMENTAL INTERPRETATION OF "SPECIAL SETTLER" EXPERIENCE

An investigation of the environmental contours of special-settler experience needs to begin by reintegrating a wide range of aspects firmly entrenched in existing knowledge about Stalinist social conditions into their natural contexts. Issues of housing, clothing, food, and hygiene, for instance, have obvious natural dimensions. Plants and animals nourish humans and supply materials; climatic phenomena and geographical features shape the needs, limitations, and possibilities of habitation. In the case of the Khibiny Mountains the long and snowy polar winter, the limited presence of building materials, the infertility of the soil, the dearth of flora and fauna for human foraging, the steep mountain relief of the worksite, the system of waterways, and the distance of the region from supply sources significantly affected the housing situation, the availability of basic domestic supplies, and special settlers' access to food and water. Nature occasionally exacerbated the situation as industrial activities caused

26. Viola, *The Unknown Gulag*, pp. 92–96; GAMO, f. 773, op. 1, d. 6, ll. 230–232.

27. V.Ia. Shashkov, *Spetspereselentsy na Murmane: Rol' spetspereselentsev v razvitii proizvoditel'nykh sil na Kol'skom poluostrove (1930–1936 gg.)* (Murmansk, 1993), p. 32; idem, *Spetspereselentsy v istorii Murmanskoi oblasti* (Murmansk, 2004), pp. 108–113.

28. *Idem, Raskulachivanie v SSSR i sud'by spetspereselentsev, 1930–1954 gg.* (Murmansk, 1996), p. 167.

29. Petrova *et al., Kirovsk v dokumentakh i faktakh*, pp. 94–96.

environmental changes such as pollution and increased avalanches, which in turn further influenced the living conditions of the special settlers.

In what follows, I examine the vulnerable situation created by state policy. I also assess the attempts of government and enterprise personnel to grapple with an environment not under their complete control and the ways that special settlers coped in harsh natural conditions.

The habitat that first greeted the forced migrants to the Khibiny region consisted of snowy mountain tundra with ad hoc housing of tents, mud huts, and *shalmany*. A hierarchical allocation of better accommodation first to freely recruited laborers meant that special settlers lived in these temporary dwellings longest. At one point in late 1930 after the winter had begun, close to 12,000 of 14,000 residents in the Khibinogorsk region lived in these types of houses.[30] As numerous human families crowded into these dirty living spaces, pathogens causing diseases such as measles, typhus, typhoid fever, and tuberculosis spread throughout the population.

A condemning report from December 1930 by the regional inspector of housing and communal sanitation, I.A. Tikhomirov, claimed that the large portion of the current housing stock that "consists of *shalmanov*, mud huts, and tents, which act as surrogates of housing, is unacceptable for the conditions of the polar winter". Tikhomirov's overall assessment was that "the housing conditions of the population, particularly during an epidemic situation, are extremely unfavorable". The mud huts seem not to have survived the winter of 1931 here, but the other housing types and extremely crowded conditions lasted through the first Five-Year Plan.[31] In 1934, Leningrad party boss Sergei Kirov wrote that special settlers in the Khibiny region only had 1.9 square meters of space per person, considerably less than the desired three square meters per person.[32]

Polar nature further complicated the housing situation in the Khibiny Mountains. It exacerbated the endemic problems the Soviet state had in providing basic supplies to new industrial sites.[33] The lack of suitable forest materials on the Kola Peninsula led the city to import wood from the Arkhang'elsk region.[34] The *Apatit* trust also continually failed to fulfill its own plans for housing construction.[35] The head of the enterprise,

30. A.V. Barabanov and T.A. Kalinina, *"Apatit": vek iz veka* (Apatity, 2004), p. 38.

31. Petrova *et al.*, *Kirovsk v dokumentakh i faktakh*, pp. 60–61, 67; Shashkov, *Spetspereselentsy v istorii Murmanskoi oblasti*, pp. 271–278.

32. GAMO, f. 773, op. 1, d. 9, ll. 22–23,191–193.

33. A contract between the main administration of camps of the OGPU and the *Apatit* trust from the summer of 1931 stipulated that the former had to supply funds for heating, illumination, and certain communal services for the special settlers and the latter was responsible for their housing, medical facilities, schools, and sanitation; GAMO, f. 773, op. 1, d. 6, ll. 230–232.

34. Barabanov and Kalinina, *"Apatit"*, p. 38.

35. RGASPI, f. 17, op. 120, d. 26, l. 85; GAMO, f. 773, op. 1, d. 5, l. 190; GAMO, f. 773, op. 1, d. 5, ll. 9–10; GAMO, f. 773, op. 1, d. 44, ll. 191–193.

Figure 3. These tents, where families of "special settlers" had lived during a winter period, were built directly on top of a cleared section of forest.
Source: Tararaksin, Sudeb sgorevshikh ochertan'e [Outlines of Burnt Fates], *p. 11.*

Vasilii Kondrikov, described the role of the Kola environment in inhibiting construction: "Unfortunately, large supplies of limestone on the Kola Peninsula have still not been found, there is comparatively little wood, the renewal period of which extends here up to 200 years, and until very recently there was a large deficit of clay."[36] Trust leaders also explained their failures in housing construction as partially due to the "[h]arsh climate of the polar tundra", and "the mountain relief of the location with rocky ground".[37]

Moreover, special settlers who attempted to construct their own housing could not find adequate supplies. One report from 1934 summarized the situation for the special settlers: "there are no funds and also no construction materials – this means that there are no houses".[38] The frequent forest fires along the Murmansk railroad and the near exhaustion of the limited wood supply near Lake Small Vud"iavr also limited special settlers' options for remedying the housing shortage themselves. After the production of concentrated apatite began in the fall of 1931, dust from the enrichment factory started destroying local flora, which reduced available building material even further.[39]

36. V.I. Kondrikov, "Sostoianie i perspektivy stroitel'stva v raione Khibinskikh razrabotok", *Karelo-Murmanskii krai*, 5–6 (1931), pp. 7–13, 9.
37. Petrova *et al.*, *Kirovsk v dokumentakh i faktakh*, p. 66.
38. Shashkov, *Spetspereselentsy v istorii Murmanskoi oblasti*, p. 277.
39. GAMO, f. 773, op. 1, d. 51, l. 92.

For the eight to nine months of the year when temperatures in the Khibiny Mountains were below freezing, snow acted as a dangerous environmental influence. The area had an annual average of over 160 days of snowstorms a year and significantly greater snow cover than other parts of the Kola Peninsula.[40] The mountainous terrain already made the potential for avalanches of snow and boulders especially great. The use of industrial explosions in the mines during the long winter heightened this risk.[41] From 1933 to 1938 observers recorded about 300 avalanches, which destroyed buildings and caused injuries and death.[42] A major avalanche from Mount Iuksporr on 5 December 1935 destroyed two buildings, which housed 249 people, and killed 89 individuals, including 46 special settlers.[43] State and industrial planners clearly contributed to making the migrants vulnerable to this disaster by deciding to place the settlement in an area known to be avalanche-prone.[44] This catastrophe inspired an active campaign in the city to monitor and prevent avalanches, but their continued threat limited the locations of new settlements in the long run.[45]

The special settlers also often lacked basic items necessary for survival in such a cold climate. The government had stripped them of most of their property except for a bit of money and some clothing and equipment for agriculture, construction, and cooking. The frequently violent expropriations of the de-*kulak*ization campaign left many peasant families with much less than the sanctioned norms.[46] To augment the clothing and tools brought by the migrants, the trust and the city government petitioned for special winter clothing, set up occasional open fairs, and established a few stores. The supply system in the Khibiny region managed to procure a somewhat reasonable level of some of the required clothing such as

40. B.K. Odovenko and R.M. Gamberg, "Sovershenstvovanie tekhnologii otkrytoi razrabotki moshchnykh rudnykh zalezhei", in I.A. Turchaninov (ed.), *Osvoenie mineral'nykh bogatstv Kol'skogo poluostrova* (Murmansk, 1974), pp. 20–45, 24.

41. P.V. Vladimirov and N.S. Morev, *Apatitovyi rudnik im. S.M. Kirova* (Leningrad, 1936), pp. 120–121.

42. B.M. Belen'kii, "Iz istorii issledovaniia snega i lavin v khibinakh", in E.Ia. Zamotkin and N.M. Egorova (eds), *Priroda i khoziaistvo Severa*, II, part 2 (Apatity, 1971), pp. 305–310, 306; Vladimirov and Morev, *Apatitovyi rudnik im. S.M. Kirova*, pp. 115–121.

43. Petrova *et al.*, *Kirovsk v dokumentakh i faktakh*, pp. 101–102; S.N. Boldyrev, "Lavina s gory Iukspor", in G.I. Rakov (ed.), *Khibinskie klady: Vospominaniia veteranov osvoeniia Severa* (Leningrad, 1972), pp. 290–300.

44. G.F. Smirnov, "Obogashchenie apatito-nefelinovoi porody Khibinskogo mestorozhdeniia", in Fersman, *Khibinskie Apatity*, I, pp. 122–139; Arkhiv Rossiiskoi Akademii Nauk [hereafter, ARAN], f. 544 [Lichnyi fond A.E. Fersmana], op. 1, d. 334, ll. 1–6; GAMO, f. 773, op. 1, d. 1, ll. 107–108, 149–154.

45. Belen'kii, "Iz istorii issledovaniia snega i lavin v khibinakh", in Zamotkin and Egorova, *Priroda i khoziaistvo Severa*, II, part 2, pp. 305–310.

46. Viola, *The Unknown Gulag*, pp. 33–44.

leather shoes, felt boots, underwear, suits, coats, bags, sheets, and hats by late 1930.[47] However, as forced and voluntary migrants continued to flow to the worksite, these efforts failed to overcome the chronic lack of sufficient items needed for living, working, and staying warm in the tundra. As special settler F.B. Zubkova later summarized it succinctly: "In material terms, we lived poorly."[48]

Food shortages characterized life in the Khibiny region throughout the 1930s. They occurred despite the contractual obligations of the trust and the secret police to supply the special settlers with sufficient food provisions and the settlement's proximity to the Murmansk railroad, which facilitated food shipments.[49] The state and party organs in Khibinogorsk attempted to procure foodstuffs through several organizations, including a Closed Workers' Cooperative and a special trust to manage imports. Like elsewhere in the country, they also set up a network of cafeterias where people ate most of their meals. Far short of supplying the state-sanctioned rations, these institutions were only minimally effective in helping to prevent the population from starving.[50]

The natural conditions of this rocky polar land inhibited efforts to feed the special settlers adequately. The infertility of the soil, the region's alpine elevation, and the short growing season characteristic of such latitudes made agriculture nearly impossible here. Indeed, scientists only conclusively established the possibility of growing certain vegetables in the 1920s and grain cultivation never became a viable option.[51] Given these environmental constraints, it is hardly surprising that the initial attempts of the *Apatit* trust to organize local agriculture were largely unsuccessful. The state farm "Industriia", where a number of special settlers worked, spent its first years on land reclamation, farming only a few hectares of land. The meat and milk economy of the state farm also suffered from a lack of shelters for livestock, which caused many animals to freeze to death.[52]

Some special settlers in the Khibiny region dealt with these shortages by making use of natural elements familiar to them in a new environment. The migrants caught freshwater fish in the nearby lakes and rivers and collected mushrooms and berries in the summer. One special settler,

47. GAMO, f. 773, op. 1, d. 2, ll. 183–186; Petrova *et al.*, *Kirovsk v dokumentakh i faktakh*, pp. 64–65, 68–69.
48. F.B. Zubkova, "Opiat' nas ushchemliaiut", in *Spetspereselentsy v Khibinakh*, pp. 19–21, 20.
49. GAMO, f. 773, op. 1, d. 6, ll. 230–232.
50. Petrova *et al.*, *Kirovsk v dokumentakh i faktakh*, pp. 68–74; and GAMO, f. 773, op. 1, d. 15, ll. 76–79.
51. S.A. Diuzhilov, "Nauchnoe reshenie problemy poliarnogo zemledeliia", in P.V. Fedorov, Iu.P. Bardileva, and E.I. Mikhailov (eds), *Zhivushchie na Severe: Vyvoz ekstremal'noi srede* (Murmansk, 2005), pp. 82–86.
52. Petrova *et al.*, *Kirovsk v dokumentakh i faktakh*, pp. 54, 74–75.

L.D. Zverev, later described the tactics employed by his family at the time:

> Father made nets. We had ponds around home and there were many fish. He was a craftsman and made nets. He went into the mountains where there were already pools and caught fish. He goes out for mushrooms and fetches netting and fish. The fish is good. And there was perch where the airdrome is. He also goes there and catches. In the White River there used to be a lot of fish, only they've gone away. In this way we didn't starve.[53]

In the first years after their arrival many families supplemented their diets with aquatic fauna that they obtained outside the state-sponsored distribution system. However, in the fall of 1931 *Apatit* began dumping massive amounts of wastewater from enrichment processing into the White River.[54] This industrial pollution soon killed off the fish there and eliminated this source of food for the special settlers.[55]

A famine in 1932–1933 hit the grain-producing regions of the country, especially Ukraine, the hardest. However, the special settlements also suffered terribly both from lack of food and ruthless government action. An immediate response of the central authorities was to reduce food rations for special settlers, thereby guaranteeing further suffering among this population.[56] A 1934 report of the Khibinogorsk City Council, after ration levels had been restored, revealed a continued insufficiency in the diets of workers and their families. The lack of food led some to flee; others died of starvation. Food shortage also resulted in widespread incidents of diseases caused by malnourishment. The specific conditions of the Khibiny environment played a role here in the scurvy outbreaks and the fact that 70 per cent of children suffered from rickets in 1934. The lack of local fruits and vegetables inhibited vitamin C intake, causing scurvy, and the long sunless months and insufficient dairy consumption likely led to vitamin D deficiencies, giving rise to rickets.[57]

Impediments posed by the natural features of the Khibiny Mountains for simultaneously organizing industrial and drinking water supplies and sewage removal negatively affected the health and livelihood of the special settlers. Throughout 1930, urban and enterprise planners struggled to align their idealistic visions for the socialist city of Khibinogorsk with

---

53. L.D. Zverev, "Rasskaz o zhizni bogatoi", in *Spetspereselentsy v Khibinakh*, pp. 11–18, 16.

54. Barabanov *et al.*, *Gigant v Khibinakh*, pp. 44–59, and S.A. Diuzhilov, "'Aripelag Svobody' na Murmane (vtoraia polovina 1920–kh–1930-e g.g.)", in P.V. Fedorov *et al.* (eds), *Zhivushchie na Severe: obrazy i real'nosti* (Murmansk, 2006), pp. 93–100, 100.

55. ARAN, f. 544, op. 1, d. 161, ll. 40–42; GAMO, f. 773, op. 1, d. 51, ll. 92–94.

56. Viola, *The Unknown Gulag*, pp. 132–149.

57. Shashkov, *Spetspereselentsy v istorii Murmanskoi oblasti*, pp. 278–279; GAMO, f. R-163 [Otdel zdravookhraneniia pri ispolnitel'nom komitete Murmanskogo okruzhnogo soveta (1927–1937 gg.)], op. 1, d. 141, l. 13.

practical considerations. They wanted to use the local water system as both a source and a dump and minimize infrastructure costs.[58] None of the options they considered during that year seemed entirely satisfactory.[59] However, they eventually chose to build both the town and the enrichment plant of *Apatit* along the southern shore of Lake Large Vud"iavr. Since industrial waste would be dumped into the White River, which flowed downstream out of Lake Large Vud"iavr, enterprise leaders hoped this model would preserve the lake water as safe for drinking.[60]

When the special settlers first arrived in 1930, they immediately began drawing water from the sources closest to their settlements for drinking, cooking, cleaning, bathing, and extinguishing fires. They often filled barrels with water from lakes and rivers or built temporary pipes that froze in the winter. Furthermore, in what became a chronic problem for many years in the Khibiny region, various sources of human contamination from laundry, trash receptacles, cesspits, and used water from the bathhouses began to pollute the water supply. Even without industrial dumping, these everyday forms of pollution already made the unpurified water far from clean. As sanitation inspector Tikhomirov wrote at the end of 1930:

> Independent of the results of the study [on the bacteriologic content of the water] one can already now count all of the available sources of a water supply as to a greater or lesser degree contaminated, the mountain character of the place with a sharp incline represents an almost insuperable obstacle to the protection of them from pollution.[61]

As diseases connected to contaminated water gripped Khibinogorsk and its outlying settlements in 1931–1932, the local government attempted to regulate migrants' use of water. They often relied on draconian measures that sought to place the burden of environmental protection on the forced migrants instead of the industrial enterprise or the city's administration. One resolution of the Khibinogorsk City Council from 1931 created a 50-meter territory around Lake Large Vud"iavr that was to be on a "strict regime" of reduced human activity and construction for the sake of preserving this water source.[62] Another resolution of the City

---

58. N.N. Vorontsov, "Khibinskoe stroitel'stvo", in A.E. Fersman (ed.), *Khibinskie Apatity: Sbornik*, II (Leningrad, 1932), pp. 182–191; O.R. Munts, "Gorod Khibinogorsk i ego planirovka", in *ibid.*, pp. 192–207; GAMO, f. 773, op. 1, d. 1, ll. 107–108; Petrova *et al.*, *Kirovsk v dokumentakh i faktakh*, pp. 33–34.

59. GAMO, f. 773, op. 1, d. 1, ll. 149–154.

60. Munts, "Gorod Khibinogorsk i ego planirovka", pp. 192–207; Petrova *et al.*, *Kirovsk v dokumentakh i faktakh*, pp. 33–34; Smirnov, "Obogashchenie apatito-nefelinovoi porody Khibinskogo mestorozhdeniia", pp. 122–139.

61. Petrova *et al.*, *Kirovsk v dokumentakh i faktakh*, pp. 62–63.

62. GAMO, f. R–163, op. 1, d. 26, ll. 15–16.

Figure 4. This picture shows a group of "special settlers" gathering their laundry to wash. *Source: Tararaksin*, Sudeb sgorevshikh ochertan'e [Outlines of Burnt Fates], *p. 28.*

Council from 21 August 1931 aimed at sanitary protection of the water supply. One hundred copies of it were printed and presumably posted around the area. The decree prohibited dumping wastes on the ground, placing cafeterias, bathhouses, cesspits, lavatories, stables, and pigsties within 50 meters of any water body, doing laundry in living quarters, and taking water from a specific lake and river for any reason besides housing construction.[63] Eventually, the city began on-site chlorination of drinking water drawn from a water body that was already polluted.[64] In later years the authorities tried to limit the number of trips special settlers made to the bathhouses and accused individuals who reused their tickets of subversive behavior.[65]

The steep tundra mountains and the existing water system of the area confounded industrialists' schemes for organizing the territory's hydrology to their maximum benefit. The regime's unwillingness to prioritize sewer construction and the effects of industrial pollution added to the difficulties with arranging a water supply for the new settlement. At the

63. GAMO, f. R–163, op. 1, d. 26, l. 17.
64. Petrova *et al.*, *Kirovsk v dokumentakh i faktakh*, p. 152.
65. Shashkov, *Spetspereselentsy v istorii Murmanskoi oblasti*, p. 283.

end of 1930 the *Apatit* trust still intended to begin construction on a sewer system, water pipe, and purification station during 1931; the drinking water source in this plan would come from the river Loparki and not Lake Large Vud"iavr, which would be the source only for industrial water.[66] However, as the enterprise lagged in its production quotas, such basic municipal expenditures as the provision of a safe water service were repeatedly deferred.[67]

This postponement delayed the construction of a sewer system until after *Apatit* had polluted the water of the White River and Lake Large Vud"iavr with byproducts from enrichment. This pollution changed the chemical character of the water and made it even less suitable for domestic use by special settlers.[68] Furthermore, without a pipe system to supply water the ability to extinguish fires that arose at industrial sites or in crowded wooded housing was virtually non-existent.[69] As a City Council report put it in 1934: "There are a lot of unsanitary conditions and the fire prevention situation is unsatisfactory – there is no water."[70] By this point the party leaders in Leningrad had also become somewhat more attentive to the problems with water in the Khibiny region. Kirov wrote to the People's Commissariat of Heavy Industry and the State Planning Committee in 1934:

> In Khibinogorsk and its settlements there is a complete lack of a sewer system and it does not have an independent system of municipal water supply – the supply of the city is produced with unpurified water from Lake Large Vud"iavr through a pumping station of the industrial water supply. Further postponing the urgent construction and the sewer system might bring the population to mass diseases of an epidemic character.[71]

Construction of these services did finally begin the next year, but only near the end of the decade did they even approach completion.[72]

---

66. Petrova *et al.*, *Kirovsk v dokumentakh i faktakh*, p. 63.
67. GAMO, f. 773, op. 1, d. 5, ll. 62–70, 192–193; Barabanov *et al.*, *Gigant v Khibinakh*, p. 51; GAMO, f. 773, op. 1, d. 51, ll. 92–94.
68. GAMO, f. 773, op. 1, d. 51, ll. 84–100.
69. Ivan Kataev offers a vivid description of a fire in Khibinogorsk from this period; Ivan Kataev, "Ledianaia Ellada", in B.I. Nikol'skii and Iu.A. Pompeev (eds), *Pul's Khibin* (Leningrad, 1984), pp. 42–66, 52–53.
70. Shashkov, *Spetspereselentsy v istorii Murmanskoi oblasti*, p. 278.
71. GAMO, f. 773, op. 1, d. 9, ll. 192–193.
72. Petrova *et al.*, *Kirovsk v dokumentakh i faktakh*, pp. 143–146. The Axis powers extensively bombed Kirovsk during World War II. The destruction of the town means that most likely the sewer system only began functioning again in the late 1940s or early 1950s. On sewage issues in postwar Soviet cities, see Donald Filtzer, "Standard of Living versus Quality of Life: Struggling with the Urban Environment in Russia During the Early Years of Postwar Reconstruction", in Juliane Fürst (ed.), *Late Stalinist Russia: Society Between Reconstruction and Reinvention* (London, 2006), pp. 81–102.

THE CONSEQUENCES FOR THE "SPECIAL SETTLERS"

The species of fauna known as *homo sapiens* could not initially thrive in the habitat created by Stalinist industrialization and forced deportations. The circumstances, from the proximate cesspits to the crowded dwellings, were a nightmare for human health. As one special settler, Aleksandra Iablonskaia, recalled decades later: "Only at night could I find a place. If you arrived late, you would sleep on the edge in the cold. [...] I crept among the sick in the cold and dirt."[73]

A meeting of doctors in Khibinogorsk in September 1931 proposed limiting the number of people per tent to 40 or 45 based on their overall assessment of the situation at the special settlement at the 18-kilometer mark: "The contamination of the settlement with garbage, overcrowding, the absence of a basic stock of everyday items and the dirtiness of the area undoubtedly is a favorable atmosphere for the development of disease."[74] A few months later, in February 1932, a report on the living conditions at the mining settlements of Iuksporiok and Rasvumchorr revealed the totality of the poor sanitary conditions there: unclean barracks with poor stoves, doors, and windows, an unsafe water supply, poor illumination, freezing temperatures, and outbreaks of disease.[75]

The local environment combined with the oppressive development model of the Soviet state to produce conditions of widespread disease and death among those individuals who did not escape. Children suffered disproportionately. The new residents in the Khibiny region fell ill with diseases similar to those that hit other special settlements in the north, including typhus, typhoid fever, tuberculosis, scurvy, and measles.[76] The available data on the incidence of these diseases are largely anecdotal. Over 175 children died from measles in September and October 1930, doctors reported 55 new cases of typhoid fever in the late summer of 1931 at one of the outlying settlements, and 20 children in Iablonskaia's *shalman* died of typhus.[77] These diseases raged throughout the area into 1932 and then began to subside. Starting in this year doctors in the area managed to administer thousands of inoculations against typhoid, smallpox, and diphtheria, which primarily accounted for the improvement despite the continued lack of municipal infrastructure necessary for urban sanitation.[78]

---

73. Tat'iana Shishkina, "Iablonskie", *Khibinskii vestnik* (5 October 2006), p. 6.
74. GAMO, f. R-163, op. 1, d. 26, ll. 8–10.
75. GAMO, f. 773, op. 1, d. 15, ll. 98–101.
76. Viola, *The Unknown Gulag*, pp. 34–141, and A.A. Kiselev, "GULAG na Murmane: Istoriia tiurem, lagerei, kolonii", *Sovetskii Murman* (8 October 1992), p. 3.
77. Barabanov and Kalinina, "*Apatit*", p. 38; GAMO, f. R-163, op. 1, d. 26, ll. 8–10; Shishkina, "Iablonskie", p. 6.
78. Petrova *et al.*, *Kirovsk v dokumentakh i faktakh*, pp. 152–153.

Table 1. *Demography of Khibinogorsk/Kirovsk.*

Date	Total population	Special settler population	Total births (previous year)	Special settler births (previous year)	Total deaths (previous year)	Special settler deaths (previous year)	Deaths of children (previous year)
1 January 1932	24,485	17,756	564	420	999	864	589
1 January 1933	28,500	19,172	856	506	860	657	339
1 January 1934	34,332	19,731	717	374	850	518	352
1 January 1935	36,957	21,325	718	310	620	401	192

Source: Shashkov, *Spetspereselentsy v istorii Murmanskoi oblasti*, pp. 143, 191.

Table 2. *Birth and death rates in Khibinogorsk/Kirovsk.*

Year	Special settler birth rate (%)	Non-special settler birth rate (%)	Total birth rate (%)	Special settler death rate (%)	Non-special settler death rate (%)	Total death rate (%)
1931	2.4	2.1	2.3	4.9	2.0	4.1
1932	2.6	3.8	3.0	3.4	2.2	3.0
1933	1.9	2.3	2.1	2.6	2.3	2.5
1934	1.5	2.6	1.9	1.9	1.4	1.7

Source: Shashkov, *Spetspereselentsy v istorii Murmanskoi oblasti,* pp. 143, 191.

For many special settlers the final outcome of all of these natural phenomena of disease, hunger, cold, and filth in the Khibiny region was death. Special settler V.M. Lebedik later drew connections among these factors: "It is hard to say how many people lived in this barrack. There was no thought about hygiene. Diseases began and every morning we brought out the dead."[79] In 1935 a health inspector in the region, A.G. Friliand, noted that the mortality rate, especially for children, at this new site of socialist modernity was considerably higher than the Soviet average.[80] Aggregate figures showing overall deaths in the Khibiny region remain elusive. However, the historian Victor Shashkov has pieced together some demographic data for the city of Khibinogorsk, the population of which had a smaller percentage of special settlers than the other settlements in the region. The figures for the surrounding settlements were almost certainly worse.

The data in Table 1 show a total of 3,329 deaths, 2,440 among the population of special settlers and 1,472 children, from 1931 through 1934 in Khibinogorsk. Children made up 44.2 per cent of those who perished in these years, though this percentage declined from a particularly dreadful 59 per cent for 1931 to 31 per cent for 1934. The figures in Table 2 also reveal a general trend of improvement in the rate of mortality. Interestingly, over this period both the birth rate and death rate of settlers gradually declined. The death rates of 4.9 per cent for the special settlers for 1931 and 3.4 per cent for 1932, compared with the 2 per cent for the remaining population for 1931 and 2.2 per cent for 1932, demonstrate the disproportional suffering of these forced migrants over freely recruited laborers and enterprise administration.

CONCLUSION

In the 1930s, Soviet government embraced what was arguably the greatest economic imperative of globalization at the time, industrialization, with a

---

79. V.M. Lebedik, "Stranitsy detstva", in *Spetspereselentsy v Khibinakh*, pp. 23–25, 24.
80. GAMO, f. R–163, op. 1, d. 141, ll. 9–26.

foolhardy enthusiasm that helped lead to extreme human suffering. Its reliance on forced labor on multiple scales is a story already well told. Scholars have paid less attention, however, to how the natural environment was a fundamental component of this history.

The environment contributed to the creation of intolerable conditions for the special settlers through the imposition of relatively stable obstacles (cold weather, for instance) and through changes in response to human activity (polluted water, for example). In doing so it thwarted the intentions of state planners, who could not fully control nature despite their desires, and added to the chaos of Stalinist industrialization. One thing that the policy of forcefully sending declassed peasants to build a socialist mining town in the far north accomplished, however, was the creation of extreme vulnerability of the special settlers to hazards within their new natural environment. This perilous situation produced tragic results for many of the individuals sent to live and labor at the apatite works in the Khibiny Mountains.

IRSH 55 (2010), Supplement, pp. 175–201 doi:10.1017/S0020859010000544
© 2010 Internationaal Instituut voor Sociale Geschiedenis

"Pumpkins Just Got in There": Gender and Generational Conflict and "Improved" Agriculture in Colonial Zimbabwe*

GUY THOMPSON

Department of History and Classics, University of Alberta

E-mail: Guy.Thompson@ualberta.ca

SUMMARY: This essay explores how gender and generational dynamics in peasant communities in colonial Zimbabwe were reshaped between 1930 and 1965 by factors introduced by colonization. British rule brought dramatically greater market opportunities and access to new agricultural tools. Some peasants readily adopted ploughs, combining these new tools with indigenous methods of production and environmental management to increase output and market sales while developing new hybrid ways of working the land. These options allowed some young men to evade the demands of, and obligations to, their fathers, while the new methods often increased women's workloads, exacerbating gender tensions. In the wake of World War II, Rhodesian state agricultural programmes sought to reshape African farming practices dramatically, initiatives that were justified as protecting the environment and modernizing the peasant sector. These measures permanently allocated and demarcated peasant land, imposed onerous environmental protection measures, and encouraged peasants to follow labour-intensive production methods based on European techniques. These conditions restricted young men's access to land and imposed intense demands on women of all ages; in practice, however, these changes led to a renegotiation of gender and generational dynamics, most obviously in a wave of protests that threatened state control of the countryside.

* I would like to acknowledge gratefully financial support for this project from the Social Sciences and Humanities Research Council of Canada and the University of Alberta, as well as the Graduate School, History Department, and the MacArthur Interdisciplinary Program on Global Change, Sustainability, and Justice of the University of Minnesota. I would also like to thank the members of the Department of Economic History at the University of Zimbabwe for their input and support for my research. Finally, I would like to acknowledge the vital assistance of my research assistants in Madziwa, Rangarirai Gurure, Obert Kufinya, and Solomon Mahdi, who not only helped with introductions and translation when my Shona failed me but also provided important insights into my work.

VaJonga and Amai Jonga built their homestead in Madziwa, Zimbabwe, in the late 1950s, on a ridge overlooking a small river. Many years later I interviewed them in the shade of a mango tree along the edge of that ridge, mainly to ask how they had changed their farming practices over their lives, and what they recalled of the methods their parents used in the 1930s. VaJonga spoke more than his wife; an accomplished and materially successful farmer, he described how well he had learned the "improved" techniques promoted by the colonial state, disdaining indigenous practices such as intercropping and cultivating close to water courses as "primitive". Late in our conversation, I pointed to the river flats below, and quietly observed that the vegetable gardens that spread out from the banks of the river were very nice. Amai Jonga spoke up, pointed to one of the closely fenced plots, and said "That one, there, that's ours, it gives us lots of vegetables."[1] VaJonga rejoined the conversation, although it was his wife who mainly explained the advantages of planting in the river flats, particularly that ground water made it possible to grow vegetables year round.

This exchange captured several dimensions of the legacies of white minority rule in Zimbabwe. The gardens on the river flats were illegal under state regulations that were imposed in Madziwa in the late 1940s and remain in effect, yet peasants throughout the country defy such bans to get access not only to more land, but also to valuable areas that tap groundwater resources, reducing their dependence on the capricious rains. Moving beyond a didactic confrontation between peasants and the state, the disjuncture between VaJonga's stated approval for "improved" agriculture and his household's willing evasion of land-use restrictions may speak to the complexities of gender dynamics.

Gardens are widely considered to be women's areas, and I knew from other conversations that husbands and wives argued over many years about how to work the land, which areas to use, and what to plant, as part of the complex negotiation of gender and authority within households. I did not feel like I had a strong enough rapport with Amai Jonga and VaJonga to ask questions along these lines with both of them present, but these dynamics certainly emerged in other interviews.

This essay builds on these themes by exploring the social disruptions that intensified among Zimbabwe peasants during the colonial period, as Africans reshaped their lives around the pressures and new options brought by British rule. I am particularly interested in the shifts in gender and the generational dynamics that played out around agricultural practices, in household priorities, as well as in how people responded to state

---

1. Interview with VaJonga (male, in his eighties) and Amai Jonga (female, seventies), 3 November 1997.

restrictions and vastly greater market opportunities. Beginning in the 1930s, many households in Madziwa readily adopted European ploughs and cultivators, often combining these new tools with indigenous methods of production and environmental management to increase output and develop new hybrid ways of working the land. These options allowed some young men to evade the demands of, and obligations to, their fathers and elders, enabling them to pursue greater autonomy. However, new methods and agricultural strategies often increased women's workloads, which included particularly onerous tasks such as weeding, exacerbating gender tensions.

State intervention in the peasant sector intensified in the wake of World War II, as officials permanently allocated and demarcated peasant land, imposed onerous and often dubious environmental protection measures, and encouraged Africans to follow production methods based on modern European techniques such as mono-cropping and manuring. By restricting farmers' access to land and demanding peasants adopt labour-intensive production methods, state policies threatened most young men's options and imposed intense demands on women of all ages. In many rural communities, including Madziwa, these factors led peasants to renegotiate gender and generational dynamics as women and young men resisted the demands placed on them and older men recognized the limits of their authority.

These arguments engage a number of important themes that run through the social history of southern Africa, including the reshaping of rural gender dynamics, the onerous demands that state agricultural betterment programmes imposed on peasants, ostensibly to protect the environment, and the different forms of resistance Africans used to challenge official demands.[2] While the historiography of the region recognized the connections between social change and government environmental policies comparatively early in

2. See Allen Isaacman, "Peasants and Rural Social Protest in Africa", in Frederick Cooper *et al.* (eds), *Confronting Historical Paradigms: Peasants, Labor, and the Capitalist World System in Africa and Latin America* (Madison, WI, 1993), pp. 205–317; Terence Ranger, *Peasant Consciousness and Guerrilla War in Zimbabwe: A Comparative Study* (Berkeley, CA, 1985); William Beinart, "Soil Erosion, Conservationism and Ideas about Development: A Southern African Exploration, 1900–1960", *Journal of Southern African Studies*, 11 (1984), pp. 52–83; Michael Drinkwater, *The State and Agrarian Change in Zimbabwe's Communal Areas* (New York, 1991); Ian Phimister, "Discourse and the Discipline of Historical Context: Conservationism and Ideas about Development in Southern Rhodesia 1930–1950", *Journal of Southern African Studies*, 12 (1986), pp. 263–275; Victor Machingaidze, "Agrarian Change from Above: The Southern Rhodesia Native Land Husbandry Act and African Response", *The International Journal of African Historical Studies*, 24 (1991), pp. 557–588; Donald Moore, "The Crucible of Cultural Politics: Reworking 'Development' in Zimbabwe's Eastern Highlands", *American Ethnologist*, 26 (1999), pp. 654–689; and William Beinart and Joann McGregor (eds), *Social History and African Environments* (Oxford, 2003).

the 1980s, these arguments have generally been advanced in isolation from efforts to understand indigenous knowledge.[3]

I want to draw out the connections between these two literatures by highlighting the contradictions between indigenous understandings of agriculture and the environment and the models promoted by the white minority government of Rhodesia that were ostensibly based in Western scientific practices. I also want to push this material further by exploring how peasants actually used the new tools they adopted, as my interviews in Madziwa revealed that many Africans combined the labour advantages of ploughs and other European tools with indigenous agricultural techniques, creating not only new hybrid production methods but also means to reshape social obligations within and beyond their households. Moreover, little attention has been drawn to the importance of rural protest in Zimbabwe in the early 1960s, which is ironic as peasant opposition clearly threatened state control over the countryside – and this open resistance to government policies was deeply rooted in the generational and gender tensions within rural communities.

While I will argue that the tensions and dynamics that played out around farming practices occurred across much of Zimbabwe, this essay draws heavily on interviews I undertook with 115 elderly residents of Madziwa Communal Area, a community of roughly 30,000 people about 125 kilometres due north of Harare. In common with all the designated communal areas, Madziwa is a legacy of Rhodesian racial planning, when certain parts of the countryside were designated as "native reserves", to be the permanent homes of the black majority when they were not in waged employment in the white-controlled economy.

While the reserves are often described as isolated, dry, and lying on poor soil, this portrayal obscures wide variations in conditions between reserves, and a long history of peasant efforts to produce a marketable surplus and have some control over their engagement with the colonial economy.[4] Madziwa receives more rain than most reserves and has better than average soil, although it is far less fertile than much of the land designated for white settlers; thus it allowed at least some individuals and

---

3. See Ken Nyamapfene, "Adaptation to Marginal Land amongst the Peasant Farmers of Zimbabwe", *Journal of Southern African Studies*, 15 (1989), pp. 384–389; Ian Scoones, "Landscapes, Fields and Soils: Understanding the History of Soil Fertility Management in Southern Zimbabwe", *Journal of Southern African Studies*, 23 (1997), pp. 615–634; K.B. Wilson, "Trees in Fields in Southern Zimbabwe", *Journal of Southern African Studies*, 15 (1989), pp. 369–383; W. Wolmer and Ian Scoones, "The Science of 'Civilized' Agriculture: The Mixed Farming Discourse in Zimbabwe", *African Affairs*, 99 (2000), pp. 575–600.
4. This imagery dominates much of the older historiography, as well as ZANU-PF propaganda from the 1960s to the present. See Robin Palmer, *Land and Racial Domination in Rhodesia* (Berkeley, CA, 1977), and Henry Moyana, *The Political Economy of Land in Rhodesia* (Gweru, 1984).

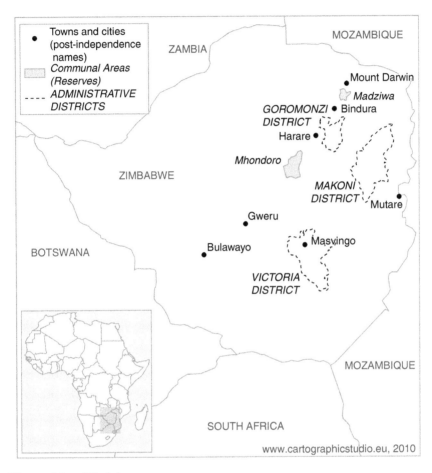

Figure 1. Map of Zimbabwe.

households not only to avoid waged labour, but also to earn significant income from crop sales, options that were much more difficult to pursue in many other reserves.

Colonial communications and state power developed comparatively slowly in Madziwa, much later than in districts such as Makoni, Goromonzi, and Victoria, which were far closer to towns and areas where European farms were concentrated.[5] This means that commercial pressures and large-scale market opportunities emerged comparatively late, in the 1930s, within the lifetime of most of the people I interviewed. Thus these peasants could describe changes in work regimes, production methods, market options, and

5. See Ian Phimister, *An Economic and Social History of Zimbabwe, 1890–1948* (London, 1988).

household dynamics that began much later than in regions close to the main areas of white settlement.

Methodologically this is important, because interviews provide the main mechanism to explore these dynamics within peasant communities. State bureaucrats, and the records they left behind, paid little attention to social and agricultural change. With a few rare exceptions, officials did not discuss generational or gender dynamics, and resorted to stereotypical descriptions of African apathy, resistance to innovation, and lack of environmental concern when they reported on agricultural developments. Thus state records reveal little about the main concerns of this essay.

However, the archival holdings in Harare do provide significant insight into the issues that preoccupied government officials, particularly the development of communications and state agricultural initiatives. They even provide some insight into how peasants responded to these efforts, including careful reports of the acts of defiance and violence that threatened government control of the countryside in the early 1960s. That said, the official records shed little light on why farmers reacted as they did; as I argue, the roots of the range of peasant responses lay in the consequences of state interventions, particularly the social disruptions, labour demands, and conflicting understandings of the environment, which emerged in my meetings with Madziwans.

All of the interviews that I conducted were open-ended conversations. While I certainly had questions in mind, I pursued interesting leads, and encouraged my research assistants to suggest questions and lines of inquiry. Several people I met clearly had strong ideas of what I needed to know, and pushed the interview in the directions they thought best. I was surprised that Madziwans readily discussed gender tensions and generational dynamics, issues I assumed could be too personal for many people. However, a number of times, peasants initially responded to my questions about the roles of men and women, and how people farmed their fields, in highly normative terms, or with assurances that they used the methods prescribed by the state. When I followed up with questions that showed I knew people often broke the rules, or that relations between husbands and wives could be complicated, many Madziwans gave much more revealing answers.

MADZIWA IN THE EARLY COLONIAL PERIOD

In accounts of their childhoods in the 1920s, the oldest farmers I met described the area as virtually untouched by colonial demands. Archival records generally support this image. Although state control of the area was established in the wake of the 1896–1897 *chimurenga* (uprising), the reserves in the district were not demarcated for another twenty years, and the dirt road that ran through Madziwa was so poor that police patrols could not enter the area for four months of the year.[6] There was no commercial development in Madziwa itself, just a few stores in Mount Darwin, 30 kilometres north. Bindura, 40 kilometres to the south, was a significant mining and farm supply centre, although getting there required climbing a high mountain pass. Taxes were certainly collected, and this meant that many men, particularly young ones, had to leave Madziwa to work in the colonial economy. Officials reported that in the early 1920s one-quarter to one-third of the men in the district left to find waged work annually; while the accuracy of this estimate is doubtful, it does indicate high levels of labour migrancy, and that the area was not as isolated as oral accounts suggest.[7]

Given the poor road and lack of stores, there was little pressure for agricultural change into the 1920s. Oral and archival records agree that farmers in Madziwa tilled the land exclusively with hoes throughout this period, growing mainly millet, but also maize, sorghum, and a wide variety of vegetables, such as beans, pumpkins, and tubers. Peasants reported that they, and their parents, used a variety of planting methods. However, there are a number of common techniques that appeared in most accounts, reflecting agricultural strategies that balanced food security, labour demands and availability, fertility, and environmental protection. These included a local system of shifting cultivation that involved clearing a new field every two or three years, working it for a few years, then leaving it fallow to allow the thin soil to recover. Fertility was also promoted by burning vegetation and crop residues. Tree stumps were left in place to reduce erosion and encourage regrowth when a field was fallowed.

Most farmers practiced intercropping, planting a range of foodstuffs and different varieties of each crop together to manage the vagaries of Zimbabwe's rainy season, which could bring prolonged dry periods and bursts of intense rain. Intermingling low growing plants such as beans and groundnuts with taller ones such as millet helped to keep moisture in the soil, while simultaneously limiting the growth of weeds. Peasants built elaborate ridges with the soil, in part to manage the flow of water, trapping light rain in their field, or directing heavy run-off away to limit erosion. Using ridges concentrated the top soil in the raised areas, making the ridges much richer and more fertile than undisturbed land. Moreover, in addition to growing crops in their conventional rain-fed fields, many households also grew rice in a wetland area, or raised vegetables and some grains on a riverbank or in a dry streambed garden, drawing on the

---

6. National Archives of Zimbabwe [hereafter, NAZ] S235/508, Report of the Native Commissioner for the Darwin District for the Year Ended 31.12.1930, p. 13.

7. NAZ S235/501, Darwin District, Report of the Native Commissioner for the Year Ending 31.12.1923, p. 4.

Figure 2. Peasants trading in Bindura in 1928. While European clothing had replaced indigenous fashions in many parts of Zimbabwe by this time, the continuation of local styles of dressing and adornment is clear in this image, reinforcing the recollections of peasants in Madziwa. *Copyright National Archives of Zimbabwe.*

accessible groundwater to produce early crops that met household needs when supplies from the previous year might be running low.[8]

The techniques that people reported using varied from household to household, but also from year to year for the same family. Peasants explained these variations in a number of ways, including their own knowledge, experience, and expectations for the coming season, but the key variable was the availability of labour. Production was organized largely along household lines, so that labour migrancy, advanced pregnancy, or illness could limit the number of hands available to work the land, leading the members of the household to adopt less demanding strategies such as extending the life of a field, undertaking little weeding, or not increasing the growing area by transplanting seedlings to new land.

During the 1920s, Madziwans used several means to draw on labour beyond the nuclear family unit. These included marrying polygynously, and expectations that adult children would continue to cultivate and plant for both sets of parents for some time after they married. The most effective mechanism peasants used to bring in extra-household labour was communal work parties, known as a *nhimbe* or *hoka* in the Shona language. These events were open to all members of the community, who would receive food and beer from the hosts in exchange for work, particularly during the demanding periods in the agricultural cycle, such as clearing a new field, weeding, and threshing. To contract another marriage, men had to pay the bride price (*lobola*) in cattle; calling a *nhimbe* required grain and meat, so that these strategies to expand household labour resources were open mainly to the relatively affluent, households that already had surplus food and animals.[9]

1930–1945: EARLY AGRARIAN CHANGE IN MADZIWA

In 1927, the local Native Commissioner (NC) reported that two ox-drawn ploughs had been sold to Madziwans, marking the beginning of a long period of agricultural and social change. In the following years, other farmers, mainly young men who had worked on white commercial farms, slowly adopted ploughs.[10] Peasants acquired ploughs for a number of reasons, but the most basic was that they made preparing fields much easier, reducing the labour involved while effectively extending the

8. Interviews with Amai Chaparira Paiena (female, sixties), 7 May 1998; Mandizva Mandizva (male, sixties), 9 May 1998; Levison Chavakaira (male, sixties), 30 May 1998; and Cyrus Nyamapfukudza (male, sixties), 28 May 1998. For a full discussion of indigenous knowledge and agricultural techniques, see my doctoral dissertation: Guy Thompson, "Cultivating Conflict: Modernism and 'Improved' Agriculture in Colonial Zimbabwe, 1920–1965" (unpublished Ph.D. dissertation, University of Minnesota, 2000).
9. Interviews with VaMusonza (male, eighties), 14 June 1998; Handidya Mazaradope (female, seventies), 6 May 1998; and Shingaidzo Madeve (female, sixties), 24 May 1998.
10. NAZ S235/505, Darwin District, Report of the Native Commissioner for the Year 1927, p. 2.

growing season as it was possible to prepare the land much more quickly, as VaKapfunde explained:

> *VaKapfunde:*   From the first day a plough was different, it was much easier to use.
>
> *Guy Thompson:*   How was it different?
>
> *VaKapfunde:*   It was different because with a hoe you could only till a small area, while with a plough you could work a big field. With a hoe it would take a month to clear the land, but with a plough only a few days.[11]

Ploughs also allowed farmers to work a larger area of land, potentially resulting in a bigger harvest.

Increased production and peasants' interest in ploughs both reflected important changes in market conditions in Madziwa. The road through the reserve was upgraded in the late 1920s, which allowed Rhodesia Railways to introduce a scheduled lorry service linking the reserve with Mount Darwin, and more importantly to the rail line in Bindura. Although both developments were primarily intended by the state to encourage the settlement of white farmers around Mount Darwin, they opened up options for Madziwans, and soon brought in itinerant traders and, in 1932, the first store in the reserve.[12] Initially sales of crops – mainly maize – were limited, but as agricultural prices improved in the late 1930s and into the 1940s sales grew dramatically. Selling crops not only brought increased income and access to consumer goods, especially cloth, ready-made clothes, sugar, tea, and bread, it also gave men in Madziwa a new option to avoid or limit labour migration.

When they acquired ploughs, peasants generally did not adopt modern European planting techniques as part of a broader technological package. During the interviews I undertook, Madziwans described how they, or their parents, blended the labour advantages of the plough with indigenous methods of production and environmental protection in the 1930s through to the early 1950s. Virtually everyone continued using shifting cultivation, fallowing, and burning. Most peasants intercropped, although some reported that they grew maize in discrete plots, on its own or mixed only with pumpkins, while intermingling millet, beans, groundnuts, and other crops in another area.

Intriguingly, most did not plant seeds in the furrows created by the plough. Some men reported that they made two passes with the plough to create a ridge, and their wives and children used hoes to plant crops in the fertile ridges, at times broadcasting seeds between the ridges. Others

---

11. Interviews with VaKapfunde (male, sixties), VaNyamapfene (male, sixties), 23 October 1997, and Mazaradope and Chavakaira.
12. NAZ S235/506, Darwin District, Report of the Native Commissioner for the Year 1928, p. 3; S481/175 Darwin to Fura Farm Road, Minister of Mines and Public Works to Chief Road Engineer, 24.11.1925, p. 1; and S235/510, Darwin District Report for the Year Ended 31.12.1932, pp. 3, 8.

simply ploughed to break up the soil and then broadcast a mixture of seeds on the tilled land, or broadcast and then used the plough to cover the seeds.[13] In either case, the raised areas would yield well in years with average rainfall, and produce something in very wet periods, while the crops in the low lying areas acted as insurance for very dry seasons. A few farmers did move closer to European practice, planting seeds deep in the furrows, a technique that was well suited to the types of white maize introduced by colonization but which did not work with millet and local varieties of maize – a crop introduced by the Portuguese in the 1500s during an earlier phase of globalization that had been indigenized.

The variation in planting methods continued to reflect different understandings of the environment and expectations for the season, but this was also deeply rooted in two new agricultural strategies opened up by peasants who adopted ploughs. The first I have identified as hybrid production, where peasants used the new tool to reduce their need for labour while drawing on a variety of indigenous techniques such as intercropping, ridging, and planting in wetlands to secure their household's food supplies regardless of the weather that year. The second strategy was maximizing production, which appealed mainly to younger male heads of households who dramatically increased the amount of land they worked and planted mainly maize because there was a much better market for it than other grains.

Peasants who sought to maximize production were much more likely to adopt modern European planting techniques such as row planting, mainly because it made it possible to use a plough like a cultivator to clear weeds between rows of plants, something that was impossible on an intercropped field. While a few men who aimed to produce on a large scale bought cultivators, planters, or other European tools, most households acquired only a plough.[14] By concentrating on maize and row planting, large-scale producers took on a much higher risk of crop failure, so some households continued to draw on indigenous techniques in part of their field or a separate area while trying to maximize production in their main field; I suspect women used indigenous methods in their part of the field as a food security strategy. While many households sold maize in this period, the small number of peasants who sought to maximize output produced the bulk of the marketed grain in the 1930s and 1940s, so that some were well know to local government officials.[15]

13. Interviews with VaMusonza, Garawa Nhembe (male, sixties), 7 October 1997; and Mazaradope and Tobias Chikuya (male, fifties), 21 May 1998.
14. Interviews with VaMusonza, Mai Kondo (female, seventies), 3 November 1997; Bowas Musonza (male, fifties), 8 November 1997; and Godfrey Reza (male, seventies), 15 May 1998.
15. NAZ S1563, Mount Darwin District Report of the Native Commissioner for the Year Ended 31.12.1934, p. 8; S235/515 Report of the Native Commissioner, Darwin, for the Year Ended 31.12.1936, pp. 3, 6.

By adopting ploughs and new agricultural strategies, peasants created different work dynamics within and beyond their households. Increasing production meant more weeding, labour that was done largely by women. While Madziwans aiming to maximize production used their cattle and equipment to clear undesirable plants between rows, women and children were generally expected to dig out the weeds between the plants within rows with hoes, so women's workloads within households following this strategy likely increased. Women who chose also to cultivate an intercropped area to secure food supplies worked even more. As men were expected to clear and prepare land for their household, some women were not able to develop separate intercropped areas or plant the crops they wanted. Mai Kondo explained:

> When a woman said "this part is where I want to plant groundnuts" and the man felt it should be for maize, then the woman was told to put her crop somewhere else. He would say "It's my field, I'll do as I want". They can discuss it, but usually it is useless.[16]

Women were not powerless in this situation, although they often had to assert themselves in indirect ways, as Amai Chipo recalled.

> *Amai Chipo*: Sometimes I asked my husband for a small portion of land for myself.
> *Guy Thompson*:   How did you ask him?
> *Amai Chipo*: It is a lot of work to get the portion, but by talking softly and politely I might get him to change his mind and give me part of the field. Sometimes I had to try very hard to get a portion released to me [laughs].[17]

Crop sales, and the growing importance of money, also fuelled conflict along gender lines. Amai Chaparira Paiena and several other people argued that commercialization in this period led men and women to lay claim to particular crops:

> *Guy Thompson:* What crops belonged to women then, and which were for men?
> *Amai Chaparira Paiena:* This idea came after people began to sell [crops]. When we made ridges [intercropped], it was hard to say these are mine. This practice came when we sold and needed money.[18]

Although most Madziwa elders disagreed with this idea, claiming that crops had always been divided along gender lines, I believe that the essence of this idea is true, that claims intensified as the value of crops grew. Peasants also presented competing attitudes, although conflict is a strong theme in many accounts.

---

16. Mai Kondo.
17. Interviews with the women of the Dambaza family (seven women married to the same man, ranging from their thirties to their sixties), 27 October 1997, and Amai Chaparira Paiena.
18. Interviews with Amai Chaparira Paiena, Simion Kagonda (male, seventies), 29 May 1998, and Morris Makaza (male, eighties), 30 October 1997.

Lillian Gurure claimed that women controlled the household's produce, and had oversight rights to men's crops and the money that came from selling them.

> If a man sold any crop without the woman's consent, then the woman would demand the money as she would be suspicious that the money had been given to another woman. In some cases, disagreements and fights erupted. It was the woman who had the right to sell the crops. If the man wanted to sell even his own crops such as maize, he had to seek his wife's consent.[19]

As struggles over crops and the proceeds of selling them continued into the present, these statements also reflect ongoing public debates about gendered roles and responsibilities, not just the dynamics of individual households.

Shifts in generational dynamics rooted in the adoption of new tools and agricultural strategies in the 1930s and 1940s are not as clear as the gendered ones. Initially it was mainly young men who acquired ploughs, often with money from migrant labour. They used their new tools and income from crop sales to assert their autonomy from their fathers, especially when it came to marital negotiations. By paying their own bride price, young men reduced their obligations to work for their father's households, or had more discretion over the timing and nature of labour.[20] Pearson Jera recounted his desire to free himself from his father's claims and to establish his own independent household in the 1940s very clearly:

> *Guy Thompson*:   How long did you stay without your own cattle?
> *Pearson Jera*:   Not very long. Father did not want me to buy cattle, he said "What about all these animals that we have here?" But this was just a way to encourage us, if a child is told that this herd is yours and believed it, he was foolish! At court, people argued about whether the cattle were theirs or ones that they had been given. Don't trust your father's wealth, it is not yours! You have to know how to clap [show deference and respect].[21]

Other men spoke of easier relationships with their fathers. VaManyika's father not only helped him pay the bride price but also gave the newly married couple a plough and cattle. However, VaManyika's description of these arrangements neatly encapsulates how ties between generations were secured by such assistance: "I did a lot of farming for my father. A man who was helped to pay bride price by his father was a trusted son. My home was close to my father's home as I was still required to help him with work."[22] As older men acquired ploughs, and those who had

19. Interview with Lillian Gurure (female, seventies), 29 May 1998.
20. Interviews with Mazaradope and Amai Chaparira Paiena.
21. Interview with the Jera family (three men, in their forties, sixties and eighties, one woman in her forties), 16 May 1998.
22. Interviews with VaManyika (male, nineties), 14 May 1998, and Nyamapfukudza.

acquired the new tools aged, cattle and ploughs became a mechanism by which older men reasserted claims on their sons. As young men sought to marry and establish their own independent households, fathers loaned cattle and equipment as a way to help the new household, but also to draw on labour from their son and members of his household, especially his son's wife.[23]

Social dynamics within the wider community also shifted in important ways in this period, particularly as the new tools and farming strategies reduced labour needs, creating new options for plough users. Producers who followed hybrid strategies reduced their need to call on extra-household labour without endangering food security. As Mai Matumba explained, "After ploughs were introduced, life got better. A family of three could finish work in the field early."[24] These households were therefore able to get through one of the crunch periods in the labour cycle without calling on relatives or others to assist them. Thus, farmers following this strategy were also able to pursue greater household autonomy, reducing their need for, and obligations to, parents, relatives, and community members, so that new farming strategies opened up new social options.

Peasants who worked large areas to maximize output continued to draw upon extra-household labour, but the conditions of these work arrangements changed. Most continued to call *nhimbe* during the 1930s and 1940s, but these now took two different forms. The first was a restricted work-group called to prepare the fields, limited to plough owners; only people who were directly invited could participate, rather than the entire community. This shift meant that large-scale farmers effectively created a closed mutual assistance group among those who were looking to maximize production. Often it was the sons of prominent men who did the actual work of tilling the soil while the older men relaxed. Participants received beer and food, including chicken or some other kind of meat.[25] The second type of work-group was called for weeding and harvesting. These events remained open to all members of the community, but participants received only beer as payment. No solid food was provided. Thus, a clear distinction appeared between ploughing groups and harvesting or weeding parties, a distinction that was reinforced as it became increasingly common for women to organize weeding groups that were restricted to women.[26]

These changes in work-groups reflected the desire of households looking to maximize output to maximize too their returns on their

---

23. Interviews with Amai Bowas Musonza (woman, seventies), 8 November 1997, and Mazaradope.
24. Interview with Mai Matumba (female, nineties), 17 October 1997.
25. Interviews with Nhembe, Mazaradope, Chikuya, and Mazivaramwe Kanyerere (male, seventies), 2 June 1998.
26. Interviews with Mai Matumba, Kanyerere, and Reza.

investment in beer and food supplied to workers from beyond the household. Open work-groups were hard to control and discipline, as Amai Manderere explained:

> *Guy Thompson*: Were there problems with *nhimbe*?
> *Amai Manderere*:   Aha! Yes, because everyone would know there was a work party. How could people not know and come? Then perhaps you will see that this one is a lazy person. Have you seen a lazy man who has been drinking beer?
> *Guy Thompson*: Would you give such a man beer?
> *Amai Manderere*:   Oh yes, yes you would. That is what was done.[27]

Labour discipline was often difficult; convenors could not exclude people and could not impose rigid work discipline when there was an open invitation.[28] Members of restricted communal groups, where reciprocal work on participants' fields was common, were more likely to work hard, especially when young men laboured under the supervision of their fathers.

These changes in labour patterns marked an important shift in large-scale producers' attitudes, as they became more concerned with income and financial returns than social prominence or acquiring influence over other members of the community through work parties and generosity.[29] For the poor, this change marked a significant loss, as open work-groups became less common, and the labour opportunities open to them were more closely supervised than they had been earlier. Moreover, the growing importance of the money economy that underlay the focus of materially successful peasants on production for the market reflected a fundamental shift in the bases of power within Madziwa. Income and material success gradually displaced other forms of social influence, as peasants were drawn into globalized markets and the values that underpinned them.

1945–1961: STATE INTERVENTION AND AGRARIAN CHANGE IN MADZIWA

The shifts in agricultural strategies and social dynamics that flowed from new tools and market opportunities continued through the 1940s and 1950s, but they were overshadowed by another dimension of colonial control, the growing interest of the white minority government in directing peasant production and conditions of life. State agricultural

27. Interview with Amai Manderere (female, seventies), 7 May 1998.
28. Interviews with Amai Bowas Musonza and Reza.
29. Jojo Mandaza and VaMakombe both tied the declining interest in *nhimbe* to the spread of money and the desire to acquire it; interviews with Jojo Mandaza (male, roughly 100), Mai Sophia (female, eighties), Mai Rita (female, seventies), 16 October 1997, and VaMakombe (male, sixties), 24 October 1997.

extension efforts in the reserves began in 1926, but remained small scale through the 1930s because of opposition from white farmers concerned about black competition, particularly during the depression. In the late 1930s, white alarmism about environmental degradation in the reserves, and its potential spread to European areas, grew dramatically, leading to calls for regulation and state intervention. These concerns continued to grow during the war, so that by 1944 officials were arguing:

> As is to be expected, the Native is rarely alive to the importance of conserving the soil; his concern is to get crops, with the consequence that the disease of erosion is spreading at an alarming pace where the primitive methods of agriculture have given place to the plough. [...] In some districts, the Natives' quest for more and more land has transformed once beautifully clad hills into gaunt spectres of ruin. One trustworthy witness instanced a hill, formerly covered with grass and trees, losing every atom of soil after having been attacked by Native cultivation.[30]

Environmental alarmism among officials and the white community more broadly were reinforced by calls for greater state direction of economic and social change in Europe and metropolitan demands tied to reconstruction after World War II. The colonies were called upon to increase outputs, exports, and productivity to support the devastated economies of Britain and France. Low and Lonsdale famously described these dynamics as the second colonial occupation, a new regime marked by government planning and economic intervention by the colonial state, public and private sector investment, and demand for increased productivity and output in African territories in particular.[31]

In much of Africa, the new postwar planning regime focused on labour stabilization, that is, as Fred Cooper argued in *Decolonization and African Society*, improving wages and working conditions for formal sector workers to boost productivity.[32] In Southern Rhodesia, however, white anxieties about African urbanization and the potential erosion of racial segregation blocked such efforts. State officials concentrated instead on restructuring peasant production. In part these efforts reflected ongoing environmental alarmism, but officials also promoted state intervention as a means to stimulate peasant output of basic foodstuffs to meet the dramatically increased demand within the colony.

The Rhodesian economy grew rapidly in the late 1940s and early 1950s, fuelled by mineral and tobacco exports that were vital for British imperial priorities, as well as industrialization to meet local demands. However,

---

30. Southern Rhodesia, *Report of the Native Production and Trade Commission* (Salisbury, 1944), pp. 12, 19.
31. D. Low and J. Lonsdale, "Introduction: Towards the New Order, 1945–1963", in D. Low and A. Smith (eds), *Oxford History of East Africa*, III (Oxford, 1976), pp. 1–64.
32. Frederick Cooper, *Decolonization and African Society: The Labor Question in French and British Africa* (Cambridge, 1996).

shortages of basic agricultural goods and the high prices that resulted were seen as significant economic constraints, as were problems with the labour supply that drove up wages and encouraged militancy among black workers. Officials promoted state intervention in the peasant sector under the rubric of rural stabilization, presenting it as a solution to both problems. By restructuring landholding and production practices, state officials argued they could increase production and the marketed output of foodstuffs, while encouraging African men to devote themselves to farming or waged work, thereby increasing the labour supply. As *What the NLHA Means to the Rural African and to Southern Rhodesia*, the white minority regime's major propaganda booklet promoting state intervention in the countryside, explained:

> Many thousands of land users [defined as male] who are no better than sub-sistence squatters will be given the choice of entering the market economy through proper land use or of seeking a livelihood in the expanding industries of the Colony, and the majority of them will be attracted by the opportunity to develop their stake in the land. [...] They [labour migrants] will find their long absences from the Reserves make it impossible to meet the farming responsi-bilities which the acceptance of farming rights entail.[33]

White opposition to investment in African agriculture diminished because of these promises to redress the labour and food shortages, but Europeans were much more strongly influenced by official pronouncements that intervening in the reserves would allow more Africans to live in them, thereby deepening racial segregation. These arguments had particular saliency in the context of the growing European immigration and the government's desire to make space for new white settlers by forcibly relocating the 135,000 black households occupying designated white land in the late 1940s.[34] Officially decried as squatters, the 600,000 Africans living on white farms represented not only roughly 20 per cent of the colony's black population, but a number 10 times the size of the European community.

The key means state planners in Southern Rhodesia developed to allow the reserves to accommodate more Africans and thereby support forced relocations and white settlement was the 1951 Native Land Husbandry Act [NLHA]. This law gave officials new coercive powers and consolidated earlier agricultural "improvement" mechanisms into a single plan. Native Affairs Department administrators could now proclaim permanent arable, grazing, and residential areas within the reserves, bringing an end to shifting

---

33. Southern Rhodesia, *What the NLHA Means to the Rural African and to Southern Rhodesia* (Salisbury, 1955), p. 13.
34. Phimister, *Economic and Social History of Zimbabwe*, pp. 267–268; Southern Rhodesia Development Coordinating Commission, *First Interim Report* (Salisbury, 1948), p. 10; Ranger, *Peasant Consciousness and Guerrilla War in Zimbabwe*, pp. 42–51; and Cooper, *Decolonization and African Society*, pp. 10–13.

cultivation. Once the land was consolidated, peasants would receive an arable plot, grazing rights, and residential areas based on their existing holdings; in areas with reasonable rainfall such as Madziwa, the formula was six acres and six cattle. Most reserves, however, were already too crowded to give every current resident a full plot, and many farmers faced a significant reduction in their stock holdings. Moreover, most households had to move to new fields and build a new house on their assigned residential plot, with no control over who their new neighbours would be.

The law also gave officials a variety of powers that were justified as environmentally necessary, including banning planting in wetlands and near watercourses, and imposing occupancy conditions on arable land that required plot holders to construct massive drainage ditches and contour ridges to control erosion. These requirements were enforced by various means of punishment, including fines and eventual confiscation of a peasant's arable land for repeat violations. Under the NLHA, officials were also supposed to promote state-sanctioned methods of working the land, although they did not have coercive powers to enforce these techniques.[35] While officials argued they were bringing modern scientific methods of production to the reserves, the interventions they promoted had been developed by missionaries in the late nineteenth and early twentieth centuries, and had received limited input from agronomists.[36]

Although the NLHA was only partially enacted in most reserves, including Madziwa, it significantly disrupted peasant livelihoods and social dynamics. The measure represented a massive extension of state power into rural people's lives that Africans deeply resented; as the law was enacted, it provoked large-scale resistance throughout the country-side. The NLHA cut off many of the mechanisms of rural accumulation such as crop sales and strategies to maximize output, while threatening dramatic cuts in individual stock holdings – even if many peasants evaded these provisions. Further, in many areas young men were told they would not receive landholdings once the law was enacted, forcing them onto the waged labour market. The permanent allocation of individual arable plots also forced peasants to adopt a different agricultural regime, one that was much more labour-intensive. Ensuring the fertility of the soil presented a

---

35. The following discussion of the main provisions of the NLHA is based on Southern Rhodesia, "The Native Land Husbandry Act", in Southern Rhodesia, *The Statute Law of Southern Rhodesia, 1951* (Salisbury, 1952), pp. 893–922; A. Pendered and W. von Memerty, "Native Land Husbandry Act of Southern Rhodesia", *Journal of African Administration*, 7 (1955), pp. 99–109; and J.E.S. Bradford, "Survey and Registration of African Land Units in Southern Rhodesia", *Journal of African Administration*, 7 (1955), pp. 165–170.

36. Jean Comaroff and John Comaroff, *Of Revelation and Revolution* (Chicago, IL, 1989); Beinart, "Soil Erosion, Conservationism and Ideas about Development"; Drinkwater, *The State and Agrarian Change in Zimbabwe's Communal Areas*, pp. 39–52; Donald Moore, *Suffering For Territory: Race, Place, and Power in Zimbabwe* (Durham, 2005), pp. 80–83.

Figure 3. Hilltop photograph of peasant fields in Madziwa. The distinct boundaries around each household's plot are the contour ridges prescribed by state planners.
Photograph by the author.

particular challenge, as the solution promoted by the state required moving to a household's fields one to two tons of cattle manure every year from the pens where stock were confined at night.[37]

Peasants clearly recognized the demands of this new agricultural system, and contested its assumptions verbally and in practice. Some peasants, such as Handidya Mazaradope, voiced overt complaints: "People felt that the agricultural demonstrators were being very unfair when they made them dig contours. It was just too much hard work for us! We started asking them why contours were needed, we did not use them in the past, but we still got good harvests."[38] Levison Chanikira advanced a broader critique of colonial rule in his account: "When the period of cutting the cattle ended, then came the cutting of the land. People began to see how bad the white man was because of the shortage of land and because they were left with few cattle."[39] As the post-independence Zimbabwean government has continued to promote the same agricultural

37. Interviews with VaMusonza, Dahwa Gono (male, eighties), 22 May 1998; NAZ S2827/2/2/ 3, I, Report of the Native Commissioner, Mount Darwin, for the Year Ended 31.12.1955, p. 6; NAZ S2797/4539, Meeting of the Madziwa Reserve Native Council, 28.9.1948, p. 2.
38. Interview with Mazaradope.
39. Interview with Chavakaira.

models as the colonial state, most Madziwans were more cautious in their direct statements. However, many spoke openly about their farming methods and encouraged me to visit their fields, gardens, and other arable plots, where there was clear evidence of people rejecting the new agricultural practices imposed on them and state restrictions on land use, as Amai Jonga and VaJonga did with their garden on the river flats.

While state intervention through the NLHA disrupted virtually all peasants' lives, its implications were particularly serious for young people and women in general, so that implementation of the law deepened gender and generational tensions. Much of the demanding work of moving manure, digging drainage ditches, and building contour ridges fell on them, given the expectations of parents and in-laws. Moreover, their future livelihoods were threatened by the NLHA. The new individual arable plots could be inherited only by a son or male relative, and so widows and any other sons would be left landless, their only options lying in the low-wage white-controlled economy. Restrictions on cattle holdings and arable areas made it difficult to accumulate resources to pay the bride price, so that the prospects to marry and establish independent households were threatened for an entire generation of young people.[40]

The state's efforts to control peasant farming had important implications for household gender dynamics. Women lost access to the wetland areas that they controlled under the centralization mechanism and environmental regulations. This was, however, partially compensated for by the creation of designated garden areas under the NLHA, which were placed in locations where it was possible to dig a well to allow plot holders to water their crops.[41] Gardens were readily accepted as women's areas, but allocations were generally smaller than wetland plots, and it was not possible to grow rice in these areas. Moreover, these holdings required much more work to irrigate, as the water sources tended to be much deeper than in plots close to the river, while digging and sharing wells could cause social strife.[42]

The difficulties women encountered because of the bans on using wetlands were far more complicated than they initially appear, as the consequences were not confined to the loss of these areas. For, in combination with the restrictions on the size of state-assigned plots and changes in methods of production, these changes triggered struggles

---

40. Interviews with VaKapfunde and VaNyamapfene, Mai Matumba, and VaHore (male, seventies), 31 May 1998.
41. While the ban on tilling land close to rivers remains, some agronomists now hold that it is possible to work wetlands without causing significant environmental damage, and it is being allowed in some areas. See R. Owen *et al.* (eds), *Dambo Farming in Zimbabwe: Water Management, Cropping and Soil Potentials for Smallholder Farming in the Wetlands* (Harare, 1995).
42. Interviews with Chief Nyamaropa (male, sixties), 18 October 1997, and VaKapfunde and VaNyamapfene.

between husbands and wives over the use and allocation of arable land. Handidya Mazaradope asserted that he decided how the family holding would be used and allocated, and his wife accepted his decision. He presented this as a social norm, saying: "The women just followed what their husbands said. If he said no to something she wanted to do, she would just follow with no objection."[43] Amai Chaparira Paiena echoed his comments, saying that her husband had insisted on controlling the arable plot, and had used it exclusively for grains. She was forced to rely only on her garden plot to raise the range of crops that were needed to support the family. As she saw it, there was nothing that a woman could do in such a situation, which she tied to bride price.

> *Guy Thompson:* How did a family decide how to use their land then [after individual allocation]?
> *Amai Chaparira Paiena:* A husband said it out loud. He would say, "Wife, you are putting your crop here, or this one here. In this land I want to put such and such a crop." All the crops sold at the Grain Marketing Board were for men.
> *Guy Thompson:* What could a woman do then?
> *Amai Chaparira Paiena:* There was nothing to do, you are a prisoner. There is no answer because you were bought![44]

Many women, however, did not have to accept these kinds of restriction. Women whose husbands were away at work for protracted periods controlled the fields on their own, although some men asserted their managerial role when they visited during the rainy season.[45] A few married couples said that they continued to work the land together, and collaboratively planned how to use it each year, so that they avoided serious conflict over land use. Others divided the field peaceably; Mai Matumba said her husband regularly gave her an acre of her own to work and an additional area for groundnuts.

Some women fought back against their husband's restrictions, drawing on a variety of techniques to win concessions. These included pleading softly, as Amai Chipo explained, being obstreperous, or even threatening divorce or suicide, according to Mai Virgina.

> In some households there were problems when the husband or wife disagreed about how to divide the land or if the man refused to give his wife some of the money from the crops. Then the woman might refuse to work in the fields the next year. Some wives went so far as to commit suicide by drinking poison, and others divorced after the man squandered all the money.[46]

---

43. Interview with Mazaradope.
44. Interviews with Amai Chaparira Paiena and Mai Jessie (female, nineties), 1 November 1997, and Morris Makaza (male, eighties), 30 October 1997.
45. Interview with Amai Mazengere (female, seventies), 24 May 1998.
46. Interviews with the women of the Dambaza family, Mai Virginia (female, nineties), 19 October 1997, and Mai Jessie. Elizabeth Schmidt argues that women also used tactics such as burning the dinner, complaining publicly, singing derisive songs, or giving names to dogs and

Isaac Maviko complained that his wife was so stubborn that he had to give her part of the field after she demanded a share. This dynamic is also evident in VaKapfunde's comments about farming practice and the division of land, when he admits to allowing his wives to each control part of the field, ironically after asserting that they followed the cropping methods that he dictated: "As for me, my wives understood that I did not want to see any other crops in the field [intercropped]. I would tell them this, or give them part of the field to plant with their crops."[47]

As this comment reveals, wives and husbands also argued over how to plant and use their land. This was an area where women were able to assert their rights particularly successfully, illustrating marital negotiation and contestation very clearly. Many women who controlled part of the main field area chose to densely intercrop their own plot, even if their husbands insisted on planting the main crops separately.[48]

Madziwa residents advanced two main reasons to explain why women continued to follow indigenous methods more closely than men. One was the small size of the individual allocations. As Levison Chavakaira explained, this encouraged women to reject other dimensions of "improved" agriculture: "The demonstrators had no way to convince the mothers to change their farming, because they were irritated, and the reason was the fields were too small."[49] Amai Chipo explained that women were forced to continue to intermingle their crops because the small plots did not leave them with enough land to cultivate the range of foodstuffs that they needed to provide for their families.

> Well, it is better to grow the crops separately, you get more that way. But it takes more land, so we women could not separate the crops as the plots we were given were too small. By mixing the crops together, we could plant many different things and get everything we needed for our children.[50]

The second reason that people put forward to explain women's preference for intercropping reflected the labour demands of different cropping systems. Women wanted to continue mixing crops together, as it reduced the amount of weeding, simplifying their lives. As VaKapfunde explained: "They [his wives] wanted to mix [crops] because they said it would be easier for us to weed the same land once than to go from here to there, to the fields of the different crops, and do the weeding."[51] Many people also said that adding

---

children that made their grievances evident, although none of the women I met mentioned these strategies. See Elizabeth Schmidt, *Peasants, Traders, and Wives: Shona Women in the History of Zimbabwe, 1870–1939* (Portsmouth, 1992).
47. Interview with VaKapfunde and VaNyamapfene.
48. Interviews with Mazaradope, Levison Chavakaira, VaKapfunde, and VaNyamapfene.
49. Interview with Chavakaira.
50. Interview with the women of the Dambaza family.
51. Interview with VaKapfunde and VaNyamapfene.

manure to their fields increased the number of weeds, requiring greater maintenance, as the seeds passed through the animals' digestive tracts.

Thus the men and women in many households were advocating different farming strategies. Men who actively pursued "improved" methods wanted to maximize production, particularly of crops that could be sold, bringing cash into the household. Women who continued to extensively intermingle different crops sought to retain the benefits of intercropping, particularly for food security, labour maximization, and crop diversity.

Household conflicts over cropping methods were not confined to the parts of the field that were designated as women's areas. Some women asserted their right to have access to land prepared by their husbands as part of the marital contract, by continuing to mix their crops, particularly pumpkins, in with the male plants in the main arable area. Many men accepted this, but serious difficulties erupted, however, when men wanted to closely follow "improved" techniques, particularly if they were collaborating with the agricultural demonstrators to earn their master farmer's certificate.[52] Amai Chipo recounted how her husband, a master farmer who had been away for several weeks, returned and was infuriated to find that his wives had planted pumpkins in the maize field. After yelling at them, he went out and uprooted all the pumpkins, ordering the women to confine their crops to their plots and follow his directions in the main field.[53]

In a very masculine exchange between three men in their sixties – VaKapfunde, VaNyamapfene, and my research assistant Solomon Mahdi – and myself, VaKapfunde described similar circumstances in his household in the early 1960s:

> *Guy Thompson*: So then how did you plant your crops after the field was individually allocated?
> *VaKapfunde*: Oh, we separated them.
> *Guy Thompson*: Did you mix anything together at all?
> *VaKapfunde*: No, we planted each crop on its own, maize in its field, millet on its own, groundnuts in their own place.
> *Guy Thompson*: What about pumpkins?
> *VaKapfunde*: [laughing] Oh pumpkins, you know, pumpkins just got in there, mixed with the maize.
> *Guy Thompson*: How?
> *VaKapfunde*: Women! You know wives, they just go and do these things, what they want to do. They just don't understand. What can you do?[54]

---

52. The master farmer's certificate was a state-sponsored programme encouraging men to work with the agricultural demonstrators and to adopt approved agricultural methods. While some men who took part in the programme did see "improved" methods as superior, others took part because certification provided access to government loans; interviews with VaMusonza and Amai Chipo.
53. Interview with the women of the Dambaza family.
54. Interview with VaKapfunde and VaNyamapfene.

VaKapfunde presented his wives as irrational, reflecting the ongoing public debates about gender roles and responsibilities. However, the women's strategy worked; as VaKapfunde said, he then began allocating part of the arable plot to each of his wives to plant as they saw fit.

Similar struggles took place in the Musonza household while VaMusonza was working towards recognition as a master farmer in the late 1950s. Despite his objections, his wife continued to plant pumpkins in the maize field. VaMusonza, however, was unwilling to face the consequences of confronting his wife and declaring that she could not intercrop pumpkins. Instead, he went out at night and cut the pumpkin vines, so that the plants would mysteriously wither and die. "Clean" fields helped him to earn his master farmer's badge quickly, so that after a few years the pumpkins flourished, once the demonstrators were no longer intensely supervising the household's plot.[55] This incident is a prime example of how farming strategies of men and women differed, as well as of the subtle, shifting balance of power within a household.

While gender dynamics in this period were strongly influenced by the state's efforts to control peasant production, growing commercialization continued to play an important role, as it had in the 1930s and 1940s. The struggles over control of crops and income continued, lying at the root of many of the conflicts over allocation of the household field to different crops. Women asserted their right to plant their crops and earn income from them, while many men tried to maximize their cash returns by increasing the area planted to maize. More direct household struggles over money and resources also flared up, often tied to farming, as Morris Makaza explained. "Men and women troubled each other after they sold their crops, and men will eat [spend] some of the money drinking beer. Some ended up going to the chief and asking for divorces, especially the young couples!"[56] My conversation with VaKapfunde, VaNyamapfene, and Solomon Mahdi also illustrated these dynamics well:

> *Guy Thompson:* So how did you and your wife handle money as it became more important?
> *Solomon Mahdi:* Aha, here comes the story that results in fights! That is, how did you keep money?
> *VaKapfunde:* When I sold my crops, I would give part of the money to my wife. When she sold some of her crops, she would keep all the money and use it herself.
> *Guy Thompson:* What did she use the money for?
> *VaKapfunde:* Well she would use it for her expenses – for dresses, plates, and pots, and also for food for the family like bread.

55. Interview with Bowas Musonza.
56. Interviews with Makaza, Mai Kondo, VaHasve (male, nineties), 9 October 1997, and Amai Mushamba (female, eighties), 10 November 1997.

VaNyamapfene: Similar things happened when we were buying seed. I went to buy the seed. If I gave money to my wife to buy the seed, she would return and say, "These seeds are not yours, these are for me".[57]

Implied in these comments is the idea that claims to crops and other resources are tied to labour. Women in households that did not work the land collaboratively expected part of the income from the primary male crop, maize, as they did much of the work of planting, weeding and harvesting it. They were not, however, willing to share income from their own crops if their husband did little more than till the soil, which women considered to be part of a man's marital obligations.

1958–1965: EVASION, CONFLICT, AND RESISTANCE

When the NLHA was initially being implemented, peasants tried to evade and question bureaucrats' orders, but in the late 1950s it became clear that the state would strictly enforce the law. As the different provisions of the act were imposed in Madziwa the pressures on peasants intensified, triggering growing anger with officials. Mai Matumba recalled this shift, arguing that "They [officials] distressed us by changing where we could live. People ended up saying 'We don't want these demonstrators! We want to stay living the way we are!'."[58] As their resentment grew, residents turned to open protest and angry confrontations with agricultural officers, although complaints often focused on broader colonial restrictions, not just the provisions of the NLHA being enforced in the reserves.

Much of the initiative in Madziwa and other rural areas came from young men and women, reflecting the demands placed on them by their elders and the restrictions of the NLHA. By turning to overt resistance, young people challenged rural age and gender hierarchies, inversions that left deep rifts in communities, so that many people in Madziwa were reluctant to discuss the turmoil of the early 1960s with me. Shingaidzo Madeve, who was in her forties at the time of the demonstrations, denied that there had been confrontations:

Guy Thompson: Did people shout and chase the demonstrators when they came to cut the fields and cattle?
Shingaidzo Madeve: There was no opportunity to do that, we could only agree.
Guy Thompson: Why was that?
Shingaidzo Madeve: They were feared! A police officer, an agricultural demonstrator, a child [assistant] of the chief, we were afraid of all of them![59]

---

57. Interview with VaKapfunde and VaNyamapfene.
58. Interview with Mai Matumba.
59. Interview with Shingaidzo Madeve.

Eventually I met a few people who would discuss the protests, such as VaHore, who described how residents threatened agricultural staff.

> People resisted having to dig contour ridges as they were a lot of work, an awful lot of work. Some even chased the agricultural demonstrators, waving axes and tools so that they ran away! It was only after the Native Commissioner [NC] intervened that the agricultural demonstrators were able to come back.[60]

Some of the people who were willing to discuss these angry confrontations and the later sabotage efforts directed against white farms and state institutions in the district were relative outsiders, retired teachers, and others who had arranged to settle in Madziwa but did not have deep social ties in the community. The others were men who had taken part in the protests, who spoke with pride of their activities in their teens and early twenties. But these men generally denied that women had been involved, I think reflecting their struggles with their wives and children over the next forty years. I also suspect that these partial silences, and the general reluctance to discuss the protests, were rooted in the painful memories of the gender and generational inversions, aspects of the past that people were reluctant to share with an outsider.[61]

State records clearly show that there were a number of confrontations in Madziwa. The NC for the area reported in 1961 that: "Demonstrators and Land Development Officers were tagged with the label 'policemen' and their role as advisors was lost sight of. The [agricultural] demonstrators themselves appeared to have lost heart and were in conflict with the people."[62] Later he observed that the last two years had both seen "vicious political agitation that seeks to breed any sort of opposition to Government as a means to achieve its end".[63]

In the early 1960s, similar reports came in from forty-one of the colony's forty-four districts, involving protests, defiance of official orders, and open confrontation. The NC responsible for Mhondoro Reserve described developments there:

> More and more of what the people called "Freedom Farming" took place. This "Freedom Farming" took the form of ploughing outside demarcated areas, ploughing up and over contours, drainstrips, demarcated waterways and so on.

---

60. Interview with VaHore, 31 May 1998.

61. These painful memories also likely reflect later disruptions, as Madziwa was very deeply involved in the liberation war. Guerrillas entered the reserve in 1971 or 1972, and the area was largely under the control of ZANU forces until independence. The 1970s were therefore marked by further generational and gendered conflicts, particularly as young men joined the guerrilla forces.

62. NAZ S2827/2/2/8, III, Report of the Native Commissioner, Shamva, for the Year Ending 31.12.1961, p. 3.

63. *Ibid.*, p. 17.

Pressure of other multifarious duties prevented as much attention being paid to these matters as should have been.[64]

There were also frequent reports of sabotage directed against government institutions and other symbols of settler control, such as Land Development Officers' offices, NLHA records, cattle dips, phone lines, chiefs' courts and offices, and schools.[65]

As the protests spread in 1961, the white minority government worried that it was losing control of the countryside. It deployed the police and army in the reserves, slowed NLHA implementation, and ordered a series of sweeping policy reviews to find ways to contain opposition. In February 1962, the cabinet suspended NLHA implementation, slashed funding for African agricultural services, and gave chiefs the power to allocate arable plots in the designated grazing areas to reduce the grievances over access to land.[66] The wave of protests, defiance, and challenges to government authority slowed, partly because the state was no longer antagonizing people by trying to enforce the NLHA and "improved" farming methods.

While these protests, driven by tensions along generational and gender lines, forced the settler regime dramatically to reduce state intervention in peasant landholding and production methods, they did little to address the broader constraints – and options – brought by colonial rule. Moreover, while the protests in Madziwa and other reserves could be seen as a simple confrontation between peasants and the state, I would argue that the dynamics were much more complicated. Young men and women initiated overt resistance to challenge their elders as well as the white minority government. These protests reflected more than the uneven impact of the NLHA and "improved" agriculture; rather, their roots lay in the social disruptions brought by colonial rule and integration into global markets, which led peasants to reshape production practices, agricultural strategies, and their environmental management techniques.

64. NAZ S2827/2/2/8, II, Report of the NC Hartley, for the year ended 31.12.61, pp. 16–17.
65. NAZ S2827/2/2/8, I, Report of the NC Nkai for the Year Ended 31.12.1961, pp. 9, 15. Report of the NC Ndanga, p. 10. For other instances of sabotage including arson and attacks on dip tanks and hide sheds, see the annual reports in the three volumes of this file for Makoni, Mangwende, Shabani, and Umtali. See also Ngwabi Bhebe, "The National Struggle, 1957–62", in C. Banana (ed.), *Turmoil and Tenacity: Zimbabwe 1890–1980* (Harare, 1989), p. 97.
66. NAZ S3240/21 SRC (61) 55th Meeting of the Cabinet, 3 October 1961, pp. 6–11; NAZ S3240/21 SRC (62) 7th Meeting of the Cabinet, 2 February 1962, pp. 6–8; NAZ S3240/22, SRC (62), 16th Meeting of the Cabinet, 22 March 1962, p. 3; NAZ Records Centre Box 84526 DSD 38/1, "Special NAAB Meeting, 20–22 March 1961", pp. 1–3; Southern Rhodesia, *Financial Statements, 1961–1962* (Salisbury, 1962), p. 7; Southern Rhodesia, *Financial Statements, 1962–1963* (Salisbury, 1963), p. 7; and NAZ Records Centre Box 98229 1195/DSD.39/10/2 Working Party D Paper 8.

IRSH 55 (2010), Supplement, pp. 203–233 doi:10.1017/S0020859010000556
© 2010 Internationaal Instituut voor Sociale Geschiedenis

Hydro-businesses: National and Global Demands on the São Francisco River Basin Environment of Brazil*

LUCIGLEIDE NERY NASCIMENTO

Department of Natural Resources and the Environment,
University of New Hampshire

E-mail: LNN_UNH@hotmail.com

MIMI LARSEN BECKER

Department of Natural Resources and the Environment,
University of New Hampshire

E-mail: mimi.becker@unh.edu

SUMMARY: The São Francisco River provided very obvious, close-by forms of sustenance for local communities. Beginning in the mid-1950s, the river became the place
for large hydro-electric facilities, large-scale flooding, and population resettlement.
A decade later, the federal government began working on pilot irrigation projects that
would lead to areas described today as the Brazilian California. Hydro-power for
Brazilian cities such as Recife and Salvador and irrigation for grapes and mangoes
destined for the United States and Europe are among the eco-system services this river
supplies. The purpose of federal policies for the north-east went beyond mitigation
of the consequences of droughts, the hydraulic approach, and started to follow an
economic approach based upon development; as a consequence, river and user came
to be distant from one another. The two major intensive uses of the river, electricity
and irrigation, threaten the long-term sustainability of this system.

* The authors acknowledge the support from the American Association of University Women
for an international doctoral fellowship and from the Graduate School of the University of
New Hampshire for a dissertation year fellowship. The authors thank the Ruth Farrington
Fund of the Department of Natural Resources and the Environment, the Natural Resources and
Earth Systems Science Ph.D. Program, and the Graduate School of the University of New
Hampshire for travel support to present the first version of this paper at the First World
Congress of Environmental History, held in Copenhagen and Malmö, 4–8 August 2009. We are
grateful for the referees' suggestions for improvements. Comments and questions should be
addressed to Lucigleide Nascimento.

INTRODUCTION

"[U]nder natural conditions nothing is ever just right: it is always too big or too little, too steep or too flat, too hot or too cold, too wet or too dry." The human use of the water resources of the São Francisco River (SFR) has long shaped the environment of the basin and of cities and towns along its course. The phrase quoted above was heard by an early sanitary engineer and environmentalist, the American Herman Baity, while working on improvements in water and sanitation access in the north-east of Brazil.[1] The thought justified the transformation of nature pushed by the national elites from 1950s onward. An alleged imperfect nature provided the means for progress and development of hydro-power and irrigated agriculture. But the Brazilian journey toward perfection has negatively impacted those who inhabited the edges of this waterway.

Starting in the 1870s and lasting a century, the use of vegetation as steamboat fuel deforested and destroyed the riparian and inland forests of the Caatinga and Cerrado biomes.[2] Extensive livestock ranching, rain-fed farming, and riparian agriculture naturally fertilized by the seasonal rise and fall of the river's water existed in the valley. The local economy included fishing and gathering. Erosion resulting from the natural processes of the basin and from land use deposited sediments in the river bed. Silting has been a major problem. In addition, other sources of pollution exist. The river has been the sink for industrial and domestic discharges, nutrients and pesticides run-off, and leaching through the soil profile.

Beginning in the mid-1950s, the river became the place for large hydro-electric facilities and flooding. The construction of infrastructure for river-flow control, hydro-power generation, and a steady water flow for

---

1. Quoted in Herman G. Baity, *Relatório do Serviço Especial de Saúde Pública (SESP) sôbre o Vale do São Francisco* (Rio de Janeiro, 1951), p. 159. According to Kastleman, Herman G. Baity received the first ever doctorate in sanitary engineering in the United States. He is also seen as a pioneer environmentalist because of his recognition of the importance of clean water and sanitation systems. He spent seventeen months in Brazil working on US-funded projects to improve health and sanitation; Linda Kastleman, "H.G. Baity: A Pioneering Environmentalist", *Carolina Public Health*, Fall (2007), p. 8.

2. Caatinga occupies about 734,478 sq. km, 11 per cent of the national territory, mostly in the Brazilian north-east. A long dry season, the irregularity and low volume of rainfall (400–600 mm), and the existence of intermittent and seasonal rivers characterize this biome. Cerrado extends over about 21 per cent of the country's land area, predominantly in the nation's central zone. Temperatures range from 72°F to 81°F (22°C to 27°C) and the annual rainfall is on average 1,500 mm. The Cerrado is rich in biodiversity. See Ministério do Meio Ambiente do Brasil, *Áreas Prioritárias para Conservação, Uso Sustentável e Repartição de Benefícios da Biodiversidade Brasileira* (Brasília, 2007); Carlos A. Klink and Ricardo B Machado, "Conservation of the Brazilian Cerrado", *Conservation Biology*, 19 (2005), pp. 707–713. On the history of navigation, see Zanoni Neves, "Rio São Francisco: Os Primeiros Navegantes e o Sistema Econômico Regional", *Ciência Hoje*, 32:192 (2003), pp. 30–35, and *idem, Na Carreira do Rio São Francisco: Trabalho e Sociabilidade dos Vapozeiros* (Belo Horizonte, 2006).

irrigation, transformed the river and basin. The once freely flowing waterway was turned into a sequence of managed lakes. These environmental changes impaired fish migration, impacting aquatic species and fishing.[3] The flow alterations associated with the effects of mining and agriculture affected other uses, such as leisure-aesthetic enjoyment. For example, in Pirapora the distorted river's water and sediment turned small natural waterfalls used for social recreation into rocks covered by vegetation. In 2007, the Pirapora government dredged the river to remove silt and plants.[4]

The creation and operation of dams required resettlement, as in the case of the Sobradinho, of more than 60,000 people and the relocation of towns including Remanso and Casa Nova.[5] In-migration also impacted municipalities. Population and city growth rose in the "poles" of development and urban zones.[6] Secondary-level cities located at these clusters now host individuals and families from nearby zones who leave their homes as they are attracted by the prospect of jobs in corporate agriculture. In the past, their destinations had been mega-cities such as São Paulo.

Cities such as Juazeiro, Petrolina, and the surrounding towns of the lower-middle São Francisco River Basin (SFRB) have felt the consequences of the reshaped and reshaping environment. Between 1972 and 1978 the construction of the Sobradinho hydro-power complex interrupted navigation 40 kilometers downstream.[7] The works impacted the once busy port of Juazeiro, which had already lost some importance due to road transport and navigation problems caused by silting and low water. After its construction, the dam continued to spur the decline in navigation because the new environment of a wide, deep, windy, and wavy reservoir impaired the use of existing boats.[8] The old vessels were not suitable for the reservoir. They capsized.

3. Yoshimi Sato and Hugo P. Godinho, "Migratory Fishes of the São Francisco River", in Joachim Carolsfeld *et al.* (eds), *Migratory Fishes of South America: Biology, Fisheries and Conservation Status* (Ottawa [etc.], 2004), pp. 195–232.

4. Luiz Ribeiro, "Começa Obra de Desassoreamento do Rio São Francisco em Pirapora", *Jornal do Meio Ambiente* (Niterói, 2007), available at http://www.portaldomeioambiente. org.br, last accessed on 19 April 2010.

5. Jane L. Collins and Greta R. Krippner, "Permanent Labor Contracts in Agriculture: Flexibility and Subordination in a New Export Crop", *Comparative Studies in Society and History*, 41 (1999), pp. 510–534.

6. Instituto Brasileiro de Geografia e Estatística, *Censo Demográfico 2000: Migração e Deslocamento – Resultados da Amostra* (Rio de Janeiro, 2000); Comitê da Bacia Hidrográfica do Rio São Francisco, *Plano de Recursos Hídricos da Bacia Hidrográfica do Rio São Francisco* (Salvador, 2004).

7. Agência Nacional de Águas *et al.*, *Projeto de Gerenciamento Integrado das Atividades Desenvolvidas em Terra na Bacia do São Francisco ANA/GEF/PNUMA/OEA – Subprojeto 4.5* (São Paulo, 2003), p. 105.

8. Superintendência de Desenvolvimento do Nordeste – SUDENE, *Plano de Aproveitamento Integrado dos Recursos Hídricos do Nordeste do Brasil – Fase I – Estudo de Demandas – Navegação Interior – Anexo V* (Recife, 1980).

Inhabitants of the watershed traditionally practiced small-scale irrigation. But in 1968 the federal government began working on pilot irrigation projects that would lead to large areas being described as the Brazilian California.[9] Irrigated agriculture replaced the local vegetation with orchards. Starting in the 1970s, various regions of Brazil consumed tomatoes from the valley and manufactured tomato sauce produced from local irrigated agriculture by the food-processing industry. In the late 1980s, fruit from the basin reached international consumers. The United States and Europe began importing grapes and mangoes. The western part of Bahia state in the SFR watershed is the largest producer of soya beans in the north-east, sending that commodity overseas.[10]

In this post-1950 era, hydro-businesses, meaning the use of water for entrepreneurial purposes – hydro-power and irrigated agriculture – shaped and reshape communities and the natural setting of the SFRB. Hydro-businesses benefit from direct and indirect governmental support, in the form, for instance, of subsidies, dams, and roads. They also build upon unpaid environmental services, such as hydro-resources. In this area of Brazil, water is a limiting factor and its scarcity already poses conflicts among its users (e.g. irrigation vs hydro-power, fishing vs hydro-power). The environmental consequences are felt locally. But their origins are located in regional, national, and international contexts.

This article addresses two questions: how have local communities been transformed in order to meet national and international demands? And how have the two major uses of the river (electricity and irrigation) coexisted and influenced other activities?[11] The environmental history of

9. According to Nanne, "the waters of the São Francisco River are producing a new promised land in northeastern Brazil. Instead of milk and honey, one finds the sweetest and juiciest fruits ever grown in the country. The key to this agricultural success is irrigation, which, in a little more than a decade, has transformed Brazil's hot, arid *sertão* region into a verdant orchard. The controlled water flow makes fruit mature more quickly and allows for larger and more frequent harvests. In 1993, the region produced 80,000 tons of fruit, earning some $40 million for its 30 exporters"; Kaíke Nanne, "Notes on the Sciences: 'California' in Brazil", *World Press Review*, 41:1 (1994), p. 44. In 2008, it produced more than a million tons; Agência Sebrae, "Vale do São Francisco dobra Exportação de Frutas", in *Abanorte* (Janaúba, 2009), available at http://www.abanorte.com.br/noticias/vale-do-sao-francisco-dobra-exportacao-de-frutas, last accessed on 19 April 2010.

10. Ministério da Agricultura, Pecuária e Abastecimento – MAPA, "Agronegócio Brasileiro: Uma Oportunidade de Investimentos" (Brasília, 2004), available at http://www.agricultura.gov.br, last accessed on 19 April 2010; Tânia Bacelar de Araújo, "Northeast, Northeasts: What Northeast?", *Latin American Perspectives*, 31:2 (2004), pp. 16–41.

11. Primary data were drawn from observations of the river and the surrounding environment, and from information gathered through seventy-six open-ended interviews with river users, managers, and researchers. Secondary data have been gathered by means of virtual and in-person visits to libraries located at, among other places, federal, state, and municipal agencies, non-governmental organizations, and universities. Data triangulation provided answers for the

the SFRB reveals a stark shift in the use of the waterway. The pre-1950 period illustrates a close-knit relationship between users and the body of water, typical of a more basic survival approach. The river resources were used mainly by the local communities. In the post-1950 era, a more corporative perspective emerged and became the enforced alternative. The river yielded profits to those far away. The large urban centers of Brazil consumed hydro-power, and in the later 1980s agricultural products from irrigated zones of the valley supplied national and international markets. The idea of an "agro-exporter nation" on the path of "national development" imposed environmental (e.g. reshaped environment), economic, and social changes upon locals. The new modus operandi focused upon hydro-power to further industrialization, urbanization, and large-scale agriculture.

THE CONTEXTUAL MAP

Historically, Brazil has played the role of a primary product exporter, beginning in the sixteenth century with valuable hard woods. Over the centuries, many other agricultural products followed, including sugar, coffee, tobacco, rubber, and cocoa. The period between 1880 and 1913 marked the culmination of Brazil's long history as solely a supplier of tropical products.[12] At the beginning of the twentieth century, coffee and rubber were the most important Brazilian export items. But the collapse of the coffee export sector was one of the many consequences of the Great Depression. The world crisis worsened Brazil's financial condition. It also showed that the view of Brazil as an agro-exporter nation was not shared by all members of society. Producers (coffee and rubber interests, for instance) disagreed among themselves and some sectors wanted to modernize the nation.[13]

Indeed, the world economic crisis of the 1930s provided a crucial moment for deepening Brazil's import-substituting industrialization which had begun in the late nineteenth century. But while the agro-commercial elites fought to limit industrialization, their opponents, technocrats in state bureaucracies, aspiring industrialists, and progressive commercial strata, struggled for its protection. The collapse of the world coffee market in the 1930s can be pointed to as the defining moment of Brazil's industrial development.

Between the 1930s and the early 1990s the state provided, among other things, investment in basic inputs and infrastructure. The pro-growth

research questions. As a rule, Lucigleide Nascimento translated all the quotations from the interviews and the non-English literature.

12. Donald Coes, "Brazil", in Arthur Lewis (ed.), *Tropical Development 1880–1913* (Evanston, IL, 1970), pp. 100–127.

13. Steven Topik, "The State's Contribution to the Development of Brazil's Internal Economy, 1850–1930", *The Hispanic American Historical Review*, 65 (1985), pp. 203–228.

state developed the areas which the private sector did not want or could not undertake.[14] Some sectors were thought to be the state's business. The 1934 Constitution (Articles 118 and 119) and 1934 Water Code (Articles 43, 63, and 139) established, for instance, that industrial use of waters, such as for hydro-power, should be undertaken or overseen by the state.[15]

Between 1945 and 1979 governmental economic policy was still based upon the 1930s' idea of national development (*Nacional-desenvolvimentismo*).[16] That time frame included two major periods. From post-World War II to the beginning of the 1960s, a permit system and high tariffs imposed restrictions on imported products. The nation used an import substitution model. The second phase, between 1961 and 1979, was that of the export industrialization model, which ended up dominating until 1989. During this period, Brazil expanded its sales abroad of manufactured items.[17] The import substitution and export industrialization paradigms centered upon industrialization and urbanization, which required vast supplies of electric power.

But Brazil never stopped being an agro-exporter nation. From 1960 to the mid-1980s, the state also instigated and regulated the modernization of agriculture.[18] The federal government provided rural credit, fixed prices, and created research institutions such as the Brazilian Agricultural Research Corporation (EMBRAPA) in 1972. The support spurred the formation of agro-industrial complexes. Selected areas and programs received special concessions, such as ethanol production.[19] The nation has also fought against the protectionism of the developed nations and their domestic and export subsidies and import restrictions. In the era of climate change, biofuels became the rising star in the country's export list, though they are now coming under increasing criticism. Thus, agribusiness has continued to be an important sector of the national economy.

---

14. Jeff Frieden, "Third World Indebted Industrialization: International Finance and State Capitalism in Mexico, Brazil, Algeria, and South Korea", *International Organization*, 35 (1981), pp. 407–431.

15. Senado Federal do Brasil, *Código de Águas (1934) e Legislação Correlata* (Brasília, 2003); Presidência da República Federativa do Brasil, *Legislação: Constituição da República Federativa do Brasil de 1934*, available at http://www.presidencia.gov.br, last accessed on 19 April 2010.

16. Heloisa Conceição Machado da Silva, "Deterioração dos Termos de Intercâmbio, Substituição de Importações, Industrialização e Substituição de Exportações: A Política de Comércio Exterior Brasileira de 1945 a 1979", *Revista Brasileira de Política Internacional*, 46 (2003), pp. 39–65.

17. *Ibid.*; Frieden, "Third World Indebted Industrialization".

18. Arilson Favareto, "Agricultores, Trabalhadores: Os Trinta Anos do Novo Sindicalismo Rural no Brasil", *Revista Brasileira de Ciências Sociais*, 21 (2006), pp. 27–44.

19. *Ibid.*; Jodenir Calixto Teixeira, "Modernização da Agricultura no Brasil: Impactos Econômicos, Sociais e Ambientais", *Revista Eletrônica da Associação dos Geógrafos Brasileiros – Seção Três Lagoas*, 2:2 (2005), pp. 21–42.

THE NORTH-EAST AND THE SÃO FRANCISCO RIVER VALLEY

European explorers discovered the mouth of the SFR in 1501. Two main human currents conquered the valley from the north to the south of the basin and in the opposite direction, at the end of the sixteenth and seventeenth centuries respectively. Both waves established cattle ranches, which supported the expansion of the human population in the area.[20] Indigenous native people, white Europeans, and escaped and African slaves inhabited the basin during Brazil's colonial times.[21]

The 2,700-kilometer-long river rises in the mountains of Minas Gerais (Figure 1 overleaf). In its northern and then eastern journey to the Atlantic Ocean 168 tributaries join the São Francisco. The SFR system drains an area the size of Spain, Portugal, and Denmark, being 57 per cent located in a drought-prone semi-arid climatic zone. The scarcity of the precious resource made water into an element of concern in the valley, which contains about 8 per cent of Brazil's territory and residents. The Upper SFR in the south-east of the nation occupies 16 per cent of the area of the watershed and almost one-half of the total inhabitants of the basin, and includes the large metropolitan zone of Belo Horizonte.[22]

The significance of the SFR has included spiritual, cultural, ecological, and economic elements and meanings for the local, regional, and national populations. The cultural and social concepts relate fundamentally to the watercourse being a provider of environmental goods and services for subsistence: fish, water, and the fertility of riparian zones due to the replenishment of nutrients that the muddy water of the river leaves behind after floods. The affectionate name given to the river, "Velho Chico" (Old Francisco), captures the spiritual link. Faith and mythology have been important elements in the life of the SFRB's populations.[23]

Aquatic activities have included aesthetic enjoyment, swimming, watching steamship navigation, or simply gazing at the river. The SFR in Pirapora is Minas Gerais's beach. The state is landlocked. River transportation has been

20. Raymond E. Crist, "Cultural Crosscurrents in the Valley of the Rio São Francisco", *Geographical Review*, 34 (1944), pp. 587–612; Instituto Brasileiro de Geografia e Estatística – IBGE, *Enciclopédia dos Municípios Brasileiros – Grande Região Leste (O São Francisco)* (Rio de Janeiro, 1960); Geraldo Rocha, *O Rio São Francisco: Fator Precípuo da Existência do Brasil*, 3rd edn (São Paulo, 1983).
21. Companhia de Desenvolvimento do Vale do São Francisco – CODEVASF, *São Francisco o Rio da Unidade* (Brasília, 1978).
22. Comitê da Bacia Hidrográfica do Rio São Francisco, *Plano de Recursos Hídricos da Bacia*.
23. Daniel R. Gross, "Ritual and Conformity: A Religious Pilgrimage to Northeastern Brazil", *Ethnology*, 10 (1971), pp. 129–148; Antônio Barbosa, "Situação Geopolítica", in *idem*, *Bom Jesus da Lapa: Antes de Monsenhor Turíbio, no Tempo do Monsenhor Turíbio, Depois de Monsenhor Turíbio* (Rio de Janeiro, 1995), pp. 30–81.

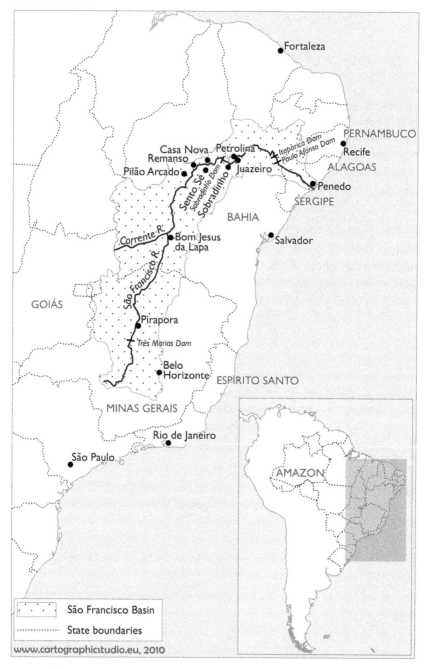

Figure 1. The extension and location of the São Francisco River and Basin in relation to the Brazilian territory.

an essential service, carrying everything: cargo, cattle, salt, fibers, mail, people, and money.[24] A variety of vessels have traveled the SFR's waters – individual canoes (*canoas*), two or more canoes tied together by leather strips (*ajoujos*), sailboats, ferries, barges, tug-boats, and ships. Manpower as oarsmen or *remeiros*, wood stokers on steamers, and the entire crew or *vapozeiros*, in combination with diesel, wind, and river currents were the driving forces behind navigation.[25] Mules in pack trains and then railroads linked the valley to the outside "developed" world.[26] In the late 1950s, Minas Gerais had the highest number of trucks in the valley. However, river navigation and animals were still the major form of transportation for the poor in the watershed area.[27] The São Francisco Basin and the hinterland of the north-east known as Sertão provided raw material and received manufactured and food products.[28] Processing and manufacture had always been a minor activity in the basin.[29]

Those living in the riparian zones, *beiradeiros*, or on the river bank's edges, *barranqueiros*, had a close link to the river.[30] In interviews, one hears how they personify the river, as described by a Pirapora fisherman: "my parents fished and grew crops with *Chico*".[31] River people regarded the river as a paternal and spiritual being. As in real life, in one of his fictional literary works, *Grande Sertão: Veredas*, Guimarães Rosa noted a canoe man requesting the river's blessing.[32] In his classic 1950s three-volume

24. Luiz Flôres de Moraes Rego, *O Valle do São Francisco: Ensaio de Monographia Geographica – Separata da Revista do Museu Paulista da Universidade de S. Paulo – Tomo XX* (São Paulo, 1936); Marcel Gautherot and Lélia Coelho Frota, *Rio São Francisco, Recôncavo e Salvador* (Rio de Janeiro, 1995).
25. Guilherme Fernando Halfeld, *Atlas e Relatório Concernente a Exploração do Rio de S. Francisco desde a Cachoeira da Pirapóra até ao Oceano Atlântico*, 2nd edn (São Paulo, 1994); Richard F. Burton, *Explorations of the Highlands of the Brazil with a Full Account of the Gold and Diamond Mines* (São Paulo, 1977); Francisco Vicente Vianna, *Memoir of the State of Bahia* (Salvador, 1893); "A Princesa do Sertão da Bahia: Um Documento da Importância de Juazeiro, a Bella Cidade sob a Coragem do São Francisco", *Bahia Illustrada*, April 1919; Murílo Carvalho and Ronaldo Kotscho, *O Vale do São Francisco: Uma Viagem de Canoa, de Minas Gerais ao Oceano Atlântico* (n.p., 1989); Zanoni Neves, *Navegantes da Integraçã: Os Remeiros do Rio São Francisco* (Belo Horizonte, 1998), and *idem*, *Na Carreira do Rio São Francisco*.
26. The E.F. Bahia–S. Francisco railroad connected Juazeiro to Salvador in 1894; see *Bahia Illustrada*, "A Princesa do Sertão da Bahia". According to President Nilo Peçanha's address to the Brazilian Congress, the Central do Brasil railroad met the São Francisco River in 1910. See José Honório Rodrigues, "Aspirações e Interesses do Brasil", *Journal of Inter-American Studies*, 3 (1961), pp. 147–185.
27. Instituto Brasileiro de Geografia e Estatística, *Enciclopédia dos Municípios Brasileiros*; Donald Pierson, *O Homem no Vale do São Francisco*, 3 vols (Rio de Janeiro, 1972), II.
28. Aroldo de Azevedo, *Brasil a Terra e o Homem: As Bases Físicas*, 2nd edn (São Paulo, 1968).
29. Pierson, *O Homem no Vale do São Francisco*, III.
30. Burton, *Explorations of the Highlands of the Brazil*; Azevedo, *Brasil a Terra e o Homem*; Maureen Bisilliat, *Terras do Rio de São Francisco* (n.p., 1986).
31. Fisherman and Fishermens' Association staff, interview, 15 May 2007, Pirapora, Minas Gerais.
32. João Guimarães Rosa, *Grande Sertão: Veredas* (São Paulo, 1983).

Figure 2. Steamboat navigation in the São Francisco River. Based upon other steamboat pictures, it is from the 1930s. The steamships carried cargo, and first- and second-class passengers. Fuel occupied a large space. Steamers made frequent stops along the river to buy wood.
Source: Agência A Tarde de Notícias, Salvador, Bahia, Brazil. Empresa Editora A Tarde S.A. Used with permission.

study of the river valley, *O Homem no Vale do São Francisco*, Pierson wrote about the transference of knowledge from adults to children.[33] Indeed, the basin has been the context for the formation of the identity of several river-related groups, such as fishermen, small-scale riparian subsistence farmers, and boatmen (including *remeiros* and *vapozeiros*). They shared the *beiradeiro/barranqueiro* values and way of life, as shown by the two illustrations from Bahia's major daily newspaper (Figures 2 and 3). The SFRB was their universe. My interviewees said that the stream is the "soul" of those who inhabit its riparian zone.[34] The waterway was their "left and right arms"[35] and "source of life" and livelihood.[36] The "traditional ecological knowledge" that was transferred throughout generations influenced their beliefs.[37]

33. Pierson, *O Homem no Vale do São Francisco*, III.
34. Historian, interview, 17 May 2007, Pirapora, Minas Gerais.
35. Fisherman 2, interview, 18 May 2007, Pirapora, Minas Gerais.
36. Small farmer in irrigated agriculture, interview, 13 June 2007, Petrolina, Pernambuco.
37. Fikret Berkes, Johan Colding, and Carl Folke, "Rediscovery of Traditional Ecological Knowledge as Adaptive Management", *Ecological Applications*, 10 (2000), pp. 1251–1262, 1252.

Figure 3. The Surubim fish, a prized native species of the São Francisco. The picture was republished on 30 March 1990. The reduction in population and size of this fish has been an indicator of the environmental degradation of local aquatic ecosystems.
Source: Agência A Tarde de Notícias, Salvador, Bahia, Brazil. Empresa Editora A Tarde S.A. Used with permission.

Interviewees' memories portray the SFR as a multiple-use resource. They especially mentioned its long history as a source of transportation, fish, and water. The recollections of older generations of the past sixty years depict a healthier, deeper, and richer fish- and shrimp-stocked river than today. It helped them survive even during difficult times. Droughts and inundations occurred, but locals understood the river. They reported that "floods used to bring fish",[38] and they also knew how, when, and where to fish, farm, and navigate *Chico*'s waters. The interviewees have observed the environmental degradation of the river, and the trend of impaired uses throughout time (in relation for instance to navigation, fishing, and the lack of flooding of lagoons – which had allowed fish growth – and of rice fields).

Nevertheless, traditional life in riparian municipalities was full of challenges. Navigation was difficult especially during droughts and low-water seasons. Boats got stranded on sandbanks and could not access docking sites. Lack of precipitation did not allow inland rain-fed fields and reduced the yields in riparian zones. The river's natural characteristics impaired navigation too. In some sections, namely Pirapora and Sobradinho,

38. Boat owner, interview, 16 January 2007, Penedo, Alagoas.

waterfalls and rapids formed the river's bed and channel. Besides, silting from deforestation and agriculture worsened the problem of the creation of sediment banks, *c'roas*. Deficient infrastructure made small-scale growers vulnerable; when not losing their crops totally, producers needed to sell the harvest for low prices due to the impossibility of access to alternative buyers. Floods used to fertilize and irrigate the land for riparian agriculture, but extreme events also destroyed fields, towns, and urban infrastructure along the waterway.[39] Federal agencies built walls to protect the locals from the river.

As in the nineteenth century, El Niños brought droughts, thus influencing the ecology and economy in the north-east of Brazil, as in various other parts of the world.[40] During the 1877–1879 and 1951 droughts, alternatives implemented for the north-east followed the technical hydraulic approach: engineering solutions to provide access to water. The federal government funded the construction of water reservoirs in different parts of the region. Nevertheless, not many people had access to the precious resource even though the SFR was one of the few steady sources of water. The semi-arid zone covered a vast area of low demographic density. Drought relief programs did not reach everyone. Besides, the resource was often diverted into the hands of few, and distributed to people on the basis of political criteria.[41] Construction of infrastructure for public water supply on private lands exemplified these irregularities.

The 1940s' and early 1950s' images and studies of the São Francisco Basin's towns and cities demonstrate the precarious access of the population to fresh water. In all too many instances, the water supply came from shallow wells, small precipitation retention reservoirs, and intermittent creeks and streams, and was produced by the labor of "*aguadeiros*" or "*botadeiras de água*", people who collected small volumes of water from the SFR and other bodies of water and sold them to households. This activity was both a necessary part of women's obligations and a paid occupation for others. Some cities had water delivered only to public fountains, *chafarizes*. Water carriers also obtained the resource from that infrastructure. They carried water in clay containers, large cans, and inside of a pumpkin-like fruit, on their head or in their hands. Mules and cattle carts carried barrels of water.[42]

---

39. Instituto Brasileiro de Geografia e Estatística, *Enciclopédia dos Municípios Brasileiros*.

40. Mike Davis, *Late Victorian Holocausts: El Niño Famines and the Making of the Third World* (London, 2001).

41. Mary Lorena Kenny, "Drought, Clientalism, Fatalism and Fear in Northeast Brazil", *Ethics, Place and Environment*, 5 (2002), pp. 123–134.

42. Gautherot and Frota, *Rio São Francisco, Recôncavo e Salvador*; Baity, *Relatório do Serviço Especial de Saúde Pública*; Pierson, *O Homem no Vale do São Francisco*, I.

Already, in the 1950s, changes in water provision arrived with the establishment of new autonomous organizations.[43] Influenced by a Brazil–United States (Rockefeller Foundation) accord, and with the support of the development agency for the valley, the Comissão do Vale do São Francisco (CVSF), the federal health agency, the Serviço de Saúde Pública (SESP), implemented partnerships with the governments of several municipalities to build or improve water treatment stations, leading to the creation of independent public water providers' systems, the Serviço Autônomo de Água e Esgoto (SAAE). Pirapora, Bom Jesus da Lapa, Juazeiro, and Penedo benefited from that intervention.[44] The Chico's water and SAAE systems still provide the resource for those riverside towns. Other arrangements existed in several places. For example, the CVSF funded the drilling of wells to supply water to rural populations.[45]

The river granted obvious, close-by forms of physical and spiritual sustenance. A local interaction of river environment and human beings existed. "The population had the natural knowledge of the time [...] the fishing time, the harvest time [...]".[46] The long-term droughts, which afflict the basin every nine to twelve years, influenced the human–river environment link. The vast literature on drought and the north-east of Brazil argues that the scarcity of water drew many to riparian zones, closer to the river.[47]

After the 1950s, federal policies for the north-east went beyond mitigation of the consequences of droughts and started to focus on other issues such as development, following a growth-based approach. A new understanding of the SFR was emerging. The geographical distance increased between the river and the users of its resources. In the 1950s, people in Salvador and Recife started to receive electric power generated by the SFR. The building of Brazil's only oil production zone, outside the city of Salvador, also required electricity.[48] The eco-system service influenced the lives of individuals living far away in growing urban zones. In population terms, Recife surged in the 1950s and 1960s.[49]

43. Elmo Rodrigues da Silva, "O Curso da Água na História" (unpublished Ph.D. dissertation, Escola Nacional de Saúde Pública, 1998).
44. Salomão Serebrenick, *O Desenvolvimento Econômico do São Francisco: Um Planejamento Regional em Marcha* (Rio de Janeiro, 1961); Pierson, *O Homem no Vale do São Francisco*, I.
45. Serebrenick, *O Desenvolvimento Econômico do São Francisco*.
46. Religious figure 1, phone interview, 13 January 2007, Barra, Bahia.
47. The literature on drought and the north-east includes: Teodoro Sampaio, *O Rio São Francisco e a Chapada Diamantina* (São Paulo, 2002); Euclides da Cunha, *Os Sertões: Campanha de Canudos* (São Paulo, 2005); and Aziz Nacib Ab' Sáber, "Sertões e Sertanejos: Uma Geografia Humana Sofrida", *Estudos Avançados: Dossiê Nordeste Seco*, 13 (1999), pp. 7–59.
48. Marc W. Herold, "Between Sugar and Petroleum: Bahia and Salvador, 1920–1960", *Revista Espaço Acadêmico*, 42 (2004), available at http://www.espacoacademico.com.br/042/42cherold_ing.htm, last accessed 6 August 2010.
49. Robert M. Levine, "Letter from Recife", *Luso-Brazilian Review*, 7 (1970), pp. 114–121.

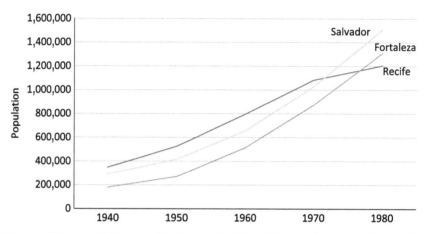

Figure 4. Urban population growth in three major cities of the coastal zone: Salvador, Recife, and Fortaleza (1940–1980).
Source: Derived from data from IBGE, 2003.

Federal censuses show that Salvador and Fortaleza even surpassed that city (Figure 4).[50]

Urban growth and industrialization created an unseen and unperceived, though strong, dependence and connection between human beings and the river environment which supplied the electrical power. In 2001, such strong dependence still existed when a drought caused a water shortage and led to urban blackouts and a mandatory electricity consumption reduction program.[51]

In addition to the policies for the north-east, the federal government planned major programs for the valley based upon its economic development even before 1950. In the late 1930s during the *New State (Estado Novo)*, President Vargas saw the valley becoming "Brazil's economic spine". The watershed would include, besides river traffic, new roads and railways. Some saw the plan as a means to nationalize Brazil's wealth.[52] Despite all the political rhetoric, no changes took place during the 1930s. World War II caused a spike in the river's importance. The waterway became the only safe water transport link between the south and the north

50. Instituto Brasileiro de Geografia e Estatística, *Estatísticas do Século XX* (Rio de Janeiro, 2003), CD-Rom and online database at http://www.ibge.gov.br/seculoxx/default.shtm, last accessed on 19 April 2010.
51. Tribuna do Norte, "CHESF Ameaça Recorrer a Apagões", *Tribuna do Norte*, 4 October 2001; Agência Brasil – Radiobras, "Sinopse – Resumo dos Jornais", *Sinopse Radiobras* (Brasília, 2001), available at http://clipping.radiobras.gov.br, last accessed on 19 April 2010.
52. Frank M. Garcia, "Vargas Seeks Help of Private Wealth", *New York Times*, 27 February 1938, pp. 1 and 27.

of the country during the war, as German U-boats attacked Brazilian coastal ocean shipping.[53]

HYDRO-BUSINESSES

Eco-systems support a wide range of human uses. In turn, those applications influence natural processes again. In the Brazilian Amazon the national government redefined and changed how locals used natural resources to employ them for developmental purposes.[54] If one compares the Amazon and the São Francisco Basin, in both cases the waterways used to be an integral part of the life of riparian communities. They used the river for fishing, natural irrigation, the fertilization of riparian lands, and for transportation. Interference from agents external to those systems produced destructive impacts – relocation of people and the elimination of areas of riparian agriculture resulting from the construction of dams and reservoirs. State development strategies redefined the Amazon, causing a move away from traditional historical roles of basic direct subsistence and into bauxite mining and hydro-power activities, turning small communities into boom towns. In the case of the SFR, the hydro-businesses of power generation and irrigation redefined and reshaped the natural system profoundly.

Hydro-power has played an important role in the provision of electricity for the nation. Before the 1920s, manufacturing depended on accessible water power, but in the first two decades of the twentieth century few had observed the nation's natural potential, as described by the following sentence: "There is enough hydraulic force available in Brazil to turn the wheels of the world but the majority of these wonderful cascades are scarcely known by name."[55]

By the 1950s, electricity shortages and a growing demand for energy were a challenge for Brazilian development.[56] Energy policy aimed at assisting the industrial development of the nation. In the north-east, governmental programs in the form of fiscal incentives, income tax exemptions, and public credit attracted industrial investment to major cities, such as Salvador and Recife. With the exception of the metropolitan area of Belo Horizonte and Pirapora in Minas Gerais state, Juazeiro in Bahia, and Petrolina in Pernambuco, industry was never the strong sector of the valley, though energy was.

53. Manoel Novaes, *Memórias do São Francisco* (Brasília, 1989); Frank D. McCann, "Brazil and World War II: The Forgotten Ally. What Did You Do in the War, Zé Carioca?", *Estudios Interdisciplinarios de America Latina y el Caribe*, 6 (1995), available at http://www.tau.ac.il/eial/VI_2/mccann.htm, last accessed 6 August 2010.
54. Paul S. Ciccantell, "It's All about Power: The Political Economy and Ecology of Redefining the Brazilian Amazon", *The Sociological Quarterly*, 40 (1999), pp. 293–315.
55. Lilian Elwyn Elliott, *Brazil Today and Tomorrow* (New York, 1917), p. 273.
56. Sam Pope Brewer, "Power Shortage Eased in Brazil", *New York Times*, 20 November 1954.

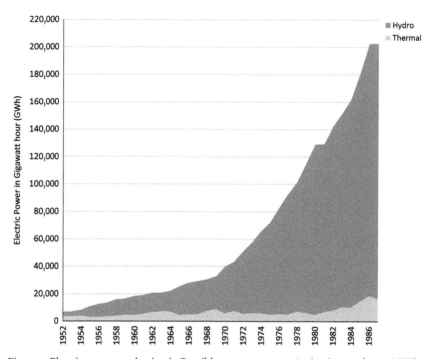

Figure 5. Electric power production in Brazil by source, 1952–1987, in gigawatt hours (GWh). *Source: Derived from data from IBGE, 2003.*

Paulo Afonso I, the first station producing electricity on a large scale in the SFRB, went online in 1954. Through power lines, electricity started to flow outward from the valley in the same year.[57] The station initially provided hydro-power to Pernambuco and Bahia. The north-east continued to expand its infrastructure, especially roads and electrical energy.[58] In the 1960s, hydro-power provided over 65 per cent of the nation's electricity, a share which steadily grew. Figure 5 displays both total Brazilian energy production and the proportion accounted for by hydro-power.[59] In the 1970s alone, four new stations started producing energy using the Velho Chico.

Nine dams control the river's flow. As with the other dams, Três Marias, the most upstream barrier holding back Chico's water, was intended to manage flooding, improve navigation, and make possible

57. Companhia Hidro Elétrica do São Francisco, *50 Anos Chesf: Companhia Hidro Elétrica do São Francisco – 1948–1998* (Recife, 1998).
58. Araújo, "Northeast, Northeasts: What Northeast?".
59. Instituto Brasileiro de Geografia e Estatística, *Estatísticas do Século XX.*

large-scale irrigation and hydro-power generation.[60] However, electricity became the principal output, followed later by water for irrigation. The damming of the SFR had quickly shifted from multiple to these dual purposes. Hydro-power infrastructure transformed the river and valley, managing the water's flow and assigning large areas of the valley as artificial lakes. The changes influenced irrigated agriculture, which helped support Brazil's role as an agro-exporter.

As already mentioned, Brazil's transnational economy has its roots in the nation's colonial past.[61] The São Francisco Basin was connected with the global economy in a variety of ways before World War II. For example, at the end of the nineteenth century the region provided hides to the United States and Germany, and goat skins for ladies' gloves, book binders' leather, and high-grade shoes.[62] Some thirty years later, a critical raw material of the valley, commercial quartz (silicon dioxide) crystal, was exported to Europe and the United States. Brazil was the only supplier of quartz, a component in the fabrication of radio station frequency controls, telephone equipment, lenses, and precision instruments.[63] After the war, scientists at Westinghouse Electric learned how to grow quartz crystals, ending the need for Brazil's natural ones. Locals also collected the wild-growing *caroá* cactus (*Neoglaziovia variegata*) for fibers. During World War II, the United States imported the fiber for the production of cordage, paper, cloth, and bags.[64]

Brazil exported agricultural products partly to obtain foreign exchange.[65] Between 1961 and 2007, with the exception of 1979 and 1986 when Brazil fell behind Colombia, the nation was the world's leading coffee exporter. It was the number one exporter of raw sugar by volume from 1998 to 2007.[66] By the 1980s, a new group of Brazilian agribusiness billionaires had emerged which included some from São Paulo: José Cutrale and Carl Fischer, producing orange juice, and the soybean king,

60. O Observador Econômico e Financeiro, *CVSF Uma Comissão Recupera um Vale: de Três Marias a Sobradinho – Separata de O Observador Econômico e Financeiro* (Rio de Janeiro, 1962).

61. J.F. Riegelhaupt and S. Forman, "Bodo was Never Brazilian", *The Journal of Economic History*, 30 (1970), pp. 100–116.

62. Marc W. Herold and Osvaldo Teixeira, "Empirical Foundations of Salvador da Bahia as Node of Commodity Networks, 1850–1914", paper presented at the XVth World Economic History Congress, Utrecht, 3–7 August 2009.

63. Robert Burnett Hall, "American Raw-Material Deficiencies and Regional Dependence", *Geographical Review*, 30 (1940), pp. 177–186.

64. George Wythe, *Brazil: An Expanding Economy* (New York, 1968).

65. Maria Auxiliadora de Carvalho and César Roberto Leite da Silva, "Vulnerabilidade do Comércio Agrícola Brasileiro", *Revista de Economia e Sociologia Rural*, 43 (2005), pp. 9–28.

66. Food and Agriculture Organization of the United Nations, "FAOSTAT Database: Trade-Exports-Countries by Commodities" (Rome, 2009), available online at http://faostat.fao.org/, last accessed on 20 April 2010.

Olacyr Francisco de Moraes.[67] During the 1970s and 1980s, in the Petrolina-Juazeiro zone of the SFR Valley, the more resource-intensive and large-scale irrigated production of tomatoes, sugar cane, and fruit was launched.[68] In the late 1980s, almost half of the irrigated land of the basin was in this zone.[69] Fruit juice and extracts from that agro-industrial area supplied the markets of a number of countries, including France and Switzerland.[70] In 1987, grapes and mangoes from the valley began carving out a niche in the international market.[71] The Netherlands, the United Kingdom, and the United States became important buyers.[72] Soybeans completed the list of the valley's export products.

Several conditions favored agricultural production in the region. The low price of land and low cost of labor gave the north-east advantages in relation to other parts of Brazil and the rest of the world.[73] In addition, the São Francisco Basin had a high annual temperature and bright sunlight.[74] Lastly, the river's water was a free natural resource for producers in the valley. In practice, free water kept prices of agricultural products low. The main costs related to infrastructure, such as powering the pumps used in irrigation.

67. "As Estrelas do Campo", *Revista Veja*, 2 June 1982, pp. 112–121, and "Pequena História de um Grupo que Gera US$ 500 Milhoes em Divisas", *Revista Veja*, 17 July 1982, pp. 40–41.
68. José Maria Alves da Silva, Alberto Martins Rezende, and Carlos Arthur Barbosa da Silva, "Condicionantes do Desenvolvimento do Pólo Agroindustrial de Petrolina/Juazeiro", *Revista Económica do Nordeste*, 31 (2000), pp. 48–64.
69. Companhia de Desenvolvimento do Vale do São Francisco, *Frutas Brasileiras: Exportação* (Brasília, 1989).
70. Silva *et al.*, "Condicionantes do Desenvolvimento".
71. Jane L. Collins, "Gender, Contracts and Wage Work: Agricultural Restructuring in Brazil's São Francisco Valley", *Development and Change*, 24 (1993), pp. 53–82, and *idem*, "Farm Size and Non Traditional Exports: Determinants of Participation in World Markets", *World Development*, 23 (1995), pp. 1103–1114.
72. Associação dos Produtores Exportadores de Hortigranjeiros e Derivados do Vale do São Francisco – Valexport, *Valexport: Há 17 Anos Unindo Forças para o Desenvolvimento do Vale do São Francisco e da Fruticultura Brasileira* (Petrolina, 2005), and *idem*, *Valexport: Há 18 Anos Unindo Forças para o Desenvolvimento do Vale do São Francisco e da Fruticultura Brasileira* (Petrolina, 2006).
73. Carlos Estêvão Leite Cardoso and José da Silva Souza, "Fruticultura Tropical: Perspectivas e Tendências", *Revista Económica do Nordeste*, 31 (2000), pp. 84–95. In the north-east of Brazil the price of an hour of work was US$ 0.75 and in California US$ 5–10 in the late 1980s; Companhia de Desenvolvimento do Vale do São Francisco e do Parnaíba – CODEVASF, "Comparações" (Brasília, 2006), available at http://www.codevasf.gov.br, last accessed on 21 April 2010.
74. Andreas Voth, "The Transformation of the São Francisco Valley (Brazil) by Changing Development Policy and Export-Oriented Fruit Production", paper presented at the Deutscher Tropentag, Berlin, 1999; Cardoso and Souza, "Fruticultura Tropical"; Empresa Brasileira de Pesquisa Agropecuária – EMBRAPA, "A Região do Vale do Rio São Francisco" (Brasília, n.d.), available at http://www.cnpma.embrapa.br/projetos/prod_int/regiaosf.html, last accessed on 20 April 2010.

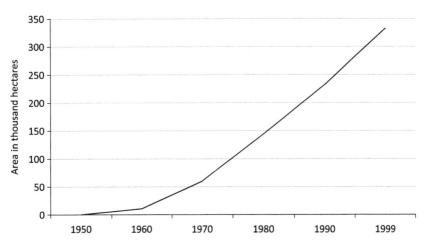

Figure 6. Irrigated land in the São Francisco River Basin.
Source: Derived from data from CODEVASF, 2008.

By 1960, 10,800 hectares of the SFRB had been irrigated. By 1999, that figure had risen to 333,000 hectares (Figure 6), representing an average annual growth rate of 9.2 per cent for that 39-year period.[75]

Irrigation allowed agricultural production beyond riparian and dry-land agriculture (*tradicional agricultura de sequeiro*).[76] Production became less dependent on the variability of the rainy periods. Irrigation permitted crop diversity, as well as spatial and temporal changes such as the location of the area of production and the time of the growing season in relation to the year. It transformed the landscape (Figures 7 and 8). Perennial and annual crops and water canals contrasted with the xerophytes and deciduous thorny scrub and trees of the semi-arid region.

Small-scale irrigated agriculture of onions and maize had operated in the riparian zones of the SFRB in the 1950s.[77] During 1950 and 1952, the CVSF, a development agency for the watershed, had financed 1,250 engines to pump water from the SFR to irrigate riparian land, especially in Bahia and Pernambuco and in the lower SFR.[78] Hydro-power infrastructure, electricity,

75. Companhia de Desenvolvimento dos Vales do São Francisco e do Parnaíba, "Irrigação: Histórico e Vantagens" (Brasília, 2008), available at http://www.codevasf.gov.br/programas_acoes/irrigacao/evolucao/, last accessed on 3 May 2010.
76. Emanoel de Souza Barros, Ecio de Farias Costa, and Yony Sampaio, "Análise de Eficiência das Empresas Agrícolas do Pólo Petrolina/Juazeiro Utilizando a Fronteira Paramétrica Translog", *Revista de Economia e Sociologia Rural*, 42 (2004), pp. 597–614.
77. Octavio Damiani, "Effects on Employment, Wages, and Labor Standards of Non-Traditional Export Crops in Northeast Brazil", *Latin American Research Review*, 38 (2003), pp. 83–112.
78. Superintendência do Vale do São Francisco – SUVALE, *Relatório – Atividades: 1948–1968* (n.p., 1968); Novaes, *Memórias do São Francisco*.

Figure 7. A vineyard at a private enterprise in Petrolina, Pernambuco, Brazil. Fruit culture is an important activity of the valley and grapes and mangoes are major products. *Photograph by Lucigleide Nascimento, 2007.*

and the construction of canals, such as the one in Figure 8, and pumping stations made possible the existence of larger-scale irrigation systems.[79]

Since the 1960s, the Companhia de Desenvolvimento dos Vales do São Francisco e do Parnaíba (CODEVASF), successor to the CVSF, and other federal agencies have been building the structural foundations for agro-industrial complexes in the valley.[80] According to a former Bahia Federal Deputy, Manoel Novaes, the projects were well planned, and were intended to boost the production of food and create jobs to meet local needs.[81] However, the projects had hidden costs, such as the overuse of water, run-off of fertilizers, salinization of soils, and ultimately a choice of products for export rather than local needs. The area in the north-east that used to grow traditional products (cotton and cassava for instance) has decreased since the 1970s.[82] In the São Francisco Valley, the higher world market prices have led to an increase in the production and importance of

79. Collins, "Gender, Contracts and Wage Work".
80. Damiani, "Effects on Employment, Wages, and Labor Standards".
81. Novaes, *Memórias do São Francisco.*
82. Araújo, "Northeast, Northeasts: What Northeast?".

Figure 8. The main water canal which is an important infrastructure of an irrigation scheme. This publically built canal is located in the lower-middle-SFR in the municipality of Petrolina, Pernambuco, Brazil.
Photograph by Lucigleide Nascimento, 2007.

non-traditional crops, such as fruit (mangoes and grapes for example), raw produce for food processing (tomatoes for instance), and sugar cane.[83]

In the governmental irrigation zones, producers paid a water bill, but it covered only the use of infrastructure and not the water itself. In practice it acted as a subsidy to lower the price of agricultural products. As already mentioned, only the costs of infrastructure in governmental irrigated areas, such as the price for the electricity used to deliver the water, was charged. The 1997 Water Policy authorized payment for the use of water resources, but the system for the SFRB has not been fully implemented.

The area of land used for extensive cattle ranching declined.[84] Irrigated agriculture reshaped and created vulnerability in the valley.[85] The dependence on international markets made the valley susceptible to global crises and

83. *Ibid.*; Silva *et al.*, "Condicionantes do Desenvolvimento"; Collins, "Farm Size and Non Traditional Exports".
84. Araújo, "Northeast, Northeasts: What Northeast?"; Silva *et al.*, "Condicionantes do Desenvolvimento"; Collins, "Farm Size and Non Traditional Exports".
85. T.K. Marsden, "Reshaping Environments: Agriculture and Water Interactions and the Creation of Vulnerability", *Transactions of the Institute of British Geographers*, new series, 22 (1997), pp. 321–337.

fluctuations in the level of demand and price. It exposed the system to international market forces and product requirements.[86] The new human uses of the valley's water have reconceptualized the good and the bad. The lack of rain was unfavorable for inland agriculture, demonstrating the vulnerability of locals to drought.[87] It also reduced the yield in riparian zones because of the decrease in the size of the area subjected to inundation, leading to a poor agricultural season. But in the irrigated, controlled model of agriculture, rain became an uncontrollable variable that can damage agricultural production.[88] Rains disrupted the planned nature of irrigated agriculture.

MIGRATION AND FORCED MIGRATION

At the end of the nineteenth century, north-easterners migrated to the Amazon during the rubber boom.[89] In the 1950s and 1960s, people left to join the labor forces of São Paulo and Rio de Janeiro and to build Brasília. Indeed, following the trend of the broader region up until the 1960s, population movement in the SFRB had been mostly outward. This out-migration was initially spurred by the recurrent devastating droughts, concentrated land ownership, and prevailing agricultural production models, then by the prospect of wage labor in urban construction and by the hope of higher living standards. Environmental refugees also sought water and shelter in the cities. Migration worsened social conditions in metropolitan zones, leading to the spread of shanty towns.[90]

In the 1950s, the number of individuals born in the north-east but living outside of it grew at an annual rate of 8.8 per cent, more than twice the corresponding rate of 3.7 per cent in the 1940s. The lower SFRB lost significant population in the 1950s and 1960s.[91] On the other hand, the north-east did not attract significant migratory inflows from other regions, except from Minas Gerais and Espírito Santo. In 1970, 99 per cent of the population in the north-east had been born there.[92]

The rural–urban migratory stream dominated in the areas of the middle and lower-middle SFRB during the 1960s.[93] In the north-east, rural to

---

86. Paulo de Queiroz Duarte, *O Nordeste na II Guerra Mundial: Antecedentes e Ocupação* (Rio de Janeiro, 1971).
87. Fernando Altenfelder Silva, *Xique–Xique e Marrecas: Duas Comunidades do Médio São Francisco* (Rio de Janeiro, 1961).
88. Marsden, "Reshaping Environments".
89. J.C. Oakenfull, *Brazil in 1912* (London, 1913).
90. Araújo, "Northeast, Northeasts: What Northeast?".
91. Hélio Augusto de Moura, "O Balanço Migratório do Nordeste no Período 1950/1970", *Revista Econômica do Nordeste*, 10 (1979), pp. 47–86.
92. *Idem*, "As Variações Migratórias no Nordeste: 1940/1970", *Revista Econômica do Nordeste*, 3 (1972), pp. 20–47.
93. *Idem*, "O Balanço Migratório do Nordeste".

urban migration continued during the 1970s and 1980s. Commerce and services attracted migrants to urban zones between 1980 and 1995, despite an economic crisis that hit the urban industrial sector harder than other areas.[94]

Migration is also associated with other causes. In some parts of the valley, the introduction of the new development approach of hydro-business destroyed the local social order of traditional ranching and agriculture, commerce, and fishing towns. The development-induced displacements disturbed the local way of life, forcing migration and adaptation to new ways of living, disconnected from the river. Hydro-power management altered aquatic eco-systems and the zones which used to be naturally subjected to the seasonal rise and fall of the waters in riparian agriculture. Irrigation led to rising land values, often resulting in expropriation. The new model altered the existing work relations in the agricultural sector by reducing or eliminating older tenancy systems. Displaced smallholders moved to cities.[95]

Good examples of this tragic situation are provided by the Sobradinho and Itaparica dams, which required the resettlement of about 65,000 and 50,000 people respectively.[96] The construction of the Sobradinho caused the relocation of four towns: Remanso, Casa Nova, Sento Sé, and Pilão Arcado. Few people ended up in the places in which they were supposed to be resettled.[97] A new way of life was imposed as riparian inhabitants resettled into inland areas. "A lot of people who used to live from onion and garlic production [...] in [seasonally inundated] fertile soils in riparian areas [...] needed to change the production system [...]. They had to shift to another activity, such as goat herding."[98] Another interviewee said that, "once these people were sent to Caatinga [...] their numbers swelled the cities [...]".[99]

In the case of the Itaparica dam, not all displaced residents received compensation. Given the informal traditional social system in which had they lived, they could not prove land ownership. The social and economic conditions of those the government resettled also often deteriorated. It took seven years for them to receive irrigation equipment to be able to farm the new lands. Violence and alcoholism increased in the community.[100]

94. Stephen G. Perz, "The Rural Exodus in the Context of Economic Crisis, Globalization and Reform in Brazil", *International Migration Review*, 34 (2000), pp. 842–881.

95. Collins and Krippner, "Permanent Labor Contracts in Agriculture".

96. *Ibid.*; Peter H. Gleick, "Water and Conflict: Fresh Water Resources and International Security", *International Security*, 18 (1993), pp. 79–112; Michael M. Cernea, "Public Policy Responses to Development-Induced Population Displacements", *Economic and Political Weekly*, 31 (1996), pp. 1515–1523.

97. Cernea, "Public Policy Responses".

98. Researcher, interview, 20 November 2006, Recife, Pernambuco.

99. Environmentalist and government staff, interview, 13 June 2007, Petrolina, Pernambuco.

100. John Horgan, "The Itaparica Dam Project in North-Eastern Brazil: Models and Reality", *Forced Migration Review*, 4 (1999), pp. 25–28.

As Hilton observed, the implementation of governmental projects would save migrants a long walk to São Paulo.[101] Irrigated agriculture attracts many to development "poles". Few find permanent work, forming a contingent workforce which finds jobs only seasonally. "Elsewhere in the region, on the periphery of the urban settlements of Petrolina and Juazeiro, settlements grew up to house the influx of migrants who formed the primary labor supply for most farms."[102] But the number of people who arrive every day is higher than towns and cities can support.

ENVIRONMENTAL CHANGE AND ECOLOGICAL SUSTAINABILITY

Ecological sustainability is critical to the long-term health and survival of both humans and non-humans.[103] Ecological sustainability requires maintaining the integrity of natural systems.[104] The protection of eco-system health and integrity means respect for the system's carrying capacity and its resilience to stress. It also implies recognition of possible limits, and prevention of future damage.[105] In the SFR case, this also means addressing water pollution and the destruction of aquatic populations, creating conditions for annual inundation to occur, as well as taking action to prevent new threats to the river's ecological sustainability.

Individual and cumulative effects on the river eco-system are many. River users, managers, and researchers from different localities have noticed the multiple changes during the last sixty years. Taking a holistic approach and comparing present with past conditions, the river has been categorized as a "sick" being or even a "dying river". Some predict that it will become a temporary river, as have many others in the semi-arid region which flow only during the rainy season. The threats to the sustainability of the SFR derive from, *inter alia*, the construction and operation of hydro-power infrastructure, urbanization and population growth (and their effects, such as the increase in raw sewage discharge), industry and mining, and agriculture and deforestation (cause and consequence). The focus here is upon electricity and irrigated agriculture, which are the forms of hydro-business in the valley.

---

101. Norman Hilton, *United Nations Special Fund Project No. 18: Survey of the São Francisco River Basin Brazil – Interim Economic Report* (n.p., 1963).

102. Collins and Krippner, "Permanent Labor Contracts in Agriculture", p. 520.

103. Ecological sustainability in this case means the preservation of the physical, chemical, and biological characteristics of the life-support system and the system's capabilities as a provider of natural goods and services (ecosystem services).

104. Mimi L. Becker, "Defining the Ecosystem Approach", in *idem, Implementing a Binational Ecosystem Management Strategy in the Great Lakes Basin* (Ann Arbor, MI, 1996).

105. Robert Costanza, Bryan G. Norton, and Benjamin D. Haskell (eds), *Ecosystem Health* (Washington DC, 1992).

Dams hold back water and sediments. An eighty-three-year-old retired boat worker, who also used to grow rice in Brejo Grande, beautifully described the changes in the river and what now takes place in the lower SFR:

> When there were floods, the entire region was full of fish, because fish and shrimp used to come. The water flooded lagoons with that yellow water, vitamin rich, which resulted from the mud [the water] removed from the river's banks. [...] People grew rice [...]. It produced important rice. Today the water seems to be filtered, isn't it? The water is kept by the dam. When the dam lets the waters go [...] the water comes clean, without the vitamins.[106]

The staff of water treatment plants in the region of the lower SFR noticed changes too, including a reduction in the level of suspended sediments.[107] The management of the river for hydro-power generation reduced the occurrence of natural floods which used to increase the level of the river seasonally and maintain riparian lagoons. Now dams prevent the flooding of such riparian water bodies.[108] In the middle SFR, starting in Pirapora and in the lower SFR, the river is surrounded by lowlands that floods used to transform into lagoons.[109] Fishing boomed in such an aquatic environment.[110] The middle SFR including Bom Jesus da Lapa was an intensive fishing center. In 1968, fishermen caught 215 tons, in 1969 the figure was 385 tons, and in 1970 the catch amounted to 366 tons of fish.[111] These numbers show the importance of the activity for the town and region.

The lack of periodic inundation inhibits fish from entering and exiting riparian lakes.[112] It isolates those water bodies from the river's main channel for long periods and prevents migratory fish from returning to spawning sites.[113] The dam itself also impairs fish migration. Many species

---

106. Retired boat worker and rice farmer, interview, 4 June 2007, Brejão-Brejo Grande, Sergipe.

107. Water treatment plant staff 1, group interview, 17 January 2007, Penedo, Alagoas.

108. M.C.C. Alvim and A.C. Peret, "Food Resources Sustaining the Fish Fauna in a Section of the Upper São Francisco River in Três Marias, MG, Brazil", *Brazilian Journal of Biology*, 64 (2004), pp. 195–202.

109. Rego, *O Valle do São Francisco*.

110. Pierson, *O Homem no Vale do São Francisco*, II.

111. Serviço Federal de Habitação e Urbanismo – SERFHAU and Superintendência de Desenvolvimento do Nordeste – SUDENE, *Relatório Preliminar de Desenvolvimento Integrado do Município de Bom Jesus da Lapa, Bahia* (n.p., 1972).

112. Jutta Gutberlet and Cristiana Simão Seixas, "Avaliação de Campo: A Situação Sócio-Econômica de Comunidades de Pesca no Alto, Médio e Baixo Rio São Francisco – Uma Avaliação Rápida e Independente" (Victoria, 2003), available at http://worldfish.org/PPA/PDFs/Semi-annual%20I%20Portuguese/1st%20s.a.%20port_C3.pdf, last accessed on 4 May 2010.

113. Paulo dos Santos Pompeu and Hugo Pereira Godinho, "Effects of Extended Absence of Flooding on the Fish Assemblages of Three Floodplain Lagoons in the Middle São Francisco River, Brazil", *Neotropical Ichthyology*, 4 (2006), pp. 427–433.

of the SFR are migratory; they include *surubim* (*Pseudoplatystoma coruscans*).[114] Fish populations have decreased. Changes in species composition have also been observed. *Surubim* has become an endangered species, and *tucunaré* (*Cichla spp.*), an invasive species, now dominates the river's waters. Locals do not know how the *tucunaré* first arrived in the SFR. It is an aggressive fish that preys on other species. In Três Marias reservoir, small-sized fish declined significantly after the introduction of *tucunaré*.[115]

The changes in fish populations have compromised the livelihood of those who depend on the river's resources. All along the SFR, especially in the middle SFR, fishermen supported local and regional markets. They formed a homogeneous group sharing social and occupational identities. They behaved in similar ways and shared similar life objectives. The destruction of fishing means the annihilation of their former way of life. In bad agricultural seasons, the inhabitants of riparian cities will fish for food and also to sell if agriculture cannot support them and their families.[116] A natural bias toward seeking subsistence from the river existed in the past, but environmental changes have increased this tendency.

The destruction of the traditional culture of fishermen does not imply that people do not fish for their sheer survival. Locals have noticed an increase in the number of fishermen.[117] In 1985, about 26,000 fishermen fished on the SFRB,[118] but many do not share the identity of the professional groups of the past. They fish for subsistence. "Today, it is difficult to sell [the fish]. There are more fishermen than buyers."[119] In various regions of the SFR, fishermen are confident that many people fish now for lack of choice, while others are still proud of their traditional way of life. For them, the river is like a good boss.[120] Unemployment, water pollution, the destruction of habitat due to the deforestation of riparian forests and the land filling of lagoons for urban and agriculture purposes, and overfishing have visibly impacted fish, fishing, and fishermen.

At the beginning of the twentieth century, an endless conflict between the river and the sea took place at the SFR's mouth.[121] The volume of

114. Gutberlet and Seixas, "Avaliação de Campo".

115. Sato and Godinho, "Migratory Fishes of the São Francisco River".

116. Pierson, *O Homem no Vale do São Francisco*, II.

117. Fisherman and Fishermens' Association staff, interview, 15 May 2007, Pirapora, Minas Gerais.

118. GEO Brasil, *O Estado do Meio Ambiente no Brasil: O Estado dos Recursos Pesqueiros – Pesca Extrativa e Aqüicultura* (Brasília, 2002).

119. Fisherman 3, interview, 18 January 2007, Penedo, Alagoas.

120. Fisherman 1, interview, 17 January 2007, Penedo, Alagoas.

121. John Casper Branner, *The Stone Reefs of Brazil, Their Geological and Geographical Relations, with a Chapter on the Coral Reefs* [Bulletin of the Museum of Comparative Zoology at Harvard] (Cambridge, MA, 1904).

water was high and swept the river's silt into the ocean. This fact did not eliminate the formation of islands and sandbanks near the SFR's mouth.[122] Today, the water is without the "vitamin", as a local from a municipality at the mouth of the SFR explained. It is "hungry water"; the sediment-starved flow sculpts the landscape, eroding, transporting, and depositing sediment.[123] At the river's mouth the load of sediment is reduced, and sea waves now accelerate beach erosion.[124] As a result, the small oceanside village of Cabeço has been completely washed out to sea.

Change in salinity affects species that grow in riparian zones. Saltwater destroys junco (*Eleocharis elegans*), a fiber-rich grass, and rice plantations. Two species of *maçunim*, shellfish, existed: one freshwater sort and the other saltwater. In the lower SFR, families spent time collecting *maçunim* on the beach up from the mouth of the river.[125] Now the salinity of the water is demonstrated by the catch of saltwater species in areas in which they were not common in the past.

Irrigated food production affects the natural system in both hydrological and ecological ways: subtracting nutrients, depleting and salinizing soils, polluting air, soil, and water due to the run-off of fertilizers and pesticides.[126] A 2002 analysis based upon qualitative information provided by environmental managers reported that about 38 per cent of the municipalities which comprise the SFRB suffered water pollution from three major causes: domestic sewage discharge, solid waste, and the use of agro-toxins and fertilizers.[127] As with irrigation, fertilizer consumption in Brazil has been increasing since the late 1960s. It jumped from 270,004 metric tons in 1961 to 7,682,000 in 2002.[128] Fertilizers are used in intensive agriculture, such as in fruit production in the north-east of Brazil. If improperly or over used, nutrients such as nitrogen can contaminate the water. Phosphorus causes eutrophication and depletion of oxygen in water bodies and the death of animal aquatic life and the impairment of human uses. Intensive irrigated

122. Pierson, *O Homem no Vale do São Francisco*, I.
123. G. Mathias Kondolf, "Hungry Water: Effects of Dams and Gravel Mining on River Channels", *Environmental Management*, 21 (1997), pp. 533–551.
124. *Ibid.*; Abílio Carlos da Silva Pinto Bittencourt *et al.*, "Wave Refraction, River Damming, and Episodes of Severe Shoreline Erosion: The São Francisco River Mouth, Northeastern Brazil", *Journal of Coastal Research*, 23 (2007), pp. 930–938.
125. Fisherwoman and Fishermens' Association staff, interview, 7 June 2007, Brejo Grande, Sergipe; Pierson, *O Homem no Vale do São Francisco*, I and II.
126. Sandra Postel, "Water and Agriculture", in Peter Gleick (ed.), *Water in Crisis* (New York, 1993), pp. 56–66; Food and Agriculture Organization of the United Nations – FAO, *Fertilizer Use by Crop in Brazil* (Rome, 2004).
127. Instituto Brasileiro de Geografia e Estatística – IBGE, *Pesquisa de Informações Básicas Municipais – Perfil dos Municípios Brasileiros: Meio Ambiente 2002* (Rio de Janeiro, 2005).
128. Food and Agriculture Organization of the United Nations – FAO, "FAOSTAT Database: Fertilizers Consumption" (Rome, 2006), available at http://faostat.fao.org, last accessed on 22 April 2010.

The effects upon these uses → The effects of these uses ↓	Navigation	Fishing	Public Water supply	Electricity	Flood control	Recreation	Traditional Agriculture	Irrigated Agriculture
Electricity	PE1, NE1	NE2	NE3	PE2	PE3	PE4	NE4	PE5, NE8
Irrigated Agriculture	NE5	NE6	NE7	NE8	–	NE9	NE10	NE11

Figure 9. This matrix shows how the two major uses of the São Francisco (to generate electricity and to irrigate agricultural fields) can affect positively (PE), negatively (NE), or both, other uses of the eco-system services of the water body (e.g. navigation and fishing).

agriculture has resulted in the salinization of soils in the valley and waterways. In the Petrolina region, the water treatment plant uptake is downstream and close to a creek which crosses irrigated land. During winter, the salinity content is particularly high.[129]

Hydro-business in the SFRB has heightened the importance of analyzing trade-offs and opportunity costs. As in the case of the redefinition of the meaning of the Velho Chico for hydro-power and irrigation, the consequences are both impaired (negative effect – NE) and improved (positive effect – PE) uses of the SFR's waters (Figure 9).

NE1: In the Sobradinho Reservoir, the new environment to provide electricity impaired navigation of older-type boats because the lake was too windy. The river was not regulated for navigation.

NE2: Electricity impaired fishing. Hydro-power infrastructure transformed the flowing river into a sequence of managed lakes. It spoiled fish migration and their reproductive cycle. Producing electricity caused a decrease in the populations of fish, in the lower SFR for instance, because those populations cannot replace themselves in the altered habitat.

NE3, NE7: The management of electricity and irrigation created concerns for public water supply, as in Penedo in the lower SFR, when air entered the water treatment plant system because the river's level was

129. Water treatment plant staff 2, interview, 14 June 2007, Petrolina, Pernambuco.

too low.[130] In Petrolina, intensive agriculture is a source of contaminants in pre-treatment drinking water.[131]

NE4: Electricity impaired traditional agriculture. The level of the river is no longer based upon natural conditions, but upon human management. Locals cannot apply their traditional knowledge to assess when the river will be high or low and when is the right time to farm and harvest.

NE5, NE6, NE7: Water withdrawn for irrigated agriculture might restrict and/or impair other uses, such as the maintenance of water to allow ecosystem life and for hydropower generation. In the basin, this use already impacts navigation and water supply for domestic uses. The Rio Salitre used to be a permanent tributary, the Rio Corrente had more flow in the past, and Minas Gerais's brooks and creeks are disappearing due to the intensive use of the water. Locals complained about the reduction in the flow of the tributaries and the contribution to the SFR. As one fisherman said, "as we need our arms, we need our legs, we need our head to govern our body; in the same way the big river needed its arms, the rivers that formed it".[132]

NE8: In future, managers will need to choose between one or the other use, water for irrigated agriculture or for electricity generation. For example, if the inter-basin water transference project (*Transposição*) of the National Integration Ministry takes place as proposed, the scheme will reduce CHESF's hydropower production by 2.4 per cent.[133] The idea for this project has existed since the time of the Brazilian emperor D. Pedro II (1840–1889). The current inter-basin project has kindled both public support and opposition, including two hunger strikes and several court cases. This new large-scale infrastructure traversing part of the basin and other regions of the north-east involves northward and eastward running canals with a total of 720 kilometers of aqueducts, reservoirs, dams, and pumping stations, which will increase hydro-business. The project exemplifies what Richard Burton noted in the nineteenth century, namely that Brazil has had a bias toward monumental constructions since times past.[134]

Climate change is another consideration relating to water use and choices in the valley. Scientists agree that changing climatic conditions will affect hydrologic cycles.[135] But the impact of those changes and our ability to cope with the problems they cause will not be distributed evenly

130. Water treatment plant staff 1, group interview, 17 January 2007, Penedo, Alagoas.
131. Water treatment plant staff 2, interview, 14 June 2007, Petrolina, Pernambuco.
132. Fisherman 1, interview, 17 January 2007, Penedo, Alagoas.
133. Ministério da Integração Nacional do Brasil, *Projeto de Integração do Rio São Francisco com Bacias Hidrográficas do Nordeste Setentrional – Relatório de Impacto Ambiental – RIMA* (Brasília, 2004), p. 16.
134. Burton, *Explorations of the Highlands of the Brazil*.
135. A.P.M. Baede *et al.*, "The Climate System: An Overview", in J.T. Houghton *et al.* (eds), *Climate Change 2001: The Scientific Basis* (Cambridge, 2001), available at http://www.grida.no/climate/ipcc_tar/wg1/pdf/TAR-01.PDF, last accessed on 22 April 2010.

around the world.[136] They might trigger extreme events such as droughts and floods, increasing or decreasing river flows, evaporation, precipitation, and infiltration. The valley is already a water-deficit zone.

NE9: Irrigated agriculture might in the future create opportunities for beneficial effects, such as aesthetic enjoyment. The visit to wineries is still an incipient activity in the Petrolina and Juazeiro regions. The negative effects are more visible in the case of Pirapora, with tourist attractions in the waterfalls area – such as the beach at Minas Gerais – being impaired.

NE10: Irrigated agricultural fields replaced areas of traditional crops and agriculture.

NE11: A limit exists to the extension of land and the size of production the SFR will be able to irrigate.

PE1: The construction of electricity-generating infrastructure, namely dams and reservoirs, improved river navigation when navigation was a high-priority use, as for example in Pirapora during the non-rainy season soon after the construction of the Três Marias dam. Then, energy became the most important river use, and the water body management focused on that.

PE2: A series of power stations and reservoirs along the river's course resulted in a better managed, fuller use of the river's flow for electricity generation.

PE3: Electricity improved flood control. Extreme floods used to submerge towns and cities more often. Now, flooding occurs only if it does not impair hydropower management priorities.

PE4: Electricity has created new means of recreation in the valley. For example, residents and tourists use the Paulo Afonso hydro-power infrastructure for aquatic sports and sunbathing on a sand beach, Prainha. The city is famous for its eco-tourism and new forms of sport. The bridge, which links Alagoas and Bahia and is supposed to save the population in the event of a dam-related disaster, is popular among bungee jumpers and rappellers.

PE5: Electricity improved irrigated agriculture. The construction of water reservoirs assured a steady supply of water and electricity to power the pumps.

CONCLUSION

The beginning of the 1950s marked a new phase in the valley: dams altering production in riparian zones, water management for hydro-power generation controlling the flooded area, and the federal government creating opportunities for irrigated agriculture in development zones. The redefinition of the uses of the SFR for hydro-power and

136. Peter H. Gleick and Michael Kiparsky, "The Water and Climate Bibliography", in Peter H. Gleick *et al.*, *The World's Water: The Biennial Report on Freshwater Resources* (Washington DC, 2004), pp. 228–233.

irrigation imposed upon locals threatened their identity as *barranqueiros* and *beiradeiros*, making their living as riparian fishermen, boatmen, and subsistence farmers more difficult. The environmental changes impaired traditional uses, namely for fishing and riparian agriculture. The new values did not correspond to the realities of their society.

Hydro-businesses favored the production of crops for export, such as fruit and soybeans, which supports Brazil's international position as an important agro-exporter at the expense of meeting the demands of local people. Large-scale hydro-business does not address the needs of subsistence farmers and other local groups. The introduction of such a form of production tends to deepen the disparity between lower and higher economic classes. Few small farmers, tenants, and sharecroppers have benefited from the hydro-businesses of the late twentieth century. As one group of fishermen and fisherwomen put it:

> A lot has changed, including the harvest we used to collect from the riparian zone where we used to grow crops after big floods. We produced a lot of cassava, watermelon, pumpkins, beans, and everything else. That came to an end [...]. Such floods [natural ones] do not exist anymore [...] the richness of food ended too [...].[137]

---

137. Fishermen and fisherwomen, group interview, 22 August 2006, Bom Jesus da Lapa, Bahia.

GUIDELINES FOR CONTRIBUTORS

Manuscripts are considered for publication on the understanding that they are not currently under consideration elsewhere and that the material – in substance as well as form – has not been previously published. Two copies of the manuscript should be submitted. Each article should be accompanied by a summary, not exceeding 100 words, outlining the principal conclusions and methods in the context of currently accepted views on the subject. All material – including quotations and notes – must be double-spaced with generous margins. Use of dot-matrix printers is discouraged. Notes should be numbered consecutively and placed at the end of the text. Spelling should be consistent throughout (e.g. Labour and Labor are both acceptable, but only one of these forms should be used in an article). Turns of phrase using masculine forms as universals are not acceptable.

Sample citation forms

Book: E.P. Thompson, *The Making of the English Working Class* (London, 1963), pp. 320–322. Journal: Walter Galenson, "The Unionization of the American Steel Industry", *International Review of Social History*, 1 (1956), pp. 8–40. Detailed instructions for contributors are available from http://www.iisg.nl/irsh/irshstyl.php. Twenty-five free offprints of each article are provided, and authors may purchase additional copies provided these are ordered at proof stage.

This book has been printed on FSC-certified paper and cover board. FSC is an independent, non-governmental, not-for-profit organization established to promote the responsible management of the world's forests. Please see www.fsc.org for information.